The Management Task

Titles in the Institute of Management Series

The Management Task

Third edition

Rob Dixon

Published in association with the Institute of Management

iM the Institute of Management

BUTTERWORTH
HEINEMANN

AMSTERDAM   BOSTON   HEIDELBERG   LONDON   NEW YORK   OXFORD
PARIS   SAN DIEGO   SAN FRANCISCO   SINGAPORE   SYDNEY   TOKYO

Butterworth-Heinemann
An imprint of Elsevier
Linacre House, Jordan Hill, Oxford OX2 8DP
200 Wheeler Road, Burlington, MA 01803

First published 1993
Reprinted 1993 (twice), 1994
Second edition 1997
Reprinted 1998, 1999, 2000, 2001, 2002

British Library Cataloguing in Publication Data
A catalogue record for this book is available from the British Library

Library of Congress Cataloguing in Publication Data
A catalogue record for this book is available from the Library of Congress

ISBN 0 7506 5985 8

For information on all Butterworth-Heinemann publications
visit our website at www.bh.com

Typeset by Keyword Typesetting Services Ltd, Wallington, Surrey
Printed and bound in Great Britain by Biddles Ltd, *www.biddles.co.uk*

BTCV
British Trust for
Conservation Volunteers

FOR EVERY TITLE THAT WE PUBLISH, BUTTERWORTH-HEINEMANN
WILL PAY FOR BTCV TO PLANT AND CARE FOR A TREE.

Contents

Series adviser's preface

This book is one of a series designed for people wanting to develop their capabilities as managers. You might think that there isn't anything very new in that. In one way you would be right. The fact that very many people want to learn to become better managers is not new, and for many years a wide range of approaches to such learning and development has been available. These have included courses leading to formal qualifications, organizationally-based management development programmes and a whole variety of self-study materials. A copious literature, extending from academic textbooks to sometimes idiosyncratic prescriptions from successful managers and consultants, has existed to aid – or perhaps confuse – the potential seeker after managerial truth and enlightenment.

So what is new about this series? In fact, a great deal – marking in some ways a revolution in our thinking both about the art of managing and also the process of developing managers.

Where did it all begin? Like most revolutions, although there may be a single, identifiable act that precipitated the uprising, the roots of discontent are many and long-established. The debate about the performance of British managers, the way managers are educated and trained, and the extent to which shortcomings in both these areas have contributed to our economic decline, has been running for several decades.

Until recently, this debate had been marked by periods of frenetic activity – stimulated by some report or enquiry and perhaps ending in some new initiatives or policy changes – followed by relatively long periods of comparative calm. But the underlying causes for concern persisted. Basically, the majority of managers in the UK appeared to have little or no training for their role, certainly far less than their counterparts in our major competitor nations. And there was concern about the nature, style and appropriateness of the management education and training that was available.

The catalyst for this latest revolution came in late 1986 and early 1987, when three major reports reopened the whole issue. The 1987 reports were The *Making of British Managers* by John Constable and Robert McCormick, carried out for the British Institute of Management and the CBI, and *The Making of Managers* by Charles Handy, carried out for the (then) Manpower Services Commission, National Economic Development Office and British Institute of Management. The 1986 report, which often receives less recognition than it deserves as a key contribution to the recent changes, was *Management Training: context and process by* Iain Mangham and Mick Silver, carried out for the Economic and Social Research Council and the Department of Trade and Industry.

It is not the place to review in detail what the reports said. Indeed, they and their consequences are discussed in several places in this series of books. But essentially they confirmed that:

- British managers were undertrained by comparison with their counterparts internationally.
- The majority of employers invested far too little in training and developing their managers.
- Many employers found it difficult to specify with any degree of detail just what it was that they required successful managers to be able to do.

The Constable/McCormick and Handy reports advanced various recommendations for addressing these problems, involving an expansion of management education and development, a reformed structure of qualifications and a commitment from employers to a code of practice for management development. While this analysis was not new, and had echoes of much that had been said in earlier debates, this time a few leading individuals determined that the response should be both radical and permanent. The response was coordinated by the newly-established Council for Management Education and Development (now the National Forum for Management Education and Development (NFMED)) under the energetic and visionary leadership of Bob (now Sir Bob) Reid, formerly of Shell UK and the British Railways Board.

Under the umbrella of NFMED a series of employer-led working parties tackled the problem of defining what it was that managers should be able to do, and how this differed for people at different levels in their organizations; how this satisfactory ability to perform might be verified; and how an appropriate structure of management qualifications could be put in place. This work drew upon the methods used to specify vocational standards in industry and commerce, and led to the development and introduction of competence-based management standards and qualifications. In this context, competence is defined as the ability to perform the activities within an occupation or function to the standards expected in employment.

It is this competence-based approach that is new in our thinking about the manager's capabilities. It is also what is new about this series of books, in that they are designed to support both this new structure of management standards, and of development activities based on it. The series was originally commissioned to support the Institute of Management's Certificate and Diploma qualifications, which were one of the first to be based on the new standards. However, these books are equally appropriate to any university, college or indeed company course leading to a certificate in management or diploma in management studies.

The standards were specified through an extensive process of consultation with a large number of managers in organizations of many different types and sizes. They are therefore employment-based and employer-supported. And they fill the gap that Mangham and Silver identified – now we do have a language to describe what it is employers want their managers to be able to do – at least in part.

If you are engaged in any form of management development leading to a certificate or diploma qualification conforming to the national management standards, then you are probably already familiar with most of the key ideas on which the standards are based. To achieve their key purpose, which is defined as achieving the organization's objectives and continuously improving its performance, managers need to perform four key roles: managing operations, managing finance, managing people and managing information. Each of these key roles has a sub-structure of units and elements, each with associated performance and assessment criteria.

The reason for the qualification 'in part' is that organizations are different, and jobs within them are different. Thus the generic management standards probably do not cover all the management competences that you may need to possess in your job. There are almost certainly additional things, specific to your own situation in your own organization, that you need to be able to do. The standards are necessary, but almost certainly not sufficient. Only you, in discussion with your boss, will be able to decide what other capabilities you need to possess. But the standards are a place to start, a basis on which to build. Once you have demonstrated your proficiency against the standards, it will stand you in good stead as you progress through your organization, or change jobs.

So how do the new standards change the process by which you develop yourself as a manager? They change the process of development, or of gaining a management qualification, quite a lot. It is no longer a question of acquiring information and facts, perhaps by being 'taught' in some classroom environment, and then being tested to see what you can recall. It involves demonstrating, in a quite specific way, that you can do certain things to a particular standard of performance. And because of this, it puts a much greater onus on you to manage your own development, to decide how you can demonstrate any particular competence, what evidence you need to present, and how you can collect it. Of course, there will always be people to advise and guide you in this, if you need help.

But there is another dimension, and it is to this that this series of books is addressed. While the standards stress ability to perform, they do not ignore the traditional knowledge base that has been associated with 'management studies'. Rather, they set this in a different context. The standards are supported by 'underpinning knowledge and understanding' which has three components:

- Purpose and context, which is knowledge and understanding of the manager's objectives, and of the relevant organizational and environmental influences, opportunities and values.
- Principles and methods, which is knowledge and understanding of the theories, models, principles, methods and techniques that provide the basis of competent managerial performance.
- Data, which is knowledge and understanding of specific facts likely to be important to meeting the standards.

Possession of the relevant knowledge and understanding underpinning the standards is needed to support competent managerial performance as specified in the standards. It also has an important role in supporting the transferability of management capabilities. It helps to ensure that you have done more than learned 'the way we do things around here' in your own organization. It indicates a recognition of the wider things which underpin competence, and that you will be able to change jobs or organizations and still be able to perform effectively.

These books cover the knowledge and understanding underpinning the management standards, most specifically in the category of principles and methods. But their coverage is not limited to the minimum required by the standards, and extends in both depth and breadth in many areas. The authors have tried to approach these underlying principles and methods in a practical way. They use many short cases and examples which we hope will demonstrate how, in practice, the principles and methods, and knowledge of purpose and context plus data, support the ability to perform as required by the management standards. In particular we hope that this type of presentation will enable you to identify and learn from similar examples in your own managerial work.

You will already have noticed that one consequence of this new focus on the standards is that the traditional 'functional' packages of knowledge and theory do not appear. The standard textbook titles such as 'quantitative methods', 'production management', 'organizational behaviour', etc. disappear. Instead, principles and methods have been collected together in clusters that more closely match the key roles within the standards. You will also find a small degree of overlap in some of the volumes, because some principles and methods support several of the individual units within the standards. We hope you will find this reinforcement useful.

Having described the positive aspects of standards-based management development, it would be wrong to finish without a few cautionary remarks. The developments described above may seem simple, logical and uncontroversial. It did not always seem that way in the years of work which led up to the introduction of the standards. To revert to the revolution analogy, the process has been marked by ideological conflict and battles over sovereignty and territory. It has sometimes been unclear which side various parties are on – and indeed how many sides there are! The revolution, if well advanced, is not at an end. Guerrilla warfare continues in parts of the territory.

Perhaps the best way of describing this is to say that, while competence-based standards are widely recognized as at least a major part of the answer to improving managerial performance, they are not the whole answer. There is still some debate about the way competences are defined, and whether those in the standards are the most appropriate on which to base assessment of managerial performance. There are other models of management competences than those in the standards.

There is also a danger in separating management performance into a set of discrete components. The whole is, and needs to be, more than the sum of the parts. Just like bowling an off-break in cricket, practising a golf swing or forehand drive in tennis, you have to combine all the separate movements into a smooth, flowing action. How you combine the competences, and build on them, will mark your own individual style as a manager.

We should also be careful not to see the standards as set in stone. They determine what today's managers need to be able to do. As the arena in which managers operate changes, then so will the standards. The lesson for all of us as managers is that we need to go on learning and developing, acquiring new skills or refining existing ones. Obtaining your certificate or diploma is like passing a mile post, not crossing the finishing line.

All the changes and developments of recent years have brought management qualifications, and the processes by which they are gained, much closer to your job as a manager. We hope these books support this process by providing bridges between your own experience and the underlying principles and methods which will help you to demonstrate your competence. Already, there is a lot of evidence that managers enjoy the challenge of demonstrating competence, and find immediate benefits in their jobs from the programmes based on these new-style qualifications. We hope you do too. Good luck in your career development.

Paul Jervis

Preface

This book was written as part of an exciting cooperative venture between Butterworth-Heinemann and the Institute of Management to provide accessible material on management, its processes and functions.

This book considers both the nature of management and the environment in which management operates. The requirements for effective, successful management techniques are explored; covering many areas from the need for planning and forecasting, leadership, motivation and communication, to control, decision-making and the management of personnel.

I would like to extend my gratitude to all those who have helped in the production of this book, particularly to Charlotte Ridings and Sharon Anderson for their background research and to my wife Ann for her patience.

Rob Dixon

Part One

Introduction

Part One

Introduction

CHAPTER 1

Introduction

WHAT IS 'THE MANAGEMENT TASK'?

The task of management is all about organizing groups of people to work together productively towards known, clear goals, or objectives. There are many different levels of management, from production foremen, hospital ward sisters and senior secretaries, all supervising small groups of employees, to managing directors and chief executives, responsible for directing large multinational companies and organizations. However, the basic description of the management task holds good for all managers, regardless of their seniority.

Unfortunately, management is not quite as simple as that! The manager's job is very wide ranging. Mintzberg (1973) analysed the roles managers have to adopt during their work and listed seven major ones, as follows:

1 The entrepreneur: the manager as planner and risk-taker.
2 The resource allocator: the manager as organizer and co-ordinator.
3 The figurehead/leader: the manager as motivator and co-ordinator.
4 The liaisor/disseminator: the manager as coordinator and communicator.
5 The monitor: the manager as controller.
6 The spokesperson/negotiator: the manager as motivator and communicator.
7 The disturbance-handler: the manager as motivator and coordinator.

Thus we can see that the manager's job is to plan, take decisions, motivate, lead and organize the employees that he/she is responsible for, communicate with them and control and coordinate their work. In Part Two these management processes of planning, motivating, etc., will each be looked at in detail.

WHY MANAGEMENT IS IMPORTANT

Good management is vital if a business or any other enterprise is to be successful. Drucker (1967) regards an effective management team as the one big advantage a company can have over its competitors:

> In a competitive economy, above all, the quality and performance of the managers determine the success of a business, indeed they determine its survival. For the quality and performance of its managers is the only effective advantage an enterprise in a competitive economy can have.

Effective management can transform an inefficient, underperforming organization into a profitable, sound business, but the reverse is also true. Ineffectual managers can ruin sound businesses by allowing them to stagnate, content to rely on past achievements rather than looking for new challenges. No doubt you can think of examples of both kinds of management in companies or just departments that you are familiar with.

THE DEVELOPMENT OF MODERN MANAGEMENT IDEAS

Before we go on to look at the processes involved in the management task, the rest of this chapter will give a little background information about the changes in management thinking over the years, which should give you an insight into how and why organizations are run in the ways they are today.

It should be remembered that, naturally, each theory reflects the thinking and attitudes of its time. But it is clear that they still have a lot of influence on today's business methods and ideas.

Theories about the best way to manage people have developed over the years from the beginning of the century. The three main schools of thought are the classical school, the human relations school, and the systems school of management. Figure 1.1 shows how the different theories have developed over time, and have built upon previous ideas.

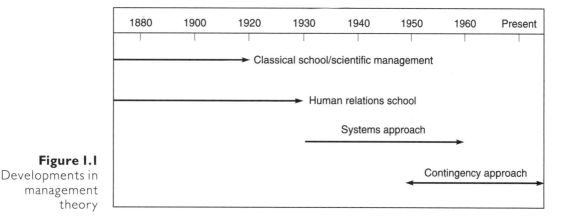

Figure 1.1
Developments in
management
theory

The classical school

The classical approach to management concentrated on trying to form general principles of management. These principles, it was hoped, could then be applied to all organizations in every business situation. Techniques of mass-production were just beginning to be widely used, and managers were concerned to find the most economical method of producing the greatest number of goods.

The solution of the classical theorists was to divide work tasks up into their constituent parts. Thus, for example, instead of a cobbler making one complete pair of shoes, from the initial cutting of the leather right through to the final buffing and polishing of the finished article, before starting afresh on a different pair, the jobs would be divided between several workers. One would cut the leather for all the shoes to be made that day, another would stretch the leather, and so on.

The main writers of the classical school were F. W. Taylor, Henri Fayol, Frank and Lillian Gilbreth, and Henry Gantt.

F. W. TAYLOR AND SCIENTIFIC MANAGEMENT

Taylor (1856-1915), whose ideas were developed when he was a manager at a steel works in the USA, was concerned with the formal structure and activities of organizations, i.e. the optimum numbers of employees that each manager should supervise, work division, etc. Taylor believed in, and pioneered the use of, scientific methods of observation and analysis in management.

THE PRINCIPLES BEHIND SCIENTIFIC MANAGEMENT

In *Principles of Scientific Management (1911)* Taylor set out the fundamental principles which he thought underlay scientific management. These can be summed up as follows:

1 Replacing rules of thumb with a true science of work. Many companies relied (and some still do!) upon information retained in the heads of employees, rather than gathering all that knowledge together and making a proper record of it. Taylor felt that without this reliance upon the 'it has always been done this way' mentality, 'every single subject, large and small, becomes the question for scientific investigation, for reduction to law' (Taylor, 1911).
2 Replacing 'chaotic individualism' with cooperation between managers and employees to the mutual benefit of all.
3 The scientific selection and progressive development of workers, i.e. workers should be given jobs which they are best suited to do, and carefully trained to do these jobs. This would be to the advantage of both companies and employees, allowing both groups to prosper.
4 Working for maximum output rather than restricted output.

Taylor's aim in his system of scientific management was to increase the efficiency of production methods, not just to lower company costs and thus increase profits, but also to enable the workers to increase their productivity and so earn higher wages. Through scientific methods of job analysis, establishing the best, most efficient way of doing the work, and through training the workers in these efficient production methods, greater productivity could, Taylor believed, be achieved. Scientific management would eliminate the ignorance on the parts of both managers and workers which led to unrealistic production targets and piece-rates of pay, and to inefficient ways of production.

Other classical theorists

Taylor was not the only proponent of scientific management. Other early supporters included Frank and Lillian Gilbreth and Henry Gantt.

THE GILBRETHS

The Gilbreths' contribution to scientific management was to develop motion study into a management tool capable of analysing work operations to establish the most efficient way of doing any particular task.

Frank Gilbreth (1917) defined motion study as 'dividing the work into the most fundamental elements possible; studying these elements separately and in relation to one another; and from these studied elements, when timed, building methods of least waste'.

Motion study was carried out using flow process charts. Symbols were used to analyse the processes of

- Operation
- Inspection
- Storage
- Transportation
- Delay

Unlike Taylor, who tended to think of pay as being the only motivator of workers and, therefore, that if workers were paid a fair piece-rate they would increase their productivity in order to maximize their earnings, the Gilbreths recognized that workforce output was dependent upon other factors as well. These included worker fatigue, poor lighting, heating and ventilation. The Gilbreths used motion studies to help reduce fatigue among workers, and they also introduced rest periods and shorter working days.

HENRY GANTT

Gantt was one of Taylor's colleagues. He, too, humanized Taylor's ideas of scientific management by introducing day-rates of pay (instead of the piece-rate system), with additional bonuses for those workers who exceeded the daily production targets. Foremen were also encouraged to train workers in their jobs by receiving a bonus for every worker who met the production targets.

Gantt is chiefly remembered today for developing a type of bar chart showing the time relationships between the stages in production processes. The Gantt chart (Figure 1.2) was originally designed to show how far a task had been achieved in comparison to the optimum target set.

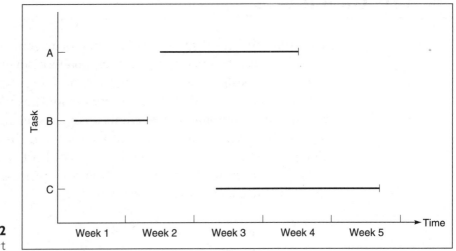

Figure 1.2
A Gantt chart

HENRI FAYOL (1841-1925)

Henri Fayol, a French industrialist, did more than anyone to popularize the idea of the 'universality of management principles': the concept that, regardless of the sort of business in question, the same broad principles of management apply. While Taylor's work was concentrated upon the shop-floor, Fayol studied management's role throughout the organization.

Fayol is known as the 'father of modern operational management theory', and, as you will see, his principles of management and his ideas on what the task of management entails are still very much in use.

FAYOL'S FUNCTIONS OF MANAGEMENT

Fayol identified five elements or functions of management (Figure 1.3): planning, organizing, commanding, coordinating and controlling.

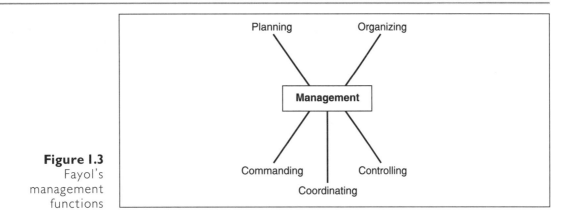

Figure 1.3
Fayol's management functions

1 *Planning.* Choosing objectives and the strategies, policies, and procedures for achieving them.
2 *Organizing.* Establishing a structure of tasks which have to be followed to achieve the organization's objectives, dividing these tasks up into jobs for individual employees, delegating authority, co-ordinating the work of different people, and setting up information and communication systems.
3 *Commanding.* Giving instructions and leadership to subordinates.
4 *Coordinating.* Harmonizing the work of different groups so that individuals are all working towards the common goals of the organization.
5 *Controlling.* Measuring, checking and correcting, if necessary, the results achieved, to ensure that they match the planned results.

FAYOL'S PRINCIPLES OF MANAGEMENT

Fayol developed his fourteen management principles from these five functions:

1 *Division of work.* The specialization of tasks, which Fayol regarded as necessary to achieve greater efficiency and productivity.
2 *Authority and responsibility.* The right to issue commands comes from authority; responsibility for the work done is also related to this authority, and in fact arises out of it.

3 *Discipline.* Fayol felt that good superiors, at all levels in the organization, were required if there was to be good company discipline.

4 *Unity of command.* Ideally, employees should only receive instructions from one superior, right up to the organization's management hierarchy.

5 *Unity of direction.* Each group of activities with the same objective should have a single plan and a single manager in charge.

6 *Subordination.* The interest of the individual should be regarded as of lesser importance than the general interest.

7 *Remuneration.* Remuneration for work should be fair both to the employees and to the employer. This means that no one should have cause for discontent.

8 *Centralization.* This is the extent to which authority is concentrated or dispersed in an organization.

9 *Scalar chain.* The 'chain of superiors', according to Fayol, extending through an organization, which should not be departed from lightly; although it could be by-passed on occasions if it would harm the company to follow the chain too closely.

10 *Order.* People and work should be organized in an orderly fashion.

11 *Equity.* Managers should be fair in their dealings with employees and situations.

12 *Stability of tenure.* Fayol could not see how a manager whose promotion prospects, or job itself, were dependent upon short-term contract or salary reviews could be expected to do his job well. Instead, there should be a proper period of training and settling in, together with freedom from interference at all times.

13 *Initiative.* This should be encouraged to the full.

14 *Esprit de corps.* Managers should build up morale and a good team spirit among the workforce.

The achievements of the classical management school

You will, hopefully, have noticed how many of the ideas of people like Taylor and Fayol are still influencing production and management approaches today: the division of work into its smallest, simplest elements is still very widespread in mass-production, assembly-line industries. Work studies and time-and-motion studies are also widely used, and Fayol's management principles give a more than adequate summary of what management should be about.

The classical theorists helped to bring about a far more formal and rational approach to management than there had been before, and there is no doubt that the improvements aimed for in increased productivity and workers' pay were achieved.

However, the drawbacks of this approach were the de-skilling of the work, and the increase in the boring, repetitive nature of the tasks. These are problems which are still to be solved. The classical approach also saw workers as being rational economic beings, motivated only by money. Motor manufacturing has been a classic example where workers concentrated on one routine task. More recently, companies such as Toyota and Nissan have introduced task groups where workers concentrate on a number of tasks in an area.

The human relations school

While the classical management approach focused upon the structure of the organization, the human relations, or behavioural, school concentrates upon the people within the organization – their social needs, motivation and behaviour. The behavioural approach really began in earnest during the 1920s and 1930s, when it became clear that classical management theories were not preventing a fall in levels of production.

The first really influential writer on the behavioural approach was Elton Mayo (1880-1949), who studied productivity levels and working conditions at the Hawthorne plant of the Western Electric Company in Chicago, between 1927 and 1932. However, a few writers had begun thinking along similar lines earlier: a French sociologist, Emile Durkheim (1825-1917), recognized that groups of people tended to form their own values and norms of behaviour, and were able to subordinate the behaviour of individual group members to these collective values.

Mary Parker Follett (1868-1933) expanded on Durkheim's work, and saw how important it was for managers to understand how and why social groups formed, and to reconcile individual workers' needs with these group needs.

ELTON MAYO AND THE HAWTHORNE STUDIES

The Hawthorne studies proved conclusively that workers could become highly motivated simply by being part of a social/work group, and by being consulted by managers about changes in work practices, etc. However, these social groups were also capable of acting against the organization's interests by setting group norms of production levels and exerting pressure on group members to conform to these levels.

Other proponents of the behavioural management approach include Abraham Maslow, McGregor, Herzberg, and Rensis Likert. Their work will be discussed later when we look at the problems of motivating people.

The systems school of approach

Systems management theory developed during the 1950s and 1960s. The theory does not look at just one aspect of an organization, as the classical and behavioural approaches do, but attempts to explain the behaviour of the organization in terms of the complete entity – people, structure, environment and technology. The organization is seen as a collection of interrelated and interacting parts, which have to be viewed as a whole.

Systems are classed as being either open or closed. A closed system is self-supporting and does not interact with the environment in which it exists. Open systems, however, such as business organizations, do interact with their external environments. A business will receive inputs from its environment (e.g. people, finance, raw materials), which it will use to produce goods, to be sold back into the outside community (see Figure 1.4).

The contribution of systems theory

Morden (1996) defines a system as 'any entity, whether conceptual or physical, which consists of inter-related, interacting and interdependent parts'. He goes on to say that 'systems thinkers distinguish between closed and open systems. Closed systems are self-supporting and do not interact with their environment. Open systems do interact with their environment, from which they receive essential inputs such as information and energy.'

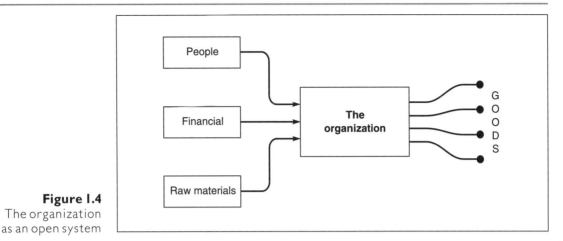

Figure 1.4
The organization
as an open system

In organizational terms a system can be either closed, i.e. not responsive to its environment, or open. Those who support the systems theory approach to management criticize classical and scientific approach thinkers for proposing a closed system approach. It is certainly difficult to imagine a management analysis that was not influenced by technology or culture. There are many studies into the impact of environment on organizations that you may wish to read about. Look for Woodward (1965) and the South Essex Studies, which looked at the impact of technology. Burns and Stalker (1961) examined the relationship between management structure and the capacity to adapt to rapidly changing market conditions. The impact of international competition was addressed by Trist *et al.* (1965), and globalization by Hofstede (1991).

Looking at the organization as an open system has achieved a number of things:

1 It has shown that managers have to consider all the elements which make up the organization – people, structure, technology, environment – as a cohesive whole, and not as separate items.

2 It has highlighted the influence that the external environment can have on the organization (something which has become more marked in recent years) precisely because open systems interact with this environment.

3 It has drawn attention to the importance of planning, because it has demonstrated how organizations have to have a purpose or *raison d'être*, and thus how it is vital for managers to plan.

4 The success of any plan depends upon the monitoring of actual results against the planned results, and then correcting any deviations, i.e. control.

The contingency approach to management

The contingency management approach is a further development of the systems approach. The systems approach emphasizes the complex nature of the organization, with its different contributory variables; contingency theory takes the idea of the complex organization a few stages further on. According to the contingency approach, the style of management and the structure of an organization should reflect and change with changes in that organization's environment.

In contrast to all the other management theories we have looked at, contingency theory does not hold with the idea that there is only one best way of management, and that the principles of this can be applied under all circumstances. Instead, contingency theorists perhaps have a more realistic approach – that the most appropriate style of management will change over time, as the circumstances of the organization change, and that the right management approach for a particular problem will not necessarily be the correct approach for a different problem. To be really effective, managers should use whatever approach is best for the organization at that particular time.

The work of contingency theorists like Woodward, and Burns and Stalker, will be discussed in detail when the effects of factors such as company size, technology, etc., on the structure of organizations are looked at later.

ASPECTS OF MANAGEMENT

Having reviewed a number of management models, it is possible to identify management roles/activities in the paragraphs below, and tie them in with models/styles of management. In this section, see if you can determine the style of management that would result from a manager who was, in paragraph (1), an innovator and keen to adapt.

1 *Innovation/adaptation*. A management style that was both innovative and willing to adapt is one that would cope well with change, and could be described as being flexible.

2 *Growth/resource acquisition*. A tendency towards growth and acquisition is still flexible, but less so than (1) above. This manager would tend towards concentration on the system's competitive position. A feature of this type is that the view can be described as looking outwards from the organization.

3 *Productivity/accomplishment*. This management group is likely to focus on increasing production levels and 'getting things done'. Still with an eye on the competitive position of the system, this style of management tends towards control rather than flexibility, and would display characteristics of motivating increased productivity and accomplishment of stated goals.

4 *Direction/goal clarity*. As with (3) there is, as the name suggests, a clear sense of direction and a real sense of what has to be done. This style is heavily into control, there is no doubt who is in charge.

5 *Stability/control*. Not a lot of change or flexibility here, but an emphasis on stability and knowing what to expect. Words like 'consolidation' and 'continuity' would feature in a description of management expectations.

6 *Documentation/information management*. The use of information is a vital part of this management group. Usually through documentation and fairly comprehensive information systems, this group focuses on making the existing system work, and maintaining what is already there.

7 *Participation/openness*. Still with a leaning towards maintaining the system, the participation model takes a step towards flexibility but is firmly focused on internal structures of the organization.

8 *Commitment/morale*. How the workforce are getting rewarded would be a high priority in this style. The development of human resources is a key aim of this group and by its nature it would tend to be flexible in approach.

Quinn's categories of management model

In *Becoming a Master Manager* (1996), R. E. Quinn *et al.* categorized four models of management thus:

1 *Rational goal*. In this model the ultimate criteria of organizational effectiveness are productivity and profit. This

means that clear direction leads to productive outcomes, so there is a continual emphasis on processes such as goal clarification, rational analysis and action taking. The manager's job is to be a 'decisive director and task-oriented producer'.

2 *Internal process.* This model is complementary to the rational goal model and is best symbolized by a pyramid, indicating stability and continuity. 'The means–ends assumption is based on the belief that routinization (*sic*) leads to stability.' Processes involved in this model are definition of responsibilities, measurement, documentation and record keeping. The structure is hierarchical and decisions may be reached by reference to existing rules, structures and traditions. The ultimate value in the internal process model is efficient work flow and the manager's job is to be a 'technically expert monitor and dependable coordinator'.

3 *Human relations.* The emphasis has shifted significantly to concepts of commitment, cohesion and morale. Here the means–ends assumption is that involvement results in commitment. Team-oriented and requiring deep involvement, the key characteristics of this model are equality, openness, conflict resolution and consensus building. This model clearly does not complement either the rational goal or the internal process models and proved to be difficult to understand and very difficult to practice.

4 *Open systems.* With the need to compete in an environment that is both ambiguous and competitive, a requirement to be adaptable and to find external support became critical. The key concepts are flexibility and responsiveness. The means–ends assumption is that 'continual adaptation and innovation lead to the acquisition and maintenance of external resources'. Quinn describes the key processes as political adaptation, creative problem solving, innovation and management of change. Common vision and shared values are very important because decisions are made quickly and risk is high. The manger 'is expected to be a creative innovator and a politically astute broker (someone who uses power and influence in the organization)'.

Quinn drew up Table 1.1 to summarise the four management models. Look carefully at this table and try to apply relevant parts of it to your own experience of organizations.

Table 1.1
The four management models

	Rational goal	Internal process	Human relations	Open systems
Criteria of effectiveness	Productivity, profit	Stability, continuity	Commitment, cohesion, morale	Adaptability, external support
Means–ends theory	Clear direction leads to productive outcomes	Routinization leads to stability	Involvement results in commitment	Continual adaptation and innovation lead to acquiring and maintaining external resources
Emphasis	Goal clarification, rational analysis and action taking	Defining responsibility, measurement, documentation	Participation, conflict resolution and consensus building	Political adaptation, creative problem-solving, innovation, change management
Climate	Rational economic: 'the bottom line'	Hierarchical	Team-oriented	Innovative, flexible
Role of manager	Director and producer	Monitor and coordinator	Mentor and facilitator	Innovator and broker

Competing values framework

Introduction

There are constant changes in the world in which the manager works. What was best practice today may be inappropriate action tomorrow. Even action taken in a situation yesterday may be found to be ineffective or worse in the same situation today. It is the desire to keep the appropriate options open, not excluding anything that might be right, that the competing values framework enables. It allows for apparent contradiction in management requirements, such as flexibility and control, external and internal focus, at the same time. There are models that share similar emphases; for example, the human relations model and the open systems model tend towards flexibility and towards decentralization and differentiation – it is not all conflict and it is perhaps easier to see in cases where similarities occur that two or more models may be in place simultaneously.

We have already identified the key areas of competence required by managers, and considered how Quinn linked them with the four key management models which he described as Rational Goal, Internal Process, Human Relations and Open Systems. Figure 1.5 arranges these competences of each model around vertical and horizontal axes, giving a figure in the form of a circle. Each model stresses the criteria shown in its relative quadrant of the circle.

There are additional features that may be added to Figure 1.5 to show general values that are associated with the relevant model. For example, the open systems model demonstrates general values of expansion and change. These are complements and are complemented by the neighbouring values of decentralization and differentiation in the adjacent sector. In this complementary state they demonstrate the general value of achieving a competitive position shown on the far right of the model. Look carefully at Figure 1.6 and observe

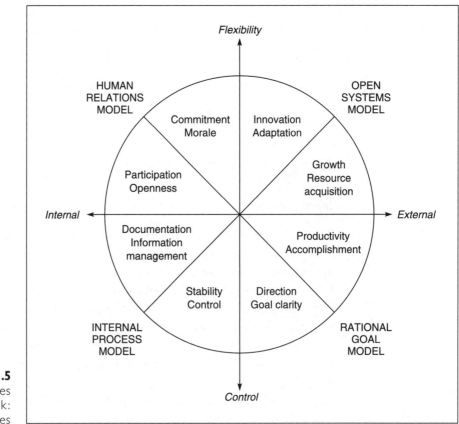

Figure 1.5
Competing values
framework:
competences

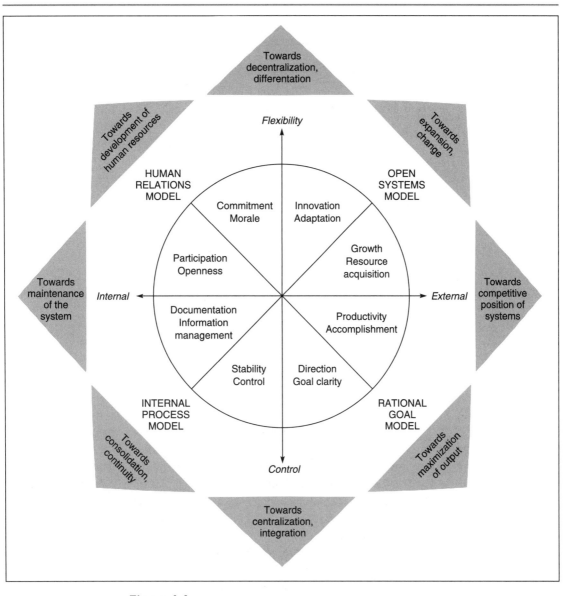

Figure 1.6
Competing values framework: general values

how adjacent values are complementary and fit within the general direction of the axes.

You should also note that there are parallels in the figure too. These are indicated by the axes. Open systems and human relations models share an emphasis on flexibility, whereas open systems and rational goal models share an emphasis on external focus. This is the 'competing values framework' (CVF).

Organizational effectiveness

Quinn argues that managers become trapped in their own particular style and the culture of the organization, perhaps making use of a single strategy in a number of situations. The design of the CVF reflects the complexity faced by managers and can be a tool to 'broaden thinking and increase choice'. However, this would only be the case if:

(a) both the strengths and the weaknesses of each model are understood;

(b) the competences required to make each model work have been acquired;

(c) the manager has the ability to integrate the competences from each model into the 'live' managerial situation.

(a) indicates knowledge = not enough, (b) and (c) indicate an increase in 'behavioural complexity'. Many studies identify a link between behavioural complexity and effective performance.

This is what Quinn says about the framework:

> We want our organizations to be adaptable and flexible, but we also want them to be stable and controlled. We want growth, resource acquisition, and external support, but we also want tight information management and formal communication. We want an emphasis on the value of human resources, but we also want an emphasis on planning and goal setting. In any real organization all of these are, to some extent, necessary.
>
> The framework does not suggest that these oppositions cannot mutually exist in a real system. It does suggest, however, that these criteria, values, and assumptions are at opposites in our minds. We tend to think about them as mutually exclusive; that is, we assume we cannot have two opposites at the same time.
>
> Moreover, in valuing one over the other we tend to devalue or discount its opposite. As we shall see, however, it is possible, in fact, desirable, to perform effectively in the four opposing models simultaneously.
>
> The four models in the framework represent the unseen values over which people, programs, policies, and organizations live and die. ... we often blindly pursue values in one of the models without considering the values in the others. As a result, our choices and our potential effectiveness are reduced.

> For managers the world keeps changing. It changes from hour to hour, day to day, and week to week. The strategies that are effective in one situation are not necessarily effective in another. Even worse, the strategies that were effective yesterday may not be effective in the same situation today. Managers tend to become trapped in their own style and in the organization's cultural values. They tend to employ very similar strategies in a wide variety of situations. The overall framework, consisting of the four models described here, can increase effectiveness. Each model in the framework suggests value in different, even opposite, strategies.

Management responsibilities and tasks vary with the point in the hierarchy at which they operate. All managers need to develop and adapt. Promotion from one level to another requires a manager to understand what remains the same in terms of manager competences, what new ones need to be learned and what old ones should be discarded. 'Effective managerial leaders are behaviourally complex and are able to integrate opposite roles' (Quinn *et al.*, 1996).

The CVF can be further developed and used as a tool to measure effectiveness both of organizations and managers. To apply the framework to organizational effectiveness it is necessary to see that the eight management roles outlined earlier in this chapter will vary intensely depending upon where in the organizational hierarchy the manager is. So a first-level manager in a broker role, say, will have different responsibilities from a senior manager in the same role. Quinn suggests that although the level of responsibility may vary, the key competences related to the manager in the broker role are common to all levels. It is also true that managers may need to learn new competences when they move to a different level in the organization. This means that as managers move from one level to another they need to identify which behaviours to keep and which new ones to learn within the competences demanded of the manager by the organization. To some degree the managerial role is a matter of balancing various skills and activities.

Managerial effectiveness

When we consider the models of management, there are challenges to our ways of thinking and operating. Each theory seemed to present an answer for the particular time or problem being posed. The more we think about organizations, though, the less it seems that any one of the models would be a suitable model to adopt. What becomes clear is that it is necessary to select bits of one and parts of another and some of a third and fourth model if the manager is to achieve the full potential of the management role.

In other words, managerial leaders behave in a complex manner and may have to be able to integrate opposite roles. There are occasions when in becoming committed to particular behaviour they become 'expert' in that role, but as a manager they would risk losing touch with the 'opposite' side of the framework and this could make them ineffective. The concept that a strength can become the source of weakness is not new, but Quinn extended the CVF to incorporate the core notion that, for a manager, low behavioural complexity may lead to unfortunate outcomes for the organization. To do this, Quinn introduces negative zones, where the outcomes are unfortunate, and a positive zone where the outcome is beneficial. Look at Figure 1.7.

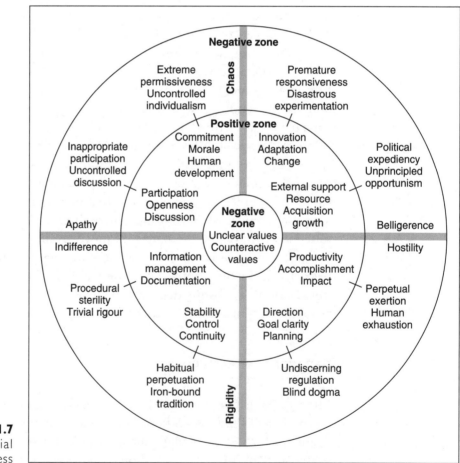

Figure 1.7
Managerial effectiveness

The lack of any key competences in managers will obviously have a detrimental effect on the organization and it will never 'get out' of the central negative zone. The ideal organization, on the chart, will be in the form of a circle firmly within the positive zone. Any over-concentration on one or more behaviour will distort the circle.

The same model type can be applied to managerial effectiveness showing effective ability in each role. So a management team would be expected to hold in 'equal' measure the skills and personnel to carry out all the roles around the perimeter of the diagram, but a lack in one area would, as before, distort the circle (see Figure 1.7).

As Quinn explores the competences required by management, he makes the following point: 'Keep in mind that [each role] is only one of the eight roles and that the ultimate goal is for you to find the appropriate balance across the competences that will allow you to operate well in a world of competing values' (Quinn *et al.*, 1996).

As with the eight roles of management in the organization, Quinn also identified three key competences related to each of the eight roles. The CVF model insists that whilst looking at individual competencces in order improve them, the overall requirement in the organization is for balance. Table 1.2 overleaf shows the eight management leadership roles and their competences, as listed by Quinn.

SUMMARY

This chapter has, of necessity, been concerned with a great deal of theory. In it we have defined the management task as consisting of organizing groups of individuals so that they work together towards common goals or, in other words, deciding what has to be done and getting other people to do it.

We have seen how the management task is achieved through the processes of planning, making decisions, organizing, leading, motivating, communicating and controlling.

We have also looked at how management theories have developed over the years, from the one-dimensional classical (or scientific) and behavioural approaches, through to the multidimensional approach of the systems school, and finally to the contingency theorists' idea of flexible management.

Table 1.2
Management leadership roles

Mentor role:	1 Understanding self and others 2 Communicating effectively 3 Developing subordinates
Facilitator role:	1 Building teams 2 Using participative decision-making 3 Managing conflict
Monitor role:	1 Monitoring individual performance 2 Managing collective performance 3 Managing organizational performance
Coordinator role:	1 Managing projects 2 Designing work 3 Managing across functions
Director role:	1 Visioning, planning and goal setting 2 Designing and organizing 3 Delegating effectively
Producer role:	1 Working productively 2 Fostering a productive work environment 3 Managing time and stress
Broker role:	1 Building and maintaining a power base 2 Negotiating agreement and commitment 3 Presenting ideas
Innovator role:	1 Living with change 2 Thinking creatively 3 Creating change

Part Two

The Management Processes

Planning

The first process of the management task that we are going to look at is planning. Planning is essential not just for successful management, but for the success of almost every activity you can think of. Planning can be defined as deciding in advance what to do, how to do this particular task, when to do it, and who is to do it.

In the context of the management task, planning involves selecting strategies from different possible courses of action, not just for the enterprise as a whole but also for every department or section of it. This requires the organization to define its objectives, and for each department or section to set its own goals and targets in order to meet these objectives, and then to find ways to achieve these goals.

If managers do not plan to some degree, they would have no idea whether or not the organization was accomplishing its purpose. How can you tell if you have reached your destination if you don't know where you want to get to when you set out?

There are four reasons why planning is important for good management:

1 Planning helps to offset the effects of uncertainty and change, on the old principle that to be forewarned is to be forearmed. This is not to say that the planning process removes, or even lessens, the presence of risk; but planning does make managers more aware of the risks involved.
2 Planning focuses attention on the organization's real objectives.
3 Planning helps to make the operations of the organization more economical.
4 Planning aids the process of control, because managers have a benchmark against which they can measure the actual results achieved.

THE DIFFERENT TYPES OF PLANS

There are four different types or levels of planning. They differ from each other, first, in the time-scale that each level covers, and, secondly, in the amount of detail they contain. As a general rule, the longer the time-period covered by the plan, the less the detail contained in the plan, and the greater the degree of uncertainty and risk involved. It is also true that the longer the time-scale of the plan, the more senior are the managers who are involved in the planning process.

The relationships between these factors are illustrated below:

Plans	Time-scale	Degree of detail	Seniority of managers
Strategic	5–10 yrs	Vague	Board level
Management	12 mths	High	Department heads
Operational	1–4 wks	Very high	Junior managers

The overall coordination and implementation of these three levels of planning is usually referred to as *corporate planning*. As its name suggests, corporate planning is concerned with planning for the company as a whole, in order to ensure that the long-term objectives of each department are compatible and do not conflict either with each other, or with the ultimate goals of the organization. Figure 2.1 shows how each planning level dovetails together to form an organized whole.

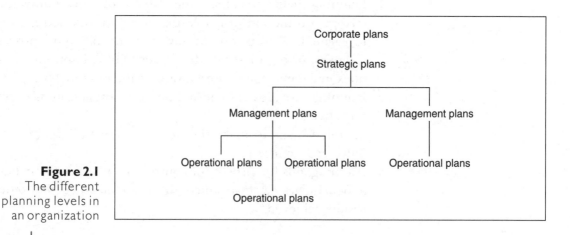

Figure 2.1
The different planning levels in an organization

Corporate planning

Peter Drucker defined corporate planning as:

The continuous process of making present risk-taking decisions systematically and with the greatest knowledge of their futurity; organizing systematically the efforts needed to carry out these decisions, and measuring the results of these decisions against the expectations through organized, systematic feedback.

The purpose of planning on a corporate basis is to define and clarify the goals of the organization as a whole. It involves making appraisals of the organization's major strengths and weaknesses, and considering the external opportunities and threats posed by the organization's environment. These will all affect which goals the organization will be able, realistically, to achieve.

Corporate planning also involves transforming long-term strategies into sufficiently detailed medium-term and operational plans (which can be changed if necessary) to help to ensure that the organization's overall objectives are achieved.

WHY CORPORATE PLANNING IS NECESSARY

A system of corporate planning, involving the coordination of plans for the entire business over a period of several years, is necessary for several reasons:

1 The importance that the real objectives of an organization are identified cannot be emphasized enough, and that, these having been identified, the whole business works towards them using co-ordinated strategies. A business with disparate goals will, at best, not perform as successfully as it could and, at worst, will tear itself apart. You can imagine the difficulties generated within conglomerates if organizations like Hanson did not have cohesive objectives.

2 The degree of competition for finite resources within an organization increases with the size of the organization, and this creates a need for central planning and control, rather than planning by individual departments or managers.

3 The ever-quickening pace of change means that organizations have to adapt and react to change *corporately* to survive, rather than on an individual departmental basis.

Strategic planning

Strategic planning is the long-range planning part of the corporate planning process. It involves establishing where the organization wants to be in five or ten years' time; where it is actually likely to be, in view of any forecast changes in its business environment; and developing long-term plans to bridge any possible gaps between where it wants to go, and where it looks like ending up.

Examples of long-term strategies are the development of new products, the opening up of new markets, and the expansion into different areas of business.

Management planning

This is a lower, intermediate level of planning. Management planning is concerned with, for example, the following areas:

1 Determining the structure of the organization.
2 Establishing functional and departmental objectives and targets, in line with the strategic plans and aims.
3 Deciding upon product/sales mixes.
4 Setting budgets, and planning staff requirements.

Operational planning

The lowest level of planning is that of operational planning, covering weekly and day-to-day planning. It involves the line manager and management at supervisory and foreman levels in setting specific tasks and key targets to help to achieve the relevant management plan. Some of these targets are expressed in financial terms; others are expressed in measures such as output per employee, the percentage utilization of machines, cost levels, etc. Once these targets have been set, they should be monitored and revised as necessary. If revisions are made in these short-term targets, then the whole plan should be altered accordingly, so that the long-term perspective is maintained but the entire plan is kept up to date.

THE PLANNING CYCLE

The successful operation of most organizations is based upon planning. This does not just happen, however. It results from a systematic process, which can be a lengthy and thought-provoking exercise. The process involved in corporate planning is designed so that organizations can establish the following:

1 What their main objectives are, and just why and for what purpose they exist.
2 What opportunities and threats are presented by their external environment.
3 What their own internal strengths and weaknesses are, especially in relation to the external environment they operate in.
4 A sound base for their strategic and operational planning.
5 Policies which will allow their employees to follow and achieve the companies' objectives.

The planning process consists of several stages, and these are shown in Figure 2.2.

Setting objectives

The first stage in the planning process is the identification and description of the organization's objectives. The importance of this step cannot be overstated. Objectives are the ends towards which the activities of an organization are directed; they give purpose and meaning to the organization's existence. For example, for a public service such as The Post Office, the primary purpose of the organization would be 'to provide a service for the community'.

There are two types of objectives. The first type includes those that lay down the overall purpose of the organization (as above). The second type includes those that set out the organization's long-term aims, defining what sort of organization it intends to be in the future, and what kind of business the organization expects to be conducting.

The traditional overall objective for businesses is to maximize profits. However, this is a rather unrealistic aim, not least because it is almost impossible to judge whether or not the company has maximized its profits! A project which was not undertaken might have yielded greater returns than one chosen in its place; there is

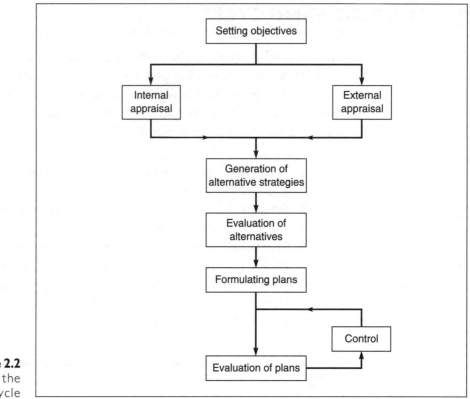

Figure 2.2
The stages in the
planning cycle

very little way of telling for sure. Maximizing profits in the short term may also reduce shareholders' returns over a longer period.

This traditional maximization of profits objective, therefore, is usually amended to the achievement of sufficient profits to ensure the company's survival and growth, and to give shareholders an acceptable return on their investment.

Cyert and March (1963) have put forward the behavioural, or stakeholder, theory of the firm. According to this, the organization is made up of a coalition of different interest groups, or stake-holders: managers, employees, shareholders, customers, suppliers, and so on. Therefore, the organization's long-term objectives are set to cover a wide variety of areas (such as market share, sales growth, public responsibility, etc.), in order to satisfy the diverse interests of these different groups. The reason why these different objectives have to be set is due to the fact that the owners of modern companies are often not the same people who control businesses in practice, because of the emergence of multiple share-holders (who are often themselves other corporate bodies) and pro-fessional managers. However, the different objectives still have to be compatible, because an organization cannot successfully operate while heading in opposite directions.

Frequently set objectives

Peter Drucker, in *The Practice of Management,* outlines seven areas in which the majority of organizations establish objectives in order to try and satisfy the differing interests of each group of stakeholders. These objectives cover the organization's profitability, market share and standing, productivity, management and employee performance, technical innovation, social responsibility, and resource management.

1 *Profitability.* The primary goal of any profit-making business has to be growth in its earnings per share ratio. When planning long-term strategies for earnings growth, aspects such as net dividends, taxation, profit and inflation have to be considered. Non-profit-making organizations, such as charities and public services, while not having to produce earnings for shareholders, still have either to keep within a budget or to generate sufficient net profit to fund their activities. Thus both these sorts of organization have to set profit-related goals.

2 *Market share and standing.* Corporate marketing objectives can cover areas such as what products are to be sold in which markets; whether or not the organization should aim to be a market leader in terms of pricing or product development; what degree of market penetration it should seek; and the standards of service required.

3 *Productivity.* Productivity is very important for an organization, as productivity and profitability are closely linked. Productivity objectives are normally expressed in terms of output per employee, and output in relation to plant, material yields, and costs.

4 *Management and employee performance.* Many businesses set objectives covering the development of good management/ employee relations, workforce training and development, and future management structure. Management performance is covered a little later in this chapter in the section on management by objectives.

5 *Technical innovation.* The company has to decide whether or not it should aim to be a technical innovator in terms of its

products, or whether it will follow the lead set by others. The organization's ability to be an innovator depends upon the technical and creative resources at its disposal. However, a technical policy should be devised, and objectives for research and development (or just development) set, in conjunction with the company's marketing and manufacturing objectives. Schmidt plc, a manufacturer of street cleaning equipment, includes in its objectives the wish to be at the forefront of technology in the industry and, to achieve this, to allocate 12 per cent of turnover to research and development.

6 *Social and public responsibility.* Organizations are increasingly setting objectives covering their social responsibilities, such as the preservation and improvement of the environment, consumer protection objectives, improvements in working conditions, and sponsorship and participation in local community activities. Unilever sets as one objective 'to contribute to a cleaner environment'. Many organizations, such as Shell, British Gas and Saab, use these objectives as part of their marketing policy.

7 *Resource utilization.* Many organizations set objectives which relate to the efficient use of physical and financial resources.

Whatever objectives are set by the organization, they must be specific goals, which the senior management team can translate into plans and strategies for action.

INVESTIGATE

Take a few minutes just to think about your own company, department, or an organization you are familiar with, and note down what you see as its objectives, under each of the above headings.

Internal appraisal

The purpose of an internal business appraisal is to allow the organization to identify just which functions it is good at, and which functions it is less successful at undertaking. This should enable the organization to forecast what might be the results in a few years' time if it continues as it is, without reducing its weaknesses and capitalizing on its strengths, i.e. a 'steady as she goes' strategy. The areas which should be examined include the following:

1 *Product mix.* The range of the company's products, together with their age, quality, and the durability of their appeal to customers, together with the company's pricing policy and competitiveness compared with rival products, should all be analysed. The company's record of introducing successful new products is also very important, especially if the company is relying upon a few elderly successful products for a large proportion of its profits.

2 *Markets.* The range of markets that the company sells its products in, as well as market share and growth rate, and the composition of each market by customer type, geographical area, and so on. If an organization is very reliant upon one particular section of the population for its market, it might consider broadening its appeal, just as Radio 2 has tried to attract younger listeners as its traditional 'market' ages.

3 *Production and* supply. The company should analyse trends in output compared to production capacity; productivity levels; the quality of finished products; wastage and spoilage rates; whether its raw material suppliers are efficient in terms of delivery times, quality, etc., or not; the efficiency of stock control methods, and so on.

4 *Research and development.* The organization's R&D policy should be compared with that of its competitors, in terms of its appropriateness for the company, its success rate in developing new products and processes, etc.

5 *Finance.* The company's finances should be examined in terms of present and projected performance, compared with past performance trends and inter-firm or industrial averages, in order to show the relative strength of the company. The effectiveness of routine financial reporting, budgeting and controls should also be looked at.

6 *Personnel.* The age, ability and skills of the company's workforce should be analysed in terms of overall productivity, together with such matters as the adequacy of staff training, and the state of industrial relations.

7 *Management.* Again, the age, ability and skills of the company's management team should be examined, plus management recruitment and promotion policies, and especially the provisions for succession to senior management posts.

8 *Organizational structure.* The suitability of the organization's structure for the company's business, for example the channels of communication, the lines of authority, the degree of independence given to managers to act, etc.

It is very important that an internal appraisal is an objective exercise, which does not seek to apportion blame for past mistakes. Constructive ideas for solving problems are obviously far more helpful than recriminations and office political point-scoring.

Having said that, it is also important that any appraisal is an honest and thorough one. The key to this is the questioning of the reasons behind every action, i.e. the vital thing is to ask just *why* something is done, and not to accept 'it's always been done this way' as a proper answer without any close examination.

INVESTIGATE

Using the appropriate areas outlined above, jot down the strengths and weaknesses of your company department, or college, as you see them.

External appraisal

An appraisal of the organization's external business environment is the counterpart of the internal appraisal. Such an external appraisal reviews the developments in the outside world in which the organization exists, and tries to forecast possible changes in it which could pose either a serious threat to the company (in which case it can take action to lessen the impact), or opportunities which can be exploited for the good of the business (Figure 2.3).

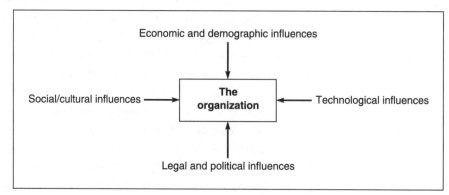

Figure 2.3 Environmental influences on the organization

The business environment is covered in more detail in Part Four; here we will just look briefly at some of those areas within the outside environment which the organization should examine during an external appraisal.

1 *The economic environment.* An organization which conducts its business exclusively in one country will need to focus on its domestic economy, while a multinational company will have to assess the international economic situation. However, both will need to collect and assess information which is relevant to their marketing plans, for example changes in the gross domestic product, changes in fixed capital information requirements, changes in consumer income and expenditure, inflation forecasts, the opening up of the European Union markets, etc.

2 *The political environment.* An organization will have to assess the political environment within which it operates, in terms of its stability and how political decisions will affect the organization's business. For example, a company operating in Hong Kong will need to review and take into consideration the uncertain political future of that place when forming its plans. On a more mundane level, an appraisal of the political environment should include such areas as government action in terms of taxation and business subsidies, spending, import duties, and the possible effects of a change of government.

3 *The legal environment.* The external appraisal will also have to examine the legal environment. The organization will be affected to some degree by, for example, the legal changes resulting from the establishment of the single European market, relating to competition rules, patents, the sale of goods, pollution controls, working regulations and industrial standards. The change to the law on Sunday trading in the UK, and the EU ban on tobacco advertising, are both examples of how the legal environment affects organizations.

4 *The social environment.* Closely linked to the political and legal environments is the social environment, because it is often thanks to pressure from certain social groups that politicians bring in new laws and regulations. The social environment has been affecting companies more and more recently, and changes in consumer tastes and perceptions can have a major impact on a business. For example, the growing awareness of

environmental matters has led to many companies having to alter their production processes and images radically. Future changes in demographic trends and in the physical make-up of the population (with the increase in numbers of pensioners and decrease in people of working age) will also affect companies in varying degrees.

5 *The technological environment.* Technological factors, i.e. changes in the supply of raw materials, production methods, and new product developments, need to be considered especially carefully in an external appraisal, because of the speed with which changes in technology are occurring.

INVESTIGATE

As with the section on internal appraisal, take a few minutes to think what threats and opportunities to your organization are posed by the external environment, and how any threats could be minimized and opportunities taken advantage of.

Clearly, the importance of each environment type varies according to the industry concerned. The social environment, will be particularly important to BAT Industries plc with significant tobacco investments, whereas the technological environment will be crucial to Amstrad Electronics.

Any external appraisal not only must examine the present situation within the environment and its on-going changes, but it should also try to assess any likely changes in the future. Such forecasting of likely environmental change is often little better than intelligent guesswork, due to the unpredictable nature of many different variables and events. However, the widespread use of computer technology to create models and 'most likely' scenarios, through the manipulation of large amounts of data, has made it easier for companies to make reasonable predictions. But it should be remembered that forecasting environmental changes will help to reduce some of the risk involved; however, uncertainty will always be present in the planning process.

Both internal and external appraisals should be concerned with identifying the few areas considered to be crucial for the organization's success or failure over the coming five or ten years. The identification of the major strengths and weaknesses of the business, and the opportunities and threats posed by its environment, is sometimes referred to as SWOT analysis.

Evaluation of alternatives

The next stage in the planning process is to choose and evaluate the possible strategies which will make the most of the organization's strengths and the business opportunities presented to it by its external environment, while correcting any major weaknesses and minimizing external threats to its survival. Hopefully, different ideas will have presented themselves during the SWOT analysis, and usually the problem is not in the generation of alternative plans, but in the reduction of the alternatives to a manageable number of those promising to be the most fruitful for the business!

The internal and external appraisals may also have thrown up a fairly large number of problems and opportunities; in this situation it is obviously better for the organization to rate them in terms of their urgency and importance and to concentrate on the three or four most vital ones.

The possible alternatives have to be examined to establish just what their effects will be on the company. They should be evaluated in terms of whether or not the company will be better off if the particular idea is adopted than if no change were made; the effect of the change on the organization's profits year by year; and whether or not the organization would be able to raise sufficient funding to meet all the anticipated expenditure required under the scheme.

The alternatives, of course, must also be evaluated in terms of meeting the organization's objectives. But it has to be borne in mind that the organization will have several objectives, and that fulfilling one objective may create constraints for the other objectives. Therefore, the organization may have to rank its objectives in order of their importance, and in the case of a clash of interests, a proposal which helps to fulfil an important objective should be chosen in preference to one which only fulfils lesser objectives.

There are three reasons why organizations do not evaluate possible alternatives in sufficient depth:

1 The large number of available alternatives often makes the task very daunting.
2 The amount of time needed for proper, detailed evaluations is regarded as excessive.
3 The uncertainty inherent in forecasting is assumed to make any detailed evaluation pointless.

However, if the alternatives are not considered properly, it invalidates the whole planning process.

The need to consider different ways of achieving given objectives on a regular basis is, generally, most keenly felt by private sector organizations, whose markets are under constant threat from competitors. However, the need also exists in the public sector, especially now that budget constraints require all managers to make the most efficient use of the resources under their control.

Formulating plans

When the different alternatives have been evaluated properly against the criteria set by the organization, and a specific course of action chosen, the point is reached at which broad strategies have to be translated into detailed plans. It is now that the implications for the various parts of the organization are made clear: specific year-by-year targets for each division and department are laid down, perhaps with an indication of the reasons for any changes from current targets; and the resources available to meet those targets are set out.

Plans vary greatly in the degree of detail contained in them. Some private sector organizations, such as the General Electric Company (GE), lay down financial targets for each individual company within the group, and then give the subsidiaries considerable freedom as to the strategies they adopt to meet those targets. However, at the other end of the spectrum, public sector organizations tend to be much more restricted in the policies which have to be adopted and the resources available to each division, with detailed budgets being set for equipment, materials, staff, etc.

The elements of commercial business plans tend to be made up in terms of particular products for various markets, and will lay down the resources required in order to implement them. The plans may include areas such as image as well as products and markets, although these latter factors usually dominate.

The coordination of short- and long-range plans

As we have seen, the strategic part of an organization's corporate plan will give a broad outline of the policies which the company intends to adopt in order to achieve its objectives. These policies are then broken down into management and operational plans, together with the establishment of key targets. It is often at this stage of the planning process that a serious error is made, in that these shorter-range plans are frequently made without reference to the long-range plans.

The integration of these long- and short-range plans is extremely important. No short-range target should be set unless it contributes to the achievement of the relevant long-range plan and overall corporate objectives. Sometimes, short-range decisions not only fail to do this, but actually impede, or require changes in, the company's strategic plans. It is part of the manager's job to consider immediate decisions and judge whether or not they contribute to the organization's long-range plans. Managers throughout the organization should be briefed regularly on its long-term plans and objectives, so that they can make decisions which are consistent with these aims.

Evaluation and control

The final stage of the planning process is that of evaluation and control. This involves the following:

1 Establishing performance targets.
2 Comparing the actual results achieved with these performance targets.
3 Analysing any deviations in the results from the acceptable tolerance limits.
4 Implementing any necessary modifications.

Effective evaluation and control needs an efficient monitoring procedure, which measures the extent of progress towards the fulfilment of set targets, and produces reports for the managers concerned with the relevant results and information, so that any problems can be remedied quickly.

Planning can be regarded as a closed loop system (Figure 2.4), with feedback on the results of the plans used to update them if necessary, and to check on their progress. Plans should never be so sacred that they cannot be changed and adapted if managers see fit.

MANAGEMENT BY OBJECTIVES

Some of you may well be familiar with the idea of 'management by objectives', and, indeed, may be working in organizations which use such a system of management. The phrase was first used by Peter

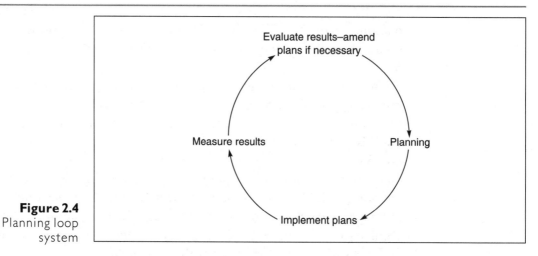

Figure 2.4
Planning loop
system

Drucker in the 1950s; management by objectives was one of his principles of management.

Both Drucker and John Humble (another advocate of management by objectives) see the process as a way of coordinating and integrating the short- and long-term plans of the organization with the goals of junior and senior managers, and the need of individual managers to be able to contribute directly to the organization's success. Drucker comments that often a common organizational target is very difficult to aim at:

> in the business enterprise managers are not automatically directed towards a common goal. On the contrary, business, by its very nature, contains three powerful factors of misdirection: in the specialised work of most managers; in the hierarchical structure of management, and in the difference in vision and work and the resultant insulation of various levels of management.

The MBO process

Under the MBO process, the jobs of managers are analysed to establish the key areas where results are necessary. Then a list of key tasks which have to be performed is drawn up from these key areas. This list normally consists of no more than eight or nine tasks, and it should be drawn up jointly by the individual managers concerned and their superiors.

The list of key tasks is used to establish certain short-term goals which are the focus for immediate priority action by each manager. Each task is given a performance standard against which attainment can be measured over a set period. These standards are either quantitative (e.g. the sales of product X should be increased by 15% over the coming year), or qualitative (e.g. the report on Y should be acceptable to the Board). Usually, control data for each task are also specified. These are sources of information against which the fulfilling of the set standards can be checked. In the first example above, the control data would be the relevant sales figures for the year.

At the end of the period, the results of the tasks should be reviewed in order to assess the manager's performance. Again, this review should be carried out jointly by both the manager concerned and the manager's superior. This allows individuals to gauge how well they are doing their jobs, and allows realistic discussions between them and their superiors about their progress and achievements. Management by objectives also allows standards and specific targets to be set for managers who do not have obviously quantifiable jobs.

The advantages of management by objectives

Management by objectives has several advantages for organizations:

1 It forces managers to think of planning for results, rather than merely planning work; this is very important, because only results-orientated planning makes any sense.
2 It increases commitment throughout the company to the aims of the organization, because everyone should be working towards definite targets which are all well coordinated.
3 It forces companies to clarify their internal structures and organizational roles.
4 It helps in the development of effective control systems, as well as leading to more effective planning.

Problems with management by objectives

1 A common cause of problems with MBO is due to senior managers not spending enough time teaching and explaining the system and the ideas behind it to the rest of the organization.

2 There is often a failure to give adequate guidelines to those managers setting their subordinates' objectives. Managers have to know what the corporate goals are and how their tasks fit in with them.

3 Another problem with MBO is that short-term targets are usually set, which risks emphasizing short-term at the expense of long-range planning.

4 Problems can arise in setting up a system that cannot adapt quickly to changes within and outside the organization. Although targets may cease to be meaningful if they are changed too often, it is none the less unwise to expect a manager to work towards a target that has been made obsolete by revised corporate objectives or changes in the environment.

WHY PLANNING SYSTEMS CAN FAIL

It is obvious that planning systems can fail. The reasons for such failure are summarized briefly below:

1 The single most important reason for the failure of planning systems is a lack of commitment to the planning process, particularly among an organization's senior management.

2 Resistance to change among middle and junior management and among the ordinary workforce.

3 The failure to set meaningful, verifiable targets, and the absence of clear aims for the business as a whole.

4 The failure to appreciate the scope of the plans and the all-encompassing nature of the planning system.

5 Over-reliance on past experiences: it is not always true that what was done in the past is likely to be appropriate in future situations.

6 Poor and inflexible control techniques. Planning cannot be effective unless those people responsible for the system know how well it is working.

7 A hostile external environment, i.e. a period of change so rapid as to require constant adjustment to plans, without it ever being possible to achieve identifiable results.

8 A lack of clear delegation in the organization. It is very difficult for people to plan if they do not know what their jobs are and how these relate to others in the organization.

A lack of clear lines of authority also makes it difficult to take decisions.

HOW PLANNING SYSTEMS CAN BE EFFECTIVE

Planning systems can be effective, however, if senior management establish a favourable climate for planning. At each level of management targets must be set, managers must be involved in the planning process throughout, reviews must be made of subordinates' plans and performances, and checks must be made to ensure that people have appropriate assistance and information. An organization's senior management team is the single most important factor in determining the success or failure of the planning system, and so the team must be committed to the planning process. Good organization is also needed; in any business which plans effectively, planning and doing are not separated.

Communication is also a vital part of planning. If planning is to be effective the goals, strategies and policies of the organization have to be communicated. Otherwise, the planning process becomes unco-ordinated and flounders.

A lack of communication can create what is known as a planning gap. In this situation the senior management understands the organization's goals and the plans; the workforce knows what it has to do each day; but the middle-level managers do not understand how their departmental goals and policies tie in with those of the organization as a whole. Effective planning is fostered when managers are given the opportunity to contribute to the plans which affect their particular areas of authority.

SUMMARY

In this chapter we have looked at the reasons why planning is so important for *all* organizations, and how a systematic, coordinated planning process can make the difference between an average business and a successful one.

We have seen that there are four different types of planning — corporate, strategic, management and operational — each of which covers a different time-span, involves different degrees of detail and uncertainty, and is carried out at different management levels.

The stages in a systematic planning process have been examined in detail, together with some of the reasons why corporate planning can fail, and what steps can be taken by managers to help to ensure its success.

The vital ingredient for a successful system of planning is the active support and backing of the senior management team in general, and the chief executive in particular, because such a system affects the entire organization and requires that everyone works towards common, well-communicated objectives and goals.

CHECKLIST: CHAPTER 2

After this chapter you will be able to identify:

1 Four types/levels of planning:
- Corporate plans
- Strategic plans
- Management plans
- Operational plans

2 That corporate planning should establish
- Objectives
- Opportunities and threats in external environment
- Strengths and weaknesses
- A sound base for strategic operational planning
- Policies to enable objectives to be achieved

3 The planning cycle:
- Setting objectives
- Internal/external appraisal
- Alternative strategies
- Evaluate alternatives
- Formulate plans
- Evaluate plans

4 Management by objectives:
- Managers' jobs analysed to identify key areas where results are needed
- The advantages and disadvantages of MBO

5 Planning failures:
- Lack of commitment
- Resistance to change
- Poor target setting

CHAPTER 3

Decision-making

Decision-making – that process of thought and action that leads to a decision – lies at the heart of management. Managers spend their time choosing between alternative courses of action on the basis of the information available to them at the time; in other words, making decisions.

Decision-making is closely linked with the management process of planning, which we h[...] is all about taking decisions about futu[...] *Ackoff* [...] 1970) writes that planning is in fact a [...] aking, with three distinguishing characteristics:

1 It is anticipatory decision-making. Planning 'is a process of deciding what to do and how to do it before action is required'. Because it takes time to decide what to do it is necessary to plan ahead.

2 Planning involves a set of interdependent decisions. This set of decisions is often too large to handle all at once, and therefore is better dealt with in stages. Decisions made in the earlier stages will affect later decisions, and vice versa; it may sometimes be necessary to alter an earlier decision in the light of decisions taken later on.

3 Planning is directed towards making decisions which would not otherwise be made.

Just as in the planning process, different levels of management have to make different types of decisions, with differing amounts of risk and uncertainty attached to them, and which are of differing time-spans.

Supervisors and junior levels of management have (usually!) fairly clear-cut decisions to make, where the problems and their solutions are routine. Decisions made at this level normally have to be made quickly. The resulting success or failure of such decisions is also quickly apparent. The time-span is short, and there is usually little uncertainty associated with this level of decision-making.

However, as managers progress up the organizational hierarchy, the decisions they have to make result in longer and longer gaps between the problems being noted and the results of their decisions becoming known. Decisions are also subject to more and more uncertainty and risk, and the consequences of wrong decisions become more and more costly. You will find that, often, senior managers delegate some problems to their subordinates in order to prepare them for this type of decision-making.

In this chapter we will look at some of the theories behind decision-making, and then go on to examine the decision-making process. Finally, we will briefly discuss some of the techniques used to analyse and evaluate possible solutions to problems.

THEORIES OF DECISION-MAKING

There are two main schools of thought underlying the decision-making process: the classical theory and the behavioural theories of writers such as Simon and Cyert and March.

The classical theory of decision-making

The classical theory of rational, economic decision-making assumes that the decision-maker:

1 Has complete knowledge of all the possible alternative courses of action.
2 Has complete knowledge of the consequences of taking every alternative.
3 Can attach definite payoffs to each possible outcome.
4 Can put each payoff in order, from the highest to the lowest payoff.

Obviously, these assumptions are fairly unrealistic and are rarely valid because of various factors, such as the following:

1 Uncertainty – possible alternative courses of action may not be known or identifiable; and the outcomes and payoffs of any individual course of action may also be uncertain.

2 The decision-maker may have many criteria, both quantifiable and unquantifiable, by which he or she wishes to value a possible course of action, and not merely the monetary payoff.

3 There may be practical limitations on the analysis of the courses of action. The decision-maker may lack the mental capacity to evaluate and compare all the possible alternatives. A search for, and evaluation of, all possible alternatives is also usually impracticable, because of the limited time and resources which can normally be devoted to any one problem.

The behavioural theory of decision-making

It was Simon (1957) who put forward the idea of 'administrative man' as a more realistic alternative to the 'rational, economic man' of the classical theorists. 'Administrative man' is a satisficer rather than a perfectionist, and his decision-making behaviour can be summed up as follows:

1 When choosing between alternatives, decision-makers look for a scheme which provides a satisfactory payoff, not the best possible payoff.

2 Decision-makers recognize that their perception of the world is only a very simplified model of the real world.

3 A satisficer can make a choice without first determining all the possible alternatives, and without ascertaining that these are actually all the alternatives.

Satisficing decisions

Simon proposed that satisficers simplify the decision-making process in various ways, in order to define the decision within the bounds of their mental capacities. In this way decision-makers limit their search to the identification of a course of action that merely satisfies some minimum set of requirements. This does not mean that large numbers of alternative schemes are not examined, but the alternatives are examined sequentially, and the first satisfactory one to be evaluated is usually the alternative selected.

THE DECISION-MAKING PROCESS

There are several steps in the decision-making process:

1 The problem must be defined – this involves diagnosing the *real* problem and not just the symptoms of it, as well as distinguishing between conditions which are 'musts' and conditions which are 'shoulds'. For example, a staffing problem can be analysed as 'We *must* employ someone who can do the job at the given salary, and they *should* fit in well with others in the organization'.

2 The relevant facts have to be gathered together and analysed – this involves finding out which people have the most experience of the problem and the most information about it.

3 Develop alternative solutions – this is a natural extension to the previous stage of fact gathering, and many possible solutions will arise naturally from it. A number of solutions should really be examined, rather than the first feasible one being chosen. This can be viewed as a compromise between the extremes of both satisficing and economic decision-making.

4 Evaluate the alternative solutions – in terms of solving the original problem and meeting the organization's overall objectives.

5 Select the best alternative – the choice will be based on the available information and will usually be a compromise solution. Drucker (1955) suggests four factors which should be used to judge potential solutions:

   (a) the risk involved compared to the expected gain;
   (b) the amount of effort that each alternative involves;
   (c) the time-span involved with each alternative; this is especially important if dramatic changes are needed immediately; and
   (d) the availability of any additional resources which may be required.

6 Analyse the possible consequences of the decision – this is important so that any anticipated problems can be dealt with

successfully. For example, there may be resistance to change within the organization, or additional funding may have to be raised.

7 Implement the decision – this will involve setting up a budget and defining responsibilities to ensure the project's completion. There will also need to be a system of checking and control to ensure that the decision is implemented correctly.

Decision-making and problem-solving

As we have seen, decision-making is closely linked to the management task of planning. It is obviously also similar to the task of problem-solving. Problem-solving and decision-making are not actually the same, although you may be forgiven for thinking that they are!

Luthans (1981) describes problem-solving as 'any goal-directed activity that must overcome some type of barrier to accomplish the goal'. Problem-solving is thus a more extensive activity than decision-making, and it is usually the need to solve a problem that creates the need for a decision. Unfortunately, in problem-solving the emphasis is too often placed exclusively on obtaining answers, when it is just as important to be sure that the right problem has been identified!

Steps in the problem-solving process

Elbing (1980) describes the management task of problem-solving as a five-step process:

1 The manager perceives a problem, perhaps without a clear, rational reason for doing so.
2 The manager responds by attempting to find out the causes of the problem.
3 In addition, the manager must attempt to define the nature of the problem.
4 The manager must select a solution, which will involve making a decision.
5 The implementation of the chosen course of action, whether or not it actually leads to a solution of the problem.

Figure 3.1 shows how the stages involved in decision-making and problem-solving combine to form a seamless process.

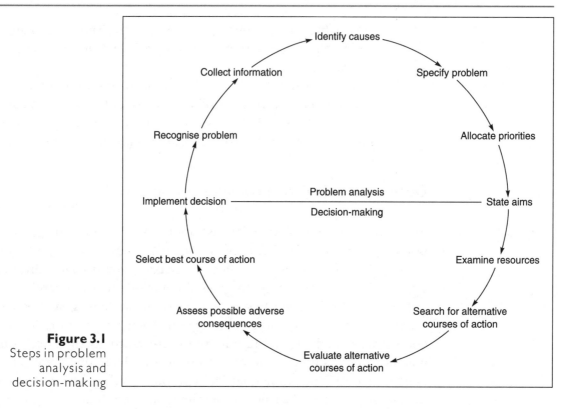

Figure 3.1
Steps in problem
analysis and
decision-making

The steps in decision-making

1 *Statement of aims.* It is very necessary to have a clear understanding of what needs to be achieved, or what the real,
underlying problem is, particularly when a number of managers are involved in the decision-making. A simple example
of the importance of identifying the underlying problem is
that of the driver who notices that her car is low on oil.
Topping it up may solve the immediate problem, but only
temporarily if there is an oil leak, and the latter could (if it
isn't fixed) result in serious engine damage.

2 *Examination of resources.* Any consideration of the available
resources should cover the three critical areas of:

    (a)   people – who is available to help; who has experience and
training which could help; how many people are available
to do any extra work involved?

    (b)   finances – what can be spent on the project, and the limits
of financial authority?

    (c)   materials and equipment – where can the work be done;
the availability of raw materials; does any specialized

equipment need to be used, and if so, is such equipment available?

3 *Searching for alternatives.* Some guidelines are suggested below which may help when alternative courses of action are being looked for:

(a) make use of any knowledge and experience which is already available; ready-made solutions often already exist, written up in reports; a little digging around in the appropriate journals can save a considerable amount of time and money later on.

(b) ask penetrating questions, don't just accept things at their face value.

(c) apply creative, lateral thinking.

4 *Evaluation of alternatives.* Evaluating the alternative solutions involves, to begin with, assessing how well each meets the desired end. The next part is concerned with assessing the advantages and disadvantages of each possible solution against one another to arrive at a balanced final decision. There are a number of techniques which can be used to evaluate alternatives. These are discussed later on in this chapter.

5 *Selecting the best course of action.* Although we can trace a sequence of logical thought processes through each stage of decision-making, at the moment of decision the logic may not be clear. The manager will, in effect, be putting a value on those factors which cannot be formally evaluated and which may, therefore, have been omitted from the earlier steps in the process. The mark of a good manager is 'flair' – that innate sense, possibly developed through long experience, of the illogicalities in human behaviour and of the element of chance in the business environment.

6 *Implementation. A* decision has no value to the business; indeed, it might be said that for all practical purposes it does not exist, until it has been put into effect. The true test of confidence in the decision-making process comes when the decision has to be converted into a plan of action; it is then that money, people and other resources are committed. A systematic approach to the whole process of problem analysis and decision-making is essential if only

for this purpose − to give managers enough confidence in the decision to initiate action.

CRITERIA FOR GOOD DECISION-MAKING

Perhaps the most serious difficulty in decision-making is the existence of objectives and aims which cannot be quantified. Janis and Mann (1977) recognized this problem and suggested making the assumption that a decision is likely to be more satisfactory when the quality of the decision-making procedure is high. They set out seven major criteria which can be used to help determine whether or not the decision-making process is of a high quality:

1 The identification of a wide range of alternative courses of action.
2 Consideration of the full range of objectives used and the values implied by this choice.
3 A careful consideration of the costs and risks of both the positive and negative consequences of each alternative.
4 A diligent search for new information for the further evaluation of possible solutions.
5 The acceptance of any new information, even when it does not support the course of action initially preferred.
6 The re-examination of the positive and negative consequences of all known alternatives, before making a final choice.
7 Making detailed plans for implementing the chosen course of action, including contingency plans in the event of various known risks actually occurring.

Janis and Mann use the term 'vigilant information processing' (VIP) to describe a decision process where all seven criteria have been met to the best of the decision-maker's ability.

DECISION ANALYSIS TECHNIQUES

There are many techniques for evaluating possible solutions, ranging from the fairly simple to complex mathematically-based techniques. The ones outlined below are some of the more common ones in use.

Marginal or incremental costing

Marginal costing compares the additional revenues which are forecasted to be generated by each possible scheme with the forecasted costs of each. It is a useful technique because it emphasizes variables instead of constants and averages. However, the drawback of marginal costing is that it can be very difficult to quantify adequately the benefits which may result from a project (especially if the project under consideration is a long-term, radical one) and all the costs which could be incurred.

Discounted cash flow appraisal

Discounted cash flow (DCF) methods of appraisal are probably the most widely used analysis techniques. They are based on the assumption that money which is received now is worth more than money which is received at some point in the future. This is because of factors such as inflation, and because cash received now can earn interest in the intervening period.

The two main methods of DCF appraisal are finding a project's net present value (NPV), and calculating its internal rate of return (IRR). Calculating the NPV involves discounting all the project's forecasted future net cash flows to their present value. The IRR of a project is the discount rate which gives an NPV of zero. In investment terms, if the IRR of a project is greater than the firm's cost of capital, then it is worth undertaking. When used to evaluate possible schemes, both methods enable projects' profitabilities over the course of their lifetimes to be compared.

Cost–benefit analysis

This evaluation technique is used when the data involved cannot be quantified, but when things like the social benefits and costs of a possible project (such as pollution or unemployment) are important in making the decision. Cost–benefit analysis works by weighing the effectiveness of each alternative in meeting the scheme's objectives against its potential costs. The major drawback of the method is its subjectiveness. However, cost–benefit analysis can be very useful, especially if used together with other, more objective, appraisal techniques.

Sensitivity analysis

Sensitivity analysis questions the assumptions behind each possible plan to see how valid they are. The dependence of the plan on each assumption is also assessed, in order to find out what degree of risk is being taken, and on how sound a basis. For example, a project which depends on a certain sum being raised by a share issue for its success should be reassessed if the probability of such a sum being raised is low. Sensitivity analysis has the advantage of being easy to use, especially with computer spreadsheet packages.

Risk analysis

Risk analysis gauges the range of each variable in a project and the probability of it occurring, for example the chances of the cost exceeding or falling below the best estimate, and by how much.

Decision tree analysis

Decision trees (such as the one shown in Figure 3.2) are conceptual maps of sequences of possible decisions and their outcomes. When the probability of each outcome occurring is added to the tree, the riskiness of each course of action can be assessed, and the possible payoffs from each can be calculated.

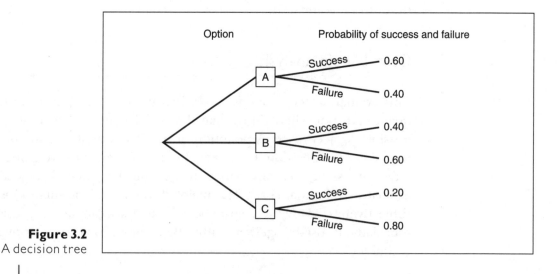

Figure 3.2
A decision tree

Linear programming

Linear programming is a mathematically based technique used to determine the best combination of limited resources which can achieve the dcsired objectives. It is especially useful when objectives can be measured and data quantified, for example when allocating tasks to machines when different tasks take different times and the machines have limits on the number of tasks they can complete in a period.

THE ADVANTAGES OF DECISION-MAKING TECHNIQUES

All the decision-making techniques detailed above try (in various ways) to attribute values or costs to different courses of action in order to provide some yardstick with which to judge possible plans against each other and against the objectives of the decision-maker. These techniques often take account of a project's risk or probability of losses. The use of decision analysis has the following advantages:

1 It focuses thinking on the critical elements of the decision.
2 It helps to structure problems and encourages organized thought.
3 It helps to uncover hidden assumptions behind a decision and clarifies its logical implications.
4 It simplifies the evaluation of alternative plans.
5 It helps to identify areas where more information is needed.
6 It provides a framework for planning contingency.

INFORMATION AND INFORMATION TECHNOLOGY

Any decisions made can only be as good as the information on which they were based. If managers receive incorrect, unclear information, or if they do not receive all the information that they need, then their decisions are liable to be poor ones. Overloading managers with information about a problem is almost as bad as not providing them with enough information. Too much data will often mean that significant information is overlooked − lost among the superfluous facts and figures.

To avoid this, the organization has to develop a good information processing system which provides its managers with relevant, timely and accurate information. This information should come both from the outside environment, and from inside the company (in the form of feedback and control reports).

Management information systems do not have to be IT based. However, microcomputer systems do allow managers to access all the information that they need instantly, and can allow them to work out the consequences of alternative solutions before making any decision, and thereby help them to avoid costly and irreversible errors of judgement. The importance of a logical information system which allows communication between components is crucial. In several large organizations, including the Health Service, there have been problems of systems not communicating and large quantities of data having to be reinput. The time and effort wasted carries a high cost. Some fund-holding general practices have gone as far as to computerize patient records to such an extent that computers assist in treatment (by identifying allergies, prior drug routines and effectiveness) and, in some cases, diagnosis.

Routine decisions dealing with routine problems can be programmed into a computer system. This will allow corrective measures to be taken quickly and easily (for example the automatic reordering of materials when items in stock fall to a certain level, thus helping to prevent expensive stock-outs), and will allow managers to concentrate on more important, non-routine decisions.

The extensive use of computers in stock control and manufacturing processes has made the application of 'Just In Time' procedures much 'cleaner' by virtue of a higher level of automation in stock levels maintenance and parts ordering.

SUMMARY

Decision-making is fundamental to the whole task of management, and is closely linked to the management processes of planning and problem-solving.

Most decisions, especially those taken by lower levels of management, are fairly routine ones, and are encountered many, many times. Some of these routine decisions can be programmed into computer systems. However, the decisions taken by senior managers are of a different nature. These involve choosing between different, often risky, strategies in order to solve ill-defined and unclear problems.

There are a variety of decision analysis techniques, and, together with a systematic approach to decision-making, they can help managers to make these second types of decisions, or at least to reduce the risk of making costly mistakes.

Good decisions are based on good information: an effective and efficient management information system should improve the quality of decisions at all levels of the organization.

CHECKLIST: CHAPTER 3

From this chapter you will have knowledge of:

1 Levels of decision-making:
   - Supervisors and junior managers see results of decisions
   - Higher management suffer a delay between the decision being made and its effects becoming clear

2 Theories of decision-making:
   - Classical theory
   - Behavioural theory
   - Satisficing

3 The decision-making process:
   - Define problem
   - Gather facts
   - Develop alternative solutions
   - Evaluate solutions
   - Select the best
   - Analyse the consequences
   - Implement decision

4 The problem-solving process:
   - Refer to Figure 3.1 for the steps in problem analysis and decision-making

5 Steps in decision-making:
   - Statement of aims
   - Examination of resources
   - Look for alternatives
   - Evaluate alternatives
   - Select the best action
   - Implement

6 Decision analysis techniques:
- Marginal or incremental costing
- DCF appraisal
- Cost-benefit analysis
- Sensitivity analysis
- Risk analysis
- Decision tree analysis
- Linear programming

7 Information and information technology

CHAPTER 4

Organizing

Organizing is that part of the manager's task which involves coordinating and directing the company's resources in such a way that the company can carry out its objectives. Managers can control very substantial resources in terms of people, money, time, materials, equipment, etc., although it is the organization of the first of these, i.e. people, which takes up most of a manager's time and attention.

In this chapter we will look at some of the ways in which organizations coordinate and arrange the work of their employees to enable all the necessary tasks to be carried out effectively. Different organizational structures and reporting relationships will be examined, together with some principles of organization. The next two chapters will cover the more 'human' topics of how managers can motivate and lead or guide their subordinates and workforce. Here we will concentrate on the physical, organizational framework of the company.

THE TASK OF ORGANIZING

Urwick (1958) defined the purpose of organizing, from the view of an administrator:

> The purpose of organisation is to sec [quote.] on and specialisation of tasks] works sm or, in other words, co-ordination.

Much of the task of organizing involves establishing a framework or structure of roles for people in the organization to fill. This means that all the tasks which have to be done to allow the company to accomplish its objectives are assigned to people who are able to carry them out competently. Organizing, therefore, involves identifying the activities which need to be done to achieve these objectives; grouping these activities together into departments; assigning such groups of activities to managers; delegating to the managers the authority to carry the tasks out; and setting up a structure for co-ordinating all these activities, both horizontally and vertically within the organization.

PRINCIPLES OF ORGANIZATIONAL STRUCTURE

There are various elements (or principles) of organizational structure which tend to be common to most businesses. One set of these principles was published by Urwick in the 1940s (which he subsequently revised in the early 1950s). They provide a useful starting point for discussion, and so are listed here:

1 *The principle of the objective.* Every part of the organization must be an expression of the purpose of the undertaking concerned, or else it is meaningless and, therefore, redundant.
2 *The principle of specialization.* The activities of every member of any organized group should be confined, as far as possible, to the performance of a single function.
3 *The principle of coordination.* The purpose of organizing, as distinguished from the purpose of the undertaking, is to facilitate co-ordination and unity of effort.
4 *The principle of authority.* In every organized group supreme authority must rest somewhere. There should be a clear line of authority from the holder of supreme authority down to every individual in the group.
5 *The principle of responsibility.* Managers have absolute responsibility for the acts of their subordinates.
6 *The principle of definition.* The content of each position (the duties involved, the authority and responsibility it contains, and the relationships with other positions) should be clearly defined in writing and given to all concerned.
7 *The principle of correspondence.* In every position the degree of responsibility it carries and the authority it confers should correspond.

8 *The principle of the span of control.* No person should supervise more than five, or at the most six, direct subordinates whose work interlocks.

9 *The principle of balance.* It is essential that the various elements of the organization should be kept in balance.

10 *The principle of continuity.* Organizing is a continuous process, and in every undertaking specific provision should be made for it (Urwick, 1952).

Unity of objectives

The importance of all parts of the organization working towards common, planned goals has already been stressed many times. Increased competition, both from domestic and international companies, together with scarce resources, mean that no company can afford the luxury of having parts of it following their own whims and not contributing to the business's objectives. This is particularly true of labour-intensive organizations in the private sector, where human resources play such a key role. It is an established part of the induction programme for new staff of Nissan Motor Company to examine in some detail corporate objectives and the importance of these objectives to the individual member of staff.

People are more likely to pursue the organization's objectives, rather than their own personal interests, if these objectives are clearly defined and widely understood. (Unfortunately, in public sector organizations political considerations often lead to objectives being blurred or, worse, constantly changed, with all the consequences of loss of efficiency that this entails.)

DELEGATION

Delegation is at the heart of the management task of organizing, and it is the process by which managers are able to get things done through other people. Delegation involves determining what has to be achieved, assigning tasks to subordinates, conferring the authority necessary to do the work upon the subordinates, and exacting responsibility for the accomplishment of the work.

To be effective, delegation has to be carefully planned. The following points are very important:

1 The subordinate must be given enough authority to carry out the task.

2 Although authority can be delegated, responsibility cannot, and so a manager cannot escape responsibility for the activities of the subordinates through delegation. However, at the same time, subordinates have an absolute responsibility to their manager for their work, once they have accepted a task and the right to carry it out.

3 Since authority is the discretionary right to carry out an assignment, and responsibility is the obligation to accomplish the task, it follows that the authority should correspond with the responsibility. For example, if a manager gives a subordinate the authority to sell certain items, that subordinate cannot be held responsible for customer complaints caused by badly designed products or faulty manufacturing.

4 The duties which are to be delegated should be clearly specified, together with a target for their achievement or a timetable. Written delegations of authority are extremely helpful both to the person who receives them and to the delegating manager. The manager will be able to see more easily any conflicts of interest or overlaps with other positions, and will also be able to identify more clearly those things for which the subordinate can and should be held responsible. Where delegation is non-specific, managers and subordinates alike are forced to feel their way and to define the authority delegated to them by trial and error. In this situation, unless they are familiar with top company policies and traditions, know the personality of their boss, and exercise sound judgement, they can be placed at a distinct and unfair disadvantage.

5 Delegated tasks should be within the capability and experience of the subordinate. If the task is too much for the subordinate, then the manager has not done the job well and has delegated badly. An adage which is often quoted is that managers get the subordinates that they deserve (and, conversely, subordinates get the managers that they deserve). A manager who delegates badly, or who does not develop subordinates to take responsibility and do their work well, will end up with subordinates who do their work badly and who cannot accept responsibility.

6 Review sessions should be held regularly, in order for the manager to monitor subordinates' performance and to

offer constructive advice. It must be noted, however, that continual checking on subordinates to make sure that no mistakes are ever made will make true delegation impossible. People often learn best by the mistakes that they make, and so a subordinate must be allowed to make errors, and their cost must be put down as investment in that person's development.

The advantages of delegation

Whatever degree of discretion a manager eventually decides to give to her subordinates the general principle is clear – senior managers should concentrate their time and effort on the major issues facing the organization. Most senior managers are overworked. Delegating tasks to subordinates whenever possible is, therefore, good management and makes business sense. The work will then often be done more cheaply; junior managers' job satisfaction will be increased (as their superiors' should be, as they will be freed from tasks which are perhaps routine to them, but which still present a challenge to their subordinates); and senior managers will be able to use their time more effectively. Delegation will also help to develop junior managers for further promotion.

The span of control

The span of control is the number of subordinates reporting directly to one manager or supervisor. There have been many different numbers suggested as the maximum number that a manager should have reporting to her. Urwick's limit is five or six, if their work interlocks. If their work does not interlock, then one manager can supervise more subordinates. However, the highest theoretical figure put forward is eight or nine people only.

Determining the span of control

The appropriate span of control does depend on a variety of factors. These include the following:

1 Whether the subordinates are qualified and capable of making decisions without constantly having to refer upwards to the manager. If they are, the number reporting to the manager can be increased.

2 Whether the manager is prepared to delegate authority to subordinates: if not, then the number of subordinates reporting to the manager cannot be very many.

3 If an organization has a well-developed, tried and tested communication system that feeds information quickly to and from senior managers, each manager is able to control and coordinate a large number of subordinates.

4 In the same way, a manager can supervise more people if the organization has a well-defined planning function and an agreed set of objectives.

5 Some organizations, particularly those in the public sector, depend a great deal on personal contact to operate effectively. These types of organizations will inevitably have small spans of control and their structures will contain many levels of managers and coordinators.

The effect of different degrees of technical sophistication on spans of control was shown by Joan Woodward in a study of 100 manufacturing companies (Woodward, 1965). The median span of control of chief executives in firms using unit production processes was four; that in mass-production companies seven; and in process production firms ten. The number of people that the first-line supervisors controlled also varied greatly, depending on the production process used: the average number in unit production firms was 23; in mass-production/large-batch firms 49; and in process production companies 13.

The 'scalar' principle

The 'scalar' principle is the idea that there is a vertical line of seniority/command from the highest to the lowest level in an organization, down which authority and responsibility run through the organization, from top to bottom.

The more clear-cut this line of authority, the more effective will be the decision-making process, and the greater the organization's efficiency. A clear understanding of this scalar principle is necessary for the proper functioning of the organization. Subordinates must know who delegates authority down to them, and to whom matters beyond their own authority must be referred.

Unity of command

Unity of command is another basic management principle. The more complete an individual's reporting relationship to a single superior, the less conflict there should be in instructions, and the greater the feeling of personal responsibility for results. In larger organizations, however, it becomes more difficult to observe this 'unity of command'. Some organizational structures, moreover, deliberately flout this principle (for example, matrix structures, which we will look at a little later on). This does create some problems, but under certain circumstances these problems are outweighed by the advantages that these types of structure bring.

TYPES OF ORGANIZATIONAL STRUCTURE

Organizational structure can be defined as 'the established pattern of relationships among the parts of the organization'. There are two types of structure, which tend to exist side-by-side: a formal structure, and an informal structure.

The formal structure

This is the organizational structure, designed by the company's senior management, to achieve the objectives of the organization, and to promote efficiency and effectiveness. Thus the design of the formal organization is guided by the principles of unity of objective (which have already been noted) and of efficiency. The principle of efficiency states that a structure is efficient if it helps people to accomplish the company's objectives with the minimum of unforeseen consequences and costs, i.e. if it promotes good management.

The formal structure of an organization is made up of the network of organizational relationships, the pattern of grouping activities into departments, and the degree to which authority and responsibility are centralized in the organization.

It must be noted that there is nothing inherently inflexible about the formal structure of an organization. On the contrary, if managers are to be able to manage well, the company structure must provide an environment in which individuals can contribute to the company goals. There should always be room for individual talents, likes and capacities, even in the most formal of organizational structures.

The informal structure

Within every organization, alongside the formal organizational structure there exists an informal one. This is based on personal relationships between individuals and groups, and as such is much more dynamic and less easily definable than the more rigid, formal structure.

In many ways, these informal structures are more powerful than the formal organizational links, because they reflect the present, real-world situation within the company. If the two structures diverge seriously, it may become necessary to formalize at least some of the informal relationships; otherwise communication channels may break down and managers could lose their freedom of action.

Introduction to Mintzberg

In beginning to look at organizational structure, there are new elements to consider. These, as identified by Mintzberg (1983, 1989), Handy (1985) and Morden (1993), include: the type of ownership; the stage of development at which the organization is; the character of individuals associated with and employed by the organization; where the power lies within the organization; and the comparative level of centralization or decentralization. Chapter 1 has considered various roles fulfilled by management; here we are looking at a bigger picture, in the sense of the overall shape of the organization as defined by the distribution and relationships between roles within it. Morden (1996) states that this 'configuration' is a function of the following variables:

- *Hierarchy*, which is the authority pattern underlying superordinate—subordinate relationships.
- *Formalization*, which is the establishment of written and enforceable management policies, procedures, rules and standing orders which prescribe action, monitor performance and record the results.
- *Standardization*, by which rules, definitions or prescriptions are used consistently in every case to which they apply.
- *Specialization*, by which operational activities are differentiated (or specialized) into various functions (for instance as described by Fayol, 1949).

- *Centralization*, which describes the location within the enterprise of the authority to make decisions and commit resources to those decisions. The issue of centralization and decentralization is dealt with in more detail below.
- *Flexibility*, which is the capacity of the enterprise to adapt to changing circumstances by making adjustments to the relevant determinant and configuration variables being described in this chapter, such that the organization structure remains congruent with, or appropriate to, the conditions of change to which the flexible response is sought.
- *Architecture*, which describes the network of relationships and contracts within and around the enterprise. The organization will establish relationships and contracts with and among its employees. This is its *internal architecture*. It will establish relationships and contracts with customers, clients, suppliers, partners and stakeholders within its external environment. This is *external architecture*.

In management terms the concept of centralization does not refer to physical location, but rather to the location of *authority* to make strategic decisions. Remember strategic decisions are those that commit people and resources.

Mintzberg (1989, p.105) notes that:

When all the power rests at a single point in an organization, we call its structure too centralized; to the extent that the power is dispersed among many individuals, we call it relatively decentralized. We can distinguish vertical decentralization — the delegation of formal power down the hierarchy to line managers — from horizontal decentralization — the extent to which formal or informal power is dispersed out of the line hierarchy to non-managers (operators, analysts, and support staff). We can also distinguish selective decentralization — the dispersal of power over different decisions to different places in the organization — from parallel decentralization — where the power over various kinds of decisions is delegated to the same place.

So centralization and decentralization are a matter of degree. The highly centralized organization holds all the power at the centre or apex, whilst the highly decentralized structure demonstrates power diffusion throughout the organization.

Mintzberg's contingency factors

Age and size

The *older* an organization, the more formalized may be its behaviour. Given its experience of a variety of more or less frequently repeated events (and its knowledge of how likely they are to occur), the enterprise can document, rationalize and institutionalize this experience.

The *larger* an organization, the more formalized its behaviour. Standardization and consistency of practice are an established hallmark of large organizations.

The *larger* an organization, the more elaborate will be its structure, that is, the more specialized will be its tasks and departments, and the more developed will be its administrative (and coordinating) components. The issues of diversity and coordination are dealt with in a later chapter. Structure may reflect historical features characteristic of the industry. Managers may be reluctant to deviate from well-established industry patterns, even if these patterns are becoming obsolete or competition is enforcing change.

Technical system

The more *regulating* the technical system, i.e. the more it controls the work of the operators, the more formalized the operating system and the more bureaucratic the management structure. This reflects Woodward's (1965) findings on the close supervision and control of large batch and mass production systems.

The more *complex* the technical system, the more elaborate and professional the support staff (and the greater the power of these staff, irrespective of their location within the hierarchy).

The automation of the operational system may transform a bureaucratic administrative structure into a more flexible or organic one. This reflects Woodward's findings on continuous flow production technology.

Mintzberg also notes:

> When unskilled work is coordinated by the standardization of work processes, we tend to get bureaucratic structure throughout the organization, because a control mentality pervades the whole system. But when the work of the operating core becomes automated, social relationships tend to change. Now it is machines, not people, that are

regulated. So the obsession with control tends to disappear — machines do not need to be watched over — and with it go many of the managers and analysts who were needed to control the operators. In their place come the [plant monitors and] support specialists to look after the machinery, coordinating their work by mutual adjustment.

The environment

The more *dynamic* an organization's environment, the more organic its structure (see Burns and Stalker, 1961; Peters and Waterman, 1982; Kanter, 1990).

The more *complex* an organization's environment, the more decentralized its structure.

The more *diversified* an organization's markets, the greater the propensity to split it into market-based units, or divisions, given favourable economies of scale and cost–volume relationships.

Extreme *hostility* or *change* in its environment may drive management to decentralize an organization's structure temporarily. This is done in order to attempt to achieve a fast and tightly coordinated response to the threat, and ensure its uniform implementation within a prescribed time scale.

Power

The greater the *external control* of an organization, the more centralized and formalized is its structure. The two most effective ways to control an organization from the outside (for instance by a parent company or government agency) are to hold its chief executive officer personally responsible for its actions, and to impose clearly defined performance standards on it (such as returns to investors, service quality, or the number of complaints). Mintzberg adds that 'moreover, external control forces the organization to be especially careful about its actions'.

A *divided* external coalition will tend to give rise to a politicized internal coalition (or management), and vice versa. That is, conflicts in one coalition may spill over into the other.

Fashion favours the structure of the day, perhaps even when inappropriate. Organizations may adopt the currently popular organization design parameters even if they are unsuitable, because of the prevailing fashion or more likely because they have been sold them by consulting firms.

From the general to the specific

Mintzberg's theory as outlined above deals in general terms with types of structure that may form all or part of an organization. There are some types of structure that, whilst exhibiting characteristics identified by Mintzberg, have become identified as distinct to a specific type of organization. For example, entrepreneurial structures are characterized as simple and informal with a lack of any significant management hierarchy. They will also be highly centralized, with authority tending to lie with the entrepreneur. Morden (1996) characterizes the development of such structures as only 'appropriate to a given level of activity'. They may become ineffective once there is an increase in scale and diversity. Under such conditions, the need for greater formalization and hierarchy, specialization and departmentalization, renders personal control by the entrepreneur ineffective. Information overloads and decision-making delay will result. At the same time there will be a growing trust–control dilemma. The entrepreneur is going to have to delegate authority and responsibility for the management of the business, and learn to trust his or her newly empowered executives. Some entrepreneurs cannot do this. Ultimately, the entrepreneur or his or her successors may face a crucial decision. How (if at all) do they want the enterprise to develop? Do they wish to keep the business small, controllable and personalized? Or do market opportunities call for an increase in scale and diversity? This in turn will call for the establishment of at least the minimum (or 'requisite') level of bureaucracy and hierarchy, and the development of a 'proper' management structure.

The entrepreneurial structure can remain small by limiting expansion. This is the option favoured by many of the independent family-owned *Mittelstand* enterprises in Germany. Family control and succession is more important than business growth. It is possible to retain entrepreneurial status and significant levels of independence and *also* seek growth through what are known as value-adding partnerships with other companies in the value chain. This is common practice in Italy, and is the basis of Benetton's manufacturing and distribution practice. The gradual development of a structure that allows for, enables and expedites increasing size and diversity is a third option.

Requisite bureaucracy has to provide the basics by which structure and competence are established so that an increased volume of transactions can be fulfilled consistently. Morden (1996) defines requisite bureaucracy as 'the minimum degree of organizational formalization, standardization, hierarchy, management structure, and functional/

operational competence needed for the enterprise to be able to cope with increasing scale, diversity and complexity'.

Further reading should include analysis of the entrepreneurial situation as considered by Drucker (1985) and Jacques (1961).

Public sector organizations, typically public service agencies, have structures that are characterized by individuals holding responsibility and being accountable. These individuals hold official positions to which they are elected, e.g. government ministers, governors. Their management behaviour will be governed by their need to control and accountability for the dispersal of public funds.

A look back at classical structures of management will reveal a number of descriptions by Weber, Fayol, and Burns and Stalker, among others. Mintzberg (1989) describes the key characteristics as:

1 The division of the total task (using the divsion of labour) into specialized roles or offices on a functional basis.
2 The allocation of these functional specialisms to departments (departmentalization).
3 The establishment of a hierarchy or ('pyramid') of operational, supervisory and management roles and offices, embodying the scalar chain. The scalar chain is used to establish a 'top-down' unity of command in which instructions flow down and feedback on results achieved flows back up the hierarchy. Communication and control processes are vertical. Decision-making will be centralized, that is, carried out at the 'top' or 'apex' of the organization (or at its corporate centre).
4 The establishment of unified and functional authority relationships. The subordinate should have only one superordinate ('boss'), and that boss should be functionally related to him or her in terms of specialization.
5 The number of subordinates who may be directly supervised is deliberately limited (for example to six or seven) by the concept of span and control. The smaller the allowed span of control, the 'taller' may be the hierarchy (that is, the greater the number of levels it will contain). Tall hierarchies are traditionally associated with information filtering and distortion and decision-making delay, but maximize the available promotion/career opportunities and pay-grading potential. Flat hierarchies are associated with wide spans of control, limited layers of management hierarchy, and delegation of authority. Flat (or 'de-layered') hierarchies were 'fashionable'

in Anglo-Saxon countries at the time when this book was written.

6 The nature of tasks and work flows may be determined by formalized processes of work study, work measurement, organization and methods, job specification and evaluation, etc. Operational activities will be standardized and routinized where they are likely to be repetitive. The work of the role or office holder will, to some degree, be based upon established and formalized policies, procedures and rules.

7 Coordination of the varied specialist and functional tasks and work flows will be carried out by management roles and information systems.

8 The delegation of responsibility and authority to managers and supervisors. Each may be held personally responsible for his or her area of responsibility as long as he or she has been allocated sufficient authority and resources to achieve the required objectives.

9 The delegation to appointed managers of the power to make decisions and command resources. While key external stakeholders such as government representatives or members of boards of directors will be closely involved in the appointment and performance appraisal of senior managers, both strategic management and the day-to-day running of the enterprise will be the responsibility of managers employed for the task.

Variations to this classical model include the use of lateral communication relationships or horizontal 'communication gangplanks' between functions to improve coordination, reduce upwards information flow, increase flexibility, and speed up operational decision-making; and the division of authority relationships into 'line', 'staff' and 'functional' categories:

■ Line authority is the direct line of authority between any boss and his or her subordinate within the scalar chain.

■ Staff authority is based upon the right to give advice, or on the possession of expert power. Line managers may be given expert advice by staff specialists (and advised to pay heed to it) but may have the right to ignore it.

■ Functional authority is the right of functional specialists to give orders in pre-specified functional areas to line managers, who must comply with these orders. Functional authority is typically used in the areas of financial control, human resource management, supply and procurement management, and health and safety management, where enterprise-wide policies are to be applied in all departments on a consistent basis.

Matrix structures

Matrix relationships involve subordinates and managers having dual responsibilities, first to their immediate superiors, and second to the specialist working groups of which they are members. Matrix structures can be set up for a limited period only – to see a particular project through, for example – or can be permanent, normal parts of the organizational structure. British Telecom's research laboratories near Ipswich are organized on a matrix structure to allow staff to work together on particular projects while allowing divisionalization for other purposes. In the 1930s Proctor & Gamble introduced brand structures in which each brand is established as a separate business unit and competes for the time and resources of the functional activities of manufacturing, sales and distribution. The NASA space programme of the 1960s formed enormous matrices from different parts of the space programme (projects) and various supplying organizations such as Rockwell and General Electric (functions).

Matrix relationships deliberately flout Urwick's unity of command principle, with people reporting to two authorities. However, the structure is the exception that proves the rule. The other main feature of matrix relationships is that they combine lateral and vertical lines of communication and authority. Matrix structures are very flexible, and can help an organization to adapt quickly to changes in its environment. They do have their disadvantages, however:

- The allocation of resources and the division of authority between project groups and functional specialists can be a potential cause of conflict, and may lead to the dilution of functional management responsibilities throughout the organization.
- There is also the possibility of divided loyalties on the part of members of project teams, in relation to their project managers and their functional superiors, because team members have to report to two bosses.

DEPARTMENTATION AND DIVISIONALIZATION

The grouping together of activities and individuals within the organization is known as 'departmentation' – or the process of dividing the business into logical, coordinated departments. The main forms of departmentation are as follows:

1 *By function.* In this form of departmentation, which is the most common one, activities are grouped around business functions such as production, marketing and finance. Occasionally, organizations also have departments set up around managerial functions such as planning and controlling. In the case of Abbey National plc, activities are split into large retailing functions with separate departments for planning and marketing. Functional departmentation has an important advantage in that it is a logical and time-proven method of organization. It is also the best way of making certain that the power and prestige of the enterprise's basic activities will be argued for by senior managers. Another advantage of functional departmentation is that it follows the principle of occupational specialization, and so encourages the efficient utilization of people. It must be noted, however, that the more numerous and specialized the various departments are, the more difficult the task of senior management becomes to coordinate and manage the business.

2 *By geographical area.* It is obviously useful to have geographically based departments whenever it is important to be close to the territory in which the organization wants to operate. For example, a company based in Britain may consider that its market is the whole of Western Europe. Rather than attempting to do everything from its head office, it may divide up the sales function (and later the production function), placing a separate operation in each country in which it sells. Many retail organizations such as W. H. Smith break operations down into small geographic areas, e.g. Northern England, and appoint a Regional Manager responsible for the outlets in the area.

3 *By product.* As organizations grow, so the range of products they offer grows. At first, all goods and services can be handled using common facilities, but there comes a time

when the volume being dealt with is so large that advantages are to be gained by treating each product as a separate division (or even company). Product is an important basis for departmentation, because it helps the organization to make the best use of economies of scale and specialized knowledge, as well as individual skills.

4 *By customer.* This form of departmentation is particularly common in service businesses, where it is felt that different kinds of customers require different treatment. One example of this is in banking, where the big clearing banks make a distinction between their business customers and their personal customers. It is also particularly common in the food manufacturing industry, where companies differentiate between the small independent shop and the large multiple supermarket chain. Thus Derwent Valley Foods will manufacture own brand snacks for Tesco, etc., but also sell Phileas Fogg through as many outlets as possible.

5 *By process or equipment.* The grouping of activities about a particular process or type of equipment is often employed by manufacturing companies. A good example of departmentation by equipment is the existence of electronic data processing departments. The purpose of such departmentation is to achieve economies of scale, although it may also be required by the nature of the equipment involved.

6 *By time.* Organizing according to time-scales, for example day and night shifts, makes sense where round-the-clock production is necessary.

7 *By numbers.* This method of departmentation involves counting off a number of people who are to perform the same duties and putting them under a manager. The essential fact of this way of departmentation is not what these people do or where they work, but that the success of the undertaking depends only upon the number of people who are doing the work. In large manufacturing operations such as Thorn EMI Lighting, groups of workers are organized into cells.

Often, several different methods of departmentation will be used within one organization. For example, a company may have a basic functional structure, but the marketing department is further divided by geographical areas, and by customer type.

Some degree of independence, authority and responsibility is allocated to the division by the corporate centre. Divisions are often established as profit centres and are responsible for the revenue and expense consequences of their operations. Alternatively they may be established as investment centres, responsible in addition for resource use and rate of return. It is then the role of the corporate centre to set the parameters within which each division is to operate, and to lay down the results expected of them. The process of divisionalization is a widely used mechanism by which to achieve some degree of decentralization. The level of divisionalization is represented by the degree to which decision-making authority and the control of resource allocation is vested in divisional rather than corporate management. This degree of decentralization may vary between:

- close monitoring, control and coordination by the corporate centre. This can be defined as controlled or coordinated decentralization; and
- full divisional responsibility and autonomy. A fully decentralized division looks and acts like an independent company.

As any organization increases in size or complexity, it becomes more difficult (and expensive) to administer and manage. Diseconomies of scale may appear. Divisionalization is widely accepted as a sensible way of dealing with these problems. The scale and complexity of any one part of the organization is reduced to a more manageable size. The division may be more market and customer focused, and 'tuned in' to other relevant situation or competition variables, or contingencies in its external environment that influence its performance. The need for complex or expensive coordinating mechanisms may be reduced. This will be of particular importance where, for instance:

- Enterprise activities are highly diversified or associated with a variety of different technologies.

■ The enterprise is involved in a wide variety of international activities, and markets an array of local, regional or global products or brands.

Divisionalization, therefore involves a significant relaxation of the limitations that may characterize a monolithic centralized structure (and particularly if the external environment is competitive and characterized by conditions of change). The process may:

■ Permit a large organization to regain the benefits of small scale while continuing to enjoy the economies of scale and experience from which it gains its cost and volume advantages.

■ Permit the division to act more rapidly and flexibly in response to market, technological and environmental influences. Divisionalized structures may be able to avoid the 'bureaucratic sluggishness' that often affects monolithic centralized hierarchies (for instance when confronted by the need for flexibility and change).

■ Permit the organization to revive entrepreneurship. This is usually defined as intrapreneurship.

■ Permit the individual performance measurement of the division as one of the strategic business units or business units of the enterprise. This practice is now widespread in the UK, for instance, whether it be in the private, public or health care sectors.

ORGANIZATIONAL RELATIONSHIPS

There are five main types of formal organizational relationship which can exist in businesses: line, staff, functional, committee and matrix relationships. All of these relationships often exist together in the same firm.

Line relationships

Line relationships describe the direct working relationships between the vertical levels of the company's structure, i.e. it is the authority that every manager exercises in respect of subordinates. This is the most common type of organizational and working relationship. It has the advantages that formal communication channels up and down the organization are clear, that authority and responsibility are agreed upon, and that instructions and information can flow up and down between the individuals concerned. Line authority is the central feature of the chain of command throughout any organization.

Staff relationships

The nature of staff relationships in an organization is an advisory one. The function of people working in a purely staff capacity (such as personnel, finance, IT and administration) is to investigate, research, and give advice to the company's line managers. It is very important to make this distinction between line and staff relationships. Both managers and their subordinates must know whether they are acting in a staff or line capacity. If they are acting in a staff capacity, their job is merely to advise their line colleagues, not to order or command. It is up to the line managers to make the decisions and issue instructions.

However, in many organizations this difference between the line and staff functions is not so clear-cut. In such companies you will often find staff manager specialists who also have line responsibility over their own subordinates. For example, in Figure 4.1 the personnel manager has a staff relationship to the managing director on personnel matters, but also has line responsibility over employees in the training, employment, recruitment and health and safety sections of the personnel department.

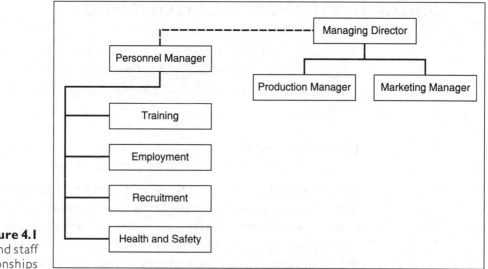

Figure 4.1
Line and staff
relationships

Functional relationships

The third type of relationship operating within an organization is the functional relationship. Functional authority is the right which an individual or department may have to control specific processes or policies, throughout the company, because of the specialist knowledge or function. So, for example, a company's finance director will be responsible for the conduct of financial matters, but may also have the authority to make line managers follow and stick to the company's financial procedures and policies. It must be noted that functional authority is not restricted to managers of a particular type of department; it can be exercised by line or staff department managers.

Committee relationships

Committee relationships also play an important part in organizations. Committees can either be formal (i.e. have a written brief and the authority to carry out a specific task), or informal. Informal committees are usually set up for a particular, temporary purpose, for example to act as a pressure valve or as a sounding board for senior management.

Matrix relationships

Finally, there are what are known as matrix relationships. A matrix relationship is a combination of the other organizational relationships already discussed. Matrix relationships involve subordinates and managers having dual responsibilities, first to their immediate superiors, and second to the specialist working groups of which they are members. Matrix structures can be set up for a limited period only — to see a particular project through, for example — or can be permanent, normal parts of the organizational structure. British Telecom's research laboratories near Ipswich are organized on a matrix structure to allow staff to work together on particular projects while allowing divisionalization for other purposes.

Matrix relationships deliberately flout Urwick's unity of command principle, with people reporting to two authorities. However, the structure is the exception which proves the rule. The other main feature of matrix relationships is that they combine lateral and vertical lines of communication and authority (see Figure 4.2).

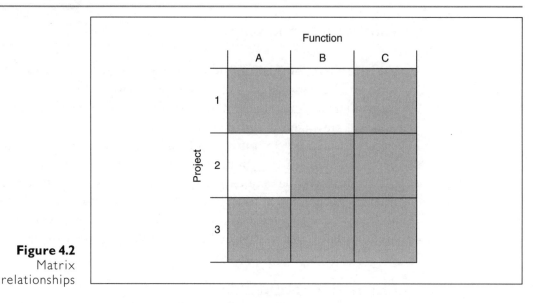

Figure 4.2
Matrix
relationships

Matrix structures are very flexible, and can help an organization to adapt quickly to changes in its environment. They do have their disadvantages, however:

1 The allocation of resources and the division of authority between project groups and functional specialists can be a potential cause of conflict, and may lead to the dilution of functional management responsibilities throughout the organization.

2 There is also the possibility of divided loyalties on the part of members of project teams, in relation to their project managers and their functional superiors, because team members have to report to two bosses.

Despite these disadvantages, the matrix organizational structure probably offers the best answer to date to the problem of handling the tension between on the one hand the need to differentiate, and on the other the need to integrate, the complex activities of the modern organization. Any difficulties which do occur with such a relationship are probably best resolved in a less rigid organization, where most problems can be sorted out by informal, quick discussions.

CENTRALIZATION OR DECENTRALIZATION?

All organizations have to decide just what degree of centralized power and authority they will have in their structure. The inevitable push towards specialization in all but the smallest of businesses leads to the diffusion of authority and accountability. The need to structure activities leads logically to the need to allocate appropriate amounts of authority to those responsible for undertaking these activities. The senior management team of every organization of any size must, therefore, consider just how much authority to delegate from the centre.

The concept of centralization can be understood in a number of ways, for example in terms of performance and also in geographical terms. But when centralization is discussed as an aspect of management, it refers to the withholding or delegating of authority for decision-making. A highly centralized organization is one where little authority (especially over major areas of the business) is exercised outside a key group of senior managers. On the other hand, a highly decentralized company is one in which the authority to organize people, money and materials is widely delegated throughout every level of the organization.

The case for centralization

Centralization has a number of advantages:

1 Support services can be provided more cheaply on an overall basis, rather than on a departmental basis.
2 The company can often employ a higher calibre of staff.
3 Tight control can be kept over the company's cash flow and expenditure.

The case for decentralization

The advantages of decentralization are as follows:

1 It prevents the overloading of top managers by freeing them from many day-to-day operational decisions, and enables them to concentrate on their more important, strategic responsibilities.
2 It allows local management to be flexible in its approach to decisions in the light of local conditions, and thus to be more adaptable in situations of rapid change.

3 It speeds up operational decisions by allowing line managers to take immediate action, without referring back to their superiors all the time.

4 It focuses attention on to important cost and profit centres within the organization, and therefore sharpens management awareness of the importance of cost-effectiveness, as well as of revenue targets.

5 It contributes to staff motivation by enabling middle and junior managers to exercise real responsibility, and by generally encouraging initiative by all employees.

In reality, few organizations are either totally centralized or completely decentralized, but most are at least partially decentralized. This is mainly because of the enormous pressures on modern business organizations to delegate more and more authority to staff at executive and specialist levels. However, it should not be thought that this is a static principle: the amount of decentralization that occurs should vary as the circumstances of the company *vary*, in order to meet the needs of the situation at the time. For example, a merger between two companies might produce a greater degree of centralization for a while, especially if one company is experiencing financial trouble (often a catalyst for mergers). The quality of the organization's middle management will also determine the amount and pace of decentralization – if they are good, the senior managers are liable to delegate more and decentralize authority more. In many organizations (such as Ford (Europe)) the Treasury function is centralized to allow funds from various activities to be aggregated and invested in higher-yielding short-term investments.

ORGANIZATIONAL PROBLEMS FOR MANAGERS

Organizing the resources under their control is one of the most difficult of managers' tasks, and, whatever the solutions and structures ultimately chosen, most managers will encounter a number of problems. The first of these often arises out of imprecise, unachievable objectives which do not have the commitment of the employees concerned. Poor delegation and vagueness of working relationships also create problems for the manager, as well as lack of feedback, inadequate communication systems, and breakdowns in the chain of command, such as the mixing up of line and staff relationships.

INNOVATIVE ORGANIZATIONS

Mintzberg (1989) uses the word 'Adhocracy' to describe an organization that is innovative in its structure, and which may be characterized as being fluid and selectively decentralized. Morden (1996) describes an adhocracy thus: 'Functional experts are deployed in multidisciplinary teams of staff, operators and managers to work on a project basis. Coordination takes place by mutual adjustment and negotiation.'

SUMMARY

We have seen how organizing involves determining the physical framework or structure of the company in order to allow staff to work most effectively and efficiently.

The formal organizational structure consists of the grouping of activities into departments (based on area, function, customer, product, equipment, time-scale, or numbers); the organizational reporting relationships which exist in the company (line, staff, functional, committee and matrix); and the degree to which authority is centralized in the organization. Alongside the formal structure, there is usually an informal structure of personal relationships, which is just as important to the smooth running of the business.

To be most effective, the organization's structure should be as flexible as possible in order to adapt to changing circumstances.

CHECKLIST: CHAPTER 4

After reading this chapter you will be able to report on:

1 The organizing task:
   ■ Framework or structure of rules
   ■ Principles of structure
      – Express the purpose of the organization
      – Each group performs a single function
      – Clear lines of authority
      – Responsibility
      – Define content of each position
      – Responsibility should correspond with authority
      – Span of control should be limited to five or six
      – Keep in balance
      – A continuous process

2 Unity of objective — a common goal

3 Delegation — at the heart of the management task:
- Give enough authority
- Responsibility *cannot* be delegated
- Authority should correspond to responsibility
- Clearly specify duties
- Within capability of subordinate
- Review sessions

4 Span of control — determination of

5 Scalar principle

6 Unity of command:
- Types of structure
  - Formal
  - Informal

7 Departmentation by:
- Function
- Geographical area
- Product
- Customer
- Process
- Time
- Numbers

8 Organizational relationship:
- Five main types:
  - Line
  - Staff
  - Functional
  - Committee
  - Matrix

9 Centralization or decentralization

CHAPTER 5

Strategy

PROCESS, CONTENT AND CONTEXT

Process is the essence of formulating – or more plainly it looks at the 'how' of strategy. *Content* indicates that the strategy must result in a 'product'. The product may be a course of action taken by an organization. Content could be viewed as the 'what' of strategy. *Context* relates the company to its surroundings or environment. The strategy of an organization would take account of both organizational and environmental contexts.

Within the 'management task' it could be argued that it is more important to understand the content and context before approaching the process itself. With this in mind, this chapter concentrates on content and context, although inevitably elements of process will arise or become evident from time to time.

ESTABLISHING A FRAMEWORK

The basic framework of a strategy is to link the organization with its environment (Figure 5.1). The strategy must adapt to surroundings as they are when the strategy is determined but also as the environment changes, and so should the strategy framework. In other words, the framework is what 'adapts' to circumstances surrounding the organization.

A basic framework, when viewed in its fundamental state, links the key characteristics of an organization with its environment. Typically the key characteristics of an organization are: goals and values, resources and capabilities, and structures and systems. Similarly,

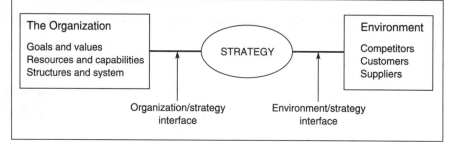

Figure 5.1
Strategy: the basic
framework

the key characteristics of the environment would be competitors, customers and suppliers.

POSITIONING APPROACH

Attention shifted towards strategy in order to achieve organizational focus on areas of greatest profitability. This focus concentrated on external environments by way of an analysis of the industry structure and competition. The key point of the 'position' is to emphasize the organization's ability to adapt to its environment, on the assumption that it is the environment that determines the organization's freedom to move and develop. Looking at the environment first and then at the organization's place within it led this approach to be dubbed the 'outside in' approach.

Figure 5.1 shows that the strategy itself is important – as opposed to the elements that led to the strategy being developed. The characteristics of a competitive strategy may be summarized:

1 Strategies are generic, common, identifiable positions in the market place.
2 The market place is economic and competitive.
3 Analytical calculation is the base for selecting 'positions' in the environment – thus leading to strategy formulation.
4 Analysts give the results of their calculations to managers, who make the choices.
5 The structure of the organization is driven by the market structure: selected strategies are articulated and then implemented.

An example of a key influence on strategy within a commercial organization would be that of market share. If market share is selected as a fundamental driver of the strategy, then information about market segment share and the growth rate of the market will directly inform strategy formulation.

GROWTH/SHARE MATRIX

The growth/share matrix plots market share against industry growth rate, and each player (or Strategic Business Unit (SBU)) in the matrix is categorized by its relative position. Figure 5.2 displays a simple growth/share matrix.

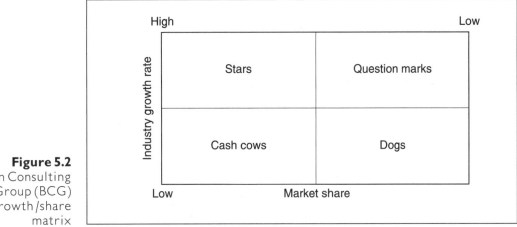

Figure 5.2
Boston Consulting Group (BCG) growth/share matrix

Key

- A *star* is a strategic business unit (SBU) enjoying high market share in a growth market. A star may have to spend heavily to be in this position but hopes that costs are reducing over time and at a faster rate than its competitors.
- A *question mark* is also in a growing market but does not have high market share; it may need to start spending heavily to increase market share, but costs are unlikely to reduce sufficiently to offset additional spending.
- A *cash cow* is a SBU with high market share but in a stable market; thus there is less need to invest heavily in the market and a cash cow should be able to maintain lower costs than its competitors. In fact the cash cow could be a cash provider.
- *Dogs* 'enjoy' a low market share of a declining market and represent the worst of all combinations on the matrix. They

may be a cash drain and are likely to use up resources beyond their capability to provide return.

Shortcomings of the growth/share matrix

- Use of the model requires a definition of the market, but the model itself provides no guidance on market definition.
- The model is used as an indicator of cash requirements of an organization. It is a clear assumption that market share is an indicator of cash requirement, whereas profits and cash flow depend on many things.
- The model does not give guidance in formulating specific strategies for a particular organization.

PORTER'S COMPETITIVE STRATEGY

Porter's competitive strategy consists of three key elements in the race for competitive advantage:

- The *five competitive forces*, which in combination determine or identify the nature of competition in the sector. The nature of the strategy is to identify how an organization can defend itself against these forces, which are:

  1 The threat of new entrants.
  2 Bargaining power of buyers.
  3 Bargaining power of suppliers.
  4 Threat of substitute products and services.
  5 Rivalry among existing competitors.

- *Generic competitive strategies*. The principal assumption here is that there are three strategies that can achieve competitive advantage. This second element makes the case for selecting one of these generic strategies in order to sustain competitive advantage. The generic competitive strategies are:

  1 Cost leadership.
  2 Differentiation.
  3 Focus.

- The *value chain*: This effectively splits an organization into activities that are relevant in a strategic context. This tool can identify what an organization does better or more cost-effectively than competitors. The value chain does this by 'disaggregating' the organization into value-added activities which in turn will assist the selection of one of the three generic strategies listed above and to identify areas of competitive advantage an organization may have in relation to the five competitive forces.

Shortcomings of the Porter theory include the fact that it is a simplistic view of organizations. Many companies were successful in implementing both cost and differentiation strategies – for example car companies offering low cost *and* differentiation in high quality. Further shortcomings include the inherent risk in extrapolating present trends and the strict process of formulating a strategy. That is to say, the theory seems to assume that once the 'environment' has been analysed, it will remain constant whilst the strategy is formulated and implemented. In reality a more flexible strategy may be required in order to respond more effectively to a fluid environment.

RESOURCE-BASED APPROACH

During the last two decades of the twentieth century there was a reaction against the positioning approach promoted by Porter. The resource-based approach shifts the emphasis from looking at the internal elements of an organization to looking at how it may adapt best to its environment.

The basic element of the resource-based approach is that superior organization resources and capabilities can allow an organization to perhaps modify the structure of the industry and even change the rules of competition. Thus the development of *individual* and *unique* resources and techniques is the basis of a good strategy.

The resource-based approach developed further with the setting down of three key concepts, which are:

1 *Core competences*. These may be described as 'the collective learning in the organization, especially how to coordinate diverse production skills and integrate multiple streams of technologies' (Hamel and Prahalad, 1980). The understanding of core competences, it is argued, allows managers and strategists to have a more rational view of future opportunities that may be beyond their existing markets. The key elements may be summarized:

- Changing opportunities in the environment require organizations to adapt quickly. To sustain a competitive advantage in such circumstances depends not on products but on factors that enable quick, flexible reactions, i.e. key competence across corporate-wide technologies and production skills.
- There is more than one key product. Core competences, like the roots of a tree, feed into more than one core product, like the trunk and major limbs of a tree, which in turn feed into more than one business unit, the smaller branches of a tree, and finally to the end products, the leaves and flowers of a tree.
- Associated organizational competences are also important.
- Core competences must be focused.
- A strategic architecture provides a mini-environment to encourage identification and development of core competences.

The key point is that for strategic analysis the important thing is what the organization *can* do rather than what it *now does*. This results in the strategic analyst looking for resources that can lead to a sustainable competitive advantage for the organization.

2 *Strategic intent.* Strategic intent is about goal, ambition, aspiration, vision and mission. The criterion for strategic intent is 'does it motivate and stimulate?' Individuals within an organization should be able to be passionate, emotional, convicted and committed to the strategy because it provides focus, sense of direction, destination and inspiration. Strategic intent may be characterized as an organization looking at where it now is and how it is to get to where it wants to be. The 'mission' is a broad statement indicating the issues that need to be addressed in order to achieve the objective expressed in 'where it wants to be'.

3 *Stretch and leverage.* Hamal and Prahalad (1980) identified a gap between an organization's resources and the goal that managers have. They supposed that the misfit between resources and aspirations creates stretch that leverages (applies pressure to) resources and effort. The 'new' strategy for management is to create this gap between ambition and resources and then determine whether the organization will survive competitively.

CHOOSING AN APPROACH

There is no exact method of determining which strategy best suits any organization. In fact some would argue that there are many 'best' ways to make a corporate strategy and that many approaches should be employed, i.e. a combination of approaches is possible.

In summary, an organization can choose a 'positioning' approach, a 'resource-based' approach, or a combination of both. The critical point is that in formulating a strategy for an organization the aim is the create a best fit between the organization and its environment.

STYLE OF COMPETITION: DENOMINATOR AND NUMERATOR MANAGEMENT

Throughout the last quarter of the twentieth century, competition tended to be based on the *cost advantage* rather than the *differentiation advantage*. Most organizations were competing head-to-head in a shrinking market and actions taken by different organizations were broadly similar. Furthermore, organizations tended to locate within markets in which they had an advantage.

Hamel and Prahalad (1980) introduced what they called the '40/30/20 rules'. This indicated that managers, on average, spend less than 3% of their time building a strategy for the future. This indicated that management is mainly concerned with today rather than tomorrow. This is described as 'denominator management'. Denominator management may be summarized as a shortcut to asset productivity – or making the most out of assets currently held – but does not create new values. This manifests itself within organizations that compete with similar products and simply attempt to achieve lower costs in order to match or beat the competition on price.

'Numerator management' is different. An organization using numerator management would raise net income by creating new wealth through innovation. Such a strategy attempts to make the competition irrelevant. As with most management tasks, the choice is not between either denominator or numerator management but rather an acceptance that both types of management need to be incorporated into the organization.

SUMMARY

We have seen how important content and context are within the management task. An organization must be linked with its environment and we have explored various types of strategy framework for forging that link. There is a variety of approaches to strategy, and we have detailed some of them. At the end of the day, the choices tend to be not so much either one strategy or approach or another, but rather the acceptance that more than one kind of management needs to be evident in an organization.

CHECKLIST: CHAPTER 5

After reading this chapter you will have knowledge of:

1 Process, content and context of management strategy
2 Strategy framework
3 The positioning approach
4 Strategic business units in the growth/share matrix
5 How an organization may best adapt to its environment

CHAPTER 6

Leading

In this chapter we will look at the management task of leading, or the directing and guiding of employees and subordinates to help them to attain the organization's objectives with the maximum application of their abilities. In the organizational context, a good leader can be regarded more as a good facilitator than as a traditional commander of people, although both types of leader benefit from a bit of charisma and the ability to inspire groups of people.

It must be noted that, although at times the terms 'leader' and 'manager' are treated as synonymous, there does need to be a distinction between leadership and management. *Leadership is* the ability to influence the attitudes and behaviour of others. *Management* is the formal process of decision and command. Leadership is one important aspect of a manager's job, but it is not all of it.

Here we will examine the importance of providing good leadership in companies, different theories about the nature of leadership, and the various styles of leadership which can be found in organizations, and their effectiveness.

THE IMPORTANCE OF LEADERSHIP

In his book, *The Practice of Management* (1955) Peter Drucker cautions against organizations relying upon leadership, instead of good management, because, although leadership is important, it is also very rare:

> Leadership is of utmost importance. Indeed there is no substitute for it ... but it cannot be taught or learned ... There is no substitute for leadership. But management cannot create leaders. It can only create the conditions under which potential leadership qualities become effective;

> or it can stifle potential leadership. The supply of leadership is much too limited and unpredictable to be depended upon for the creation of the spirit the business enterprise needs to be productive and to hold together. Management must work on creating the spirit by other means. These means may be less effective and more pedestrian. But at least they are available and within management's control. In fact, to concentrate on leadership may only too easily lead management to do nothing at all about the spirit of the organization.

Certainly, however, leadership is an important element of effective management. The functions of management undertaken by the manager will produce far greater results if they have the ingredient of effective leadership added to them. When this effective leadership, or effective direction and guidance, permeates the whole enterprise, the result is a successful organization.

THEORIES OF LEADERSHIP

We will look at the three main leadership theories here: the personality or behavioural approach; the situational approach; and the contingency theory of leadership.

Personality or behavioural traits

The earliest studies of leadership were largely based on attempts to identify the personality traits that leaders possessed. In searching for measurable leadership traits, researchers took two approaches.

The first approach was to compare the personality traits of leaders and non-leaders. This was the most common approach, but it failed to identify any traits that consistently set leaders apart from their followers. As a group, leaders were found to be taller, brighter, more extrovert and self-confident than non-leaders. However, many people who are not leaders also possess these traits, while others who are acknowledged as brilliant leaders do not! For instance, two extremely charismatic, successful leaders – Napoleon and Alexander the Great – were both well below average height! The psychologist, E. E. Jennings, perhaps understood the real value of this approach when he wrote: 'Fifty years of study have failed to produce one personality trait or set of qualities that can be used to discriminate between leaders and non-leaders'.

The second approach was to compare the personality traits of effective leaders with those of ineffective leaders. This, too, has failed to isolate any traits which are strongly associated with successful leadership.

The situational approach

It was because of the inconclusiveness of the studies into the personality traits of leaders that the situational theory of leadership developed. According to this, people follow those leaders who they think are best placed to enable them to achieve their own personal goals and objectives.

The contingency approach to leadership

According to Fiedler (1967), people become leaders not only because of their personal attributes and personalities, but also because of the interaction between them and changing situations. Therefore, an effective leader is one who can adapt and lead in all situations.

Action centred leadership

John Adair further developed the contingency approach to leadership into the idea of action centred, or functional, leadership. According to Adair there are three variables in any work situation: task needs, group needs and individual needs. The effective leader has to be able to balance each set of needs against the demands of the total situation at that point in time. The leader has to judge which should have priority and at what time. This is a very flexible approach to leadership and depends entirely upon the circumstances of the situation.

Figure 6.1 shows how the three sets of needs are interconnected.

The interconnection of each set of needs means that action taken in relation to one particular set will have an effect upon the other two. For example, if the leader concentrates on building up group motivation, his action is liable to motivate the individuals making up the group as well, and the effect of both is usually to make the accomplishment of the task easier. Conversely, if the leader neglects one section of needs, the needs of the other two will not be met fully

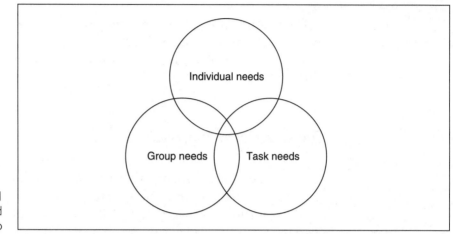

Figure 6.1
Action centred
leadership

either – if task needs are ignored, then the group will cease to have goals to aim at and the individuals will have no occupation or purpose.

LEADERSHIP STYLES

Some earlier explanations of leadership styles classified them on the basis of how leaders use their authority. These regard managers as applying one of the three basic styles:

1 *Autocratic* style. The autocratic leader is seen as a person who commands and expects compliance, who is dogmatic and positive, and who leads and directs others by an ability to give or withhold rewards or punishment.

2 *Democratic/participative style.* The leader who uses this leadership style consults with his subordinates about proposed actions and decisions and encourages them to participate in these decisions.

3 *Independent/self-motivatory style.* This third style of leadership is one in which the leader gives subordinates a substantial degree of independence in their work, leaving them to set their own goals and discover their own ways of achieving them. The leader adopting this style sees his role as one of facilitating the activities of the others by providing them with information, and acting as a contact with the group's external environment.

McGregor's theory X and theory Y

The style adopted, whether autocratic or more participative, will depend in part upon the manager's view of human nature in general, and of the ability of subordinates in particular. McGregor (1960) set out two sets of contrasting views and assumptions about human behaviour: Theory X and Theory Y.

According to Theory X:

1 The average human being has an inherent dislike of work and will avoid it if possible.
2 Because of this human characteristic of dislike of work, most people must be coerced, controlled, directed [or] threatened with punishment to get them to put forth adequate effort towards the achievement of organizational objectives.
3 The average human being prefers to be directed, wishes to avoid responsibility, has relatively little ambition, [and] wants security above all.

Theory X managers will favour autocratic or perhaps paternalistic management styles.

In contrast, according to Theory Y:

1 The expenditure of physical and mental effort in work is as natural as play or rest. The average human being does not inherently dislike work. Depending upon the controllable conditions, work may be a source of satisfaction or a source of punishment.
2 External control and the threat of punishment are not the only means for bringing about effort towards organizational objectives. People will exercise self-direction and self-control in the service of objectives to which they are committed.
3 Commitment to objectives is a [result] of the rewards associated with their achievement ...
4 The average human being learns, under proper conditions, not only to accept but to seek responsibility ...
5 The capacity to exercise a relatively high degree of imagination, ingenuity and creativity in the solution of organizational problems is widely, not narrowly, distributed in the population.
6 Under conditions of modern industrial life, the intellectual potentialities of the average human being are only partially utilized.

Theory Y thus encourages a more participative style of management, or at least consultative leadership, rather than leadership by the imposition of decisions.

Likert's styles of management leadership

Likert (1967) identified four styles of systems of management:

Style 1 Exploitative/authoritative
Style 2 Benevolent/authoritative
Style 3 Consultative
Style 4 Participative/group

1 *Exploitative–authoritative.* Managers who use this style of leadership are highly autocratic; they place little trust in subordinates and use fear and punishment as motivators, with only occasional rewards. They retain all powers of decision-making and only engage in downward communication.

2 *Benevolent/authoritative.* Managers using this style are paternalistic, placing a condescending trust and confidence in subordinates whom they motivate with rewards and some punishment. They allow some upward communication and opinions from their junior ranks and do also delegate some decision-making, although they retain close policy control.

3 *Consultative.* Managers using this leadership style seek out the opinions and ideas of subordinates and work to put them to constructive use. They also engage in communication both upwards and downwards and encourage some participation in decision-making.

4 *Participative–group.* Managers who use this system show complete confidence and trust in their subordinates in all matters. They use the ideas and opinions of subordinates and motivate them through economic rewards and participation, and involve them in setting goals and undertaking appraisals of these goals. In effect, these managers operate as part of a group consisting of both peers and subordinates.

It is this *participative–group* style of leadership which Likert regarded as the most effective for managers. Its effectiveness comes from the group/unit concept that it operates upon. All the members of the group, including the manager or leader, adopt a supportive relationship in which they feel a genuine common interest in terms of needs, values, aspirations, goals and expectations.

INVESTIGATE

Which of Likert's styles of leadership do you think is nearest to that used in an organization you are familiar with, either in that organization as a whole or by your superior or supervisor? Do they differ at all? If so, how, and why?

The managerial grid — Blake and Mouton

Blake and Mouton's managerial grid (Figure 6.2) is a two-dimensional measurement of managers' leadership styles. One axis of the grid represents how production is valued, the other represents the human element in businesses — how people are valued. Scores are allocated from one to ten along both axes (1 = low, 10 = high).

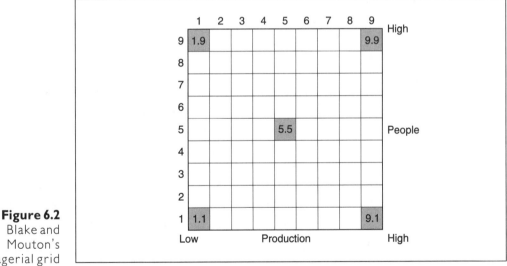

Figure 6.2
Blake and
Mouton's
managerial grid

Using this grid Blake and Mouton identified four extreme styles of management:

1 *Impoverished management.* This style of management is reflected in low scores on both axes as managers show little concern for either people or production values. They tend to be involved to a minimum in the requirements of management.

2 The antithesis of impoverished management occurs when managers are dedicated both to production values and people, scoring highly on both axes.

3 *Country club management.* Here the manager scores low on the production scale and has little concern for production values. Instead, the manager is concerned primarily for people in the managerial role, and places great emphasis on promoting a relaxed and friendly environment. The creation of such a working environment is made at the expense of any co-ordinated effort to accomplish the organization's goals.

4 *Autocratic task managers.* These managers score highly on the production scale but low on the people scale. They are concerned only with developing an efficient operation and have little or no concern for people. They tend to be quite auto-cratic in their leadership style.

EFFECTIVE LEADERSHIP

The thing to remember about all these different leadership styles is that they can all be effective, although at different times, and with different groups of people. Indeed, the best managers are those who do not use just one style all the time, but who recognize that during some situations they will have to exercise autocratic leadership, while during other circumstances they will be most effective by leaving people to work out their own goals and methods of operation.

Managers in charge of a group of research scientists would not be very effective as leaders if they used an autocratic management style, setting the group specific, daily targets to meet, and not consulting the group or listening to their opinions. Such a work situation clearly calls for a far more participative leadership style, where the manager acts as a group chairperson, facilitating the scientists' work.

On the other hand, if a hazardous chemical was released into the laboratory, the managers would not be showing particularly good leadership if they called the group together to debate what action they should take! In these circumstances, an autocratic leadership style is obviously required.

Reddin's three-dimensional theory of management effectiveness

The trouble with Blake and Mouton's managerial grid is that it is only a two-dimensional measurement of management style. It does not take into account that the four basic managerial styles can all be more-or-less effective, depending upon the particular circumstances in which the styles are used. As we have explained, the style that is most effective some of the time is not necessarily the most effective all of the time.

Therefore, to the two dimensions of Blake and Mouton's grid, Reddin (1970) has added a third, measuring 'managerial effectiveness' – or the extent to which the management style used meets the needs of the particular situation.

The Vroom–Yetton leadership model

Yetton and Vroom (1978) developed a model to show which of five management styles, ranging from autocratic to group decision-making, could be used effectively in dealing with different situations. Their work demonstrates that in practice managers do not usually just use one leadership approach or style, but do respond and adapt to circumstances (Yetton and Vroom, 1978):

> Whereas once there were only participative or autocratic managers, we now find that it makes as much sense to talk about participative and autocratic problems.

The five management styles are as follows:

A1 The manager solves the problem or makes a decision on the information available at the time.

A11 The manager gets any information needed from subordinates, and then makes a decision. The subordinates supply specific information in answer to the manager's requests; they do not define or discuss the problem at all.

C1 The manager asks the views of individual subordinates, and then makes a decision.

C11 The manager asks the views of subordinates in a group meeting, and then makes a decision.

G11 The manager shares the problem with subordinates as a group, and tries to reach a consensus decision. The manager's role here is really that of chairperson.

Vroom and Yetton then define seven situational variables, in the form of questions, which should be used with the leadership model. These are as follows:

1 Does the problem possess a quality requirement?
2 Do I have sufficient information to make a high-quality decision?
3 Is the problem structured?
4 Is the acceptance of the decision by my subordinates important for its effective implementation?
5 If I were to make the decision by myself, am I reasonably certain that it would be accepted by my subordinates?
6 Do my subordinates share the organizational goals to be attained by solving this problem?
7 Is conflict among my subordinates likely with the preferred solution?

The leadership model, showing (in the form of a decision tree) the set of managerial styles which could be used in response to the questions/variables given, is illustrated in Figure 6.3.

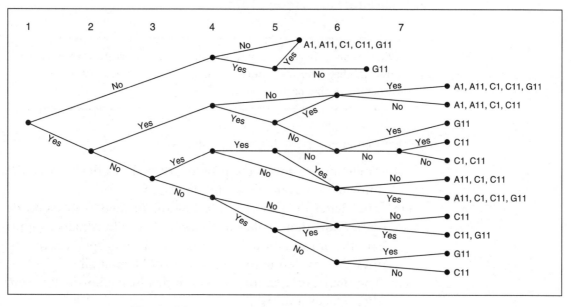

Figure 6.3
The Vroom—Yetton leadership model

Management by wandering around

Peters and Austin (1986) identify two key management roles. These are:

1 That managers must make sure that the culture and operations of the organization are orientated to taking constant care of customers.

2 That managers must endeavour to ensure that the enterprise achieves constant innovation in response to market change and technological obsolescence.

These two roles in turn call for a proper and genuine concern for people at all levels in the organization and effective leadership. Leadership is referred to by Peters and Austin as 'management by wandering around' or MBWA. The concept of MBWA was developed by the Hewlett Packard Corporation, and can be described in the following terms:

1 The basic need for the leader is to be an expert in the protection and promotion of values, and the creation of cultures.

2 The basic leadership values should comprise:

- A competitive belief in being the best.
- A belief in the need to offer superior quality and service to customers and clients, whether internal or external.
- A belief in the need for close attention to detail.
- A belief in the dignity and worth of the individual employee.
- A belief in the need for ongoing innovation and entrepreneurship.

3 An effective leader must be the master of two ends of the spectrum comprising ideas at the highest level of abstraction at one end, and actions at the most mundane level of detail at the other. The leader will first be concerned to create a broad vision of the present and future that will generate excitement and interest on the part of other people in the organization. At the same time the leader will wish to set an example and create enthusiasm through his or her daily identification with, and involvement in, detailed events of implementation. That is, the leader will want to be in on the day-to-day action, no matter how routine it is. In demonstrating a concern for routine and detail the leader will instil values through deeds not words, and through personally demonstrating the application of those values on a day-to-day basis. At the same time the leader will show his or her respect

for those ordinary employees who carry out the day-to-day routines, and demonstrate their individual importance in the wider scheme of things.

4 Success in promoting and instilling values derives from obvious, sincere and sustained personal commitment to those values. This leadership success will also require persistence in reinforcing these values through the actual process of 'wandering around' (or 'walking the job').

5 Leaders formulate their vision, create cultures and instil values by communicating with, and by being highly visible to, employees, customers, suppliers, etc. This is the process of managing by wandering around from which the concept of MBWA derives. MBWA means 'staying in touch with the action', where and when it is happening. Managers 'wander around' the field of action, maintaining close and informal communication links with employees, customers, suppliers, etc. It is the role of the manager under MBWA to 'preach' and reinforce corporate wisdom and values. This he or she does while walking the job, not while sitting in the office. MBWA implies spending much time 'down the line', particularly with junior staff and with those people who, acting in customer service type roles, most need encouragement, reinforcement and a sense of appreciation.

6 For any one manager individually to practise MBWA is not enough. MBWA must be practised by the whole of senior management. 'Setting the tone' needs to be a teamwork process. All need to speak with one voice when promoting the values and culture of the organization.

Vision and holism

Hampden-Turner and Trompenaars (1994) comment on the holistic character of French attitudes towards organization and management. The French describe such concepts as *solidarisme*. The animating principles are:

■ *L'élan vital* (the vital impulse, or spark).
■ Vision as key motivations for any organized community. Mary Parker Follett (1987) describes leadership in holistic terms when she states that it is the leader who 'can organize the experience of the group. ... It is by organizing experi-

ence that we transform experience into power. ... The task of the chief executive is to articulate the integrated unity which his business aims to be. ... The ablest administrators do not merely draw logical conclusions from the array of facts ... they have a vision of the future.'

Hampden-Turner and Trompenaars suggest that vision comes easily to the holistically operating mind, while those with an analysing bias admit, like ex-President Bush of the USA, to being not 'good at the vision thing'.

Vision can be defined as an organized perception or phenomenon. It is an imagined or perceived pattern of communal possibilities to which others can be drawn, given the necessary enthusiasm and momentum on the part of the leader who is promulgating that vision. Bennis and Nanus (1985) see the leader as the person who can transform the organization, in terms of the social architect. They define leadership in terms of the capacity to create compelling vision, to translate it into action, and to sustain it. Their 1985 study of 90 successful US public figures identified the following leadership skills:

- The creation of a vision that others can believe in and adopt as their own. Vision is about the long term. Market imperatives are short-term. The leader uses vision to build a bridge from the present to the future of the organization.
- The communication of that vision (for instance through the process of MBWA), and its translation into practicalities. Its implementation, for example, might be based on the enterprise mission statement, the organization's culture, management by wandering around, or systems of incentive and reward.
- The creation of a climate of organizational trust. Trust acts as an emotional glue that unites leaders and followers in a common purpose, and helps achieve the outcomes of that vision.

Innovation

There are a number of ways in which organizations meet the challenge of change. As part of that the manager has a role as innovator, in the sense of living with and managing change. There is an additional competence associated with the innovator role of the manager as identified in the competing value framework, and it is that of creative thinking.

Quinn *et al.* (1996) list the following statements in an attempt to assess whether you are a creative thinker.

INVESTIGATE

Listed are a series of statements describing individual behaviours or attitudes that have been found to be related to creative thinking ability. Read each statement and *tick* those items that you are surprised to see related to creativity. Then review the list, and *circle* the number of those statements that you think describe you.

1 In a group, voicing unconventional, but thought-provoking opinions.
2 Sticking with a problem over extended periods of time.
3 Getting overly enthusiastic about things.
4 Getting good ideas when doing nothing in particular.
5 Occasionally relying on intuitive hunches and the feeling of 'rightness' or 'wrongness' when moving towards the solution of a problem.
6 Having a high degree of aesthetic sensitivity.
7 Occasionally beginning work on a problem that could only dimly be sensed and not yet expressed.
8 A tendency to forget details, such as names of people, streets, highways, small towns, and so on.
9 Sometimes feeling that the trouble with many people is that they take things too seriously.
10 Feeling attracted to the mystery of life.

When we think about who is creative, our popular notions of creativity tend towards individuals whom we regard as singularly unique, gifted, talented, and just different from the rest of us. In the arts and sciences we think of people like Bach, Beethoven, Einstein and Rembrandt. In business we think of people like Steve Jobs (co-founder of Apple Computers), Jack Welch (General Electric) and Anita Roddick (The Body Shop). People rarely think of creative ability existing in the general population. More importantly, we are rarely encouraged to think or learn about being creative. It is not surprising, then, that many people underestimate their creative abilities. In fact, a very wide range of behaviours and personality traits have been found to be associated with creative ability. More important, creative thinking is a skill that each person can develop. Creativity is a way of thinking that involves the generation of new ideas and solutions.

More specifically, it is the process of associating known things or ideas into new combinations and relationships.

An example of this creative thinking utilizing existing information is that of Imation (3M). The researchers at the company had expert knowledge of adhesives and also knew that people often write themselves notes on pieces of paper. They brought the two elements together to create Post-it note pads, and had thus discovered a new association between the two elements.

Quinn *et al.* (1996) argue that 'the use of creative thinking in problem-solving allows organizations to access human resources that often go untapped'. In comparing Japanese and American organizations, Deming (1986) has argued that 'the greatest waste in America is failure to use the abilities of people.' Managers should recognize that employees' abilities are a free resource. Although most resources have extra cost factors involved, creative thinking does not. From this perspective, one could argue that no organization – public or private – can afford to waste this resource.

Beyond the overall organizational benefits, managers should recognize the personal benefits of encouraging creative thinking among their employees. Creative thinking can increase the effectiveness of the unit through better problem-solving. In addition, creative thinking can be used as a motivational tool. In the work environment of large organizations, it is sometimes easy for employees to see themselves as a replaceable cog in the giant wheel and to become demotivated. When individuals are encouraged to be creative in their thinking and problem-solving, they are more likely to feel unique, valued, and affirmed as important employees of the organization. Thus, not only are there benefits from the employees' good ideas, but individuals feel better about themselves as employees. In sum, the encouragement of employees' creative thinking can result in substantial benefits to the organization, to the work unit, and to the individuals who exercise their creative skills.

Managers often find there is significant resistance to change, and this is discussed in Chapter 12. In terms of innovation, especially innovation that is linked to new technological advances, there may be a need for what Morden (1993) calls 'a positive and deliberate emphasis on overcoming the impediments to innovation'. Morden goes on to list three key impediments, which are:

1 The 'not invented here' syndrome. Peters (1985) describes this management view as negative to external developments and suggests a three-stage solution to this attitude:

- be positive rather than negative about competitors' products;
- be positive about other industries' products and services from which you can learn;
- open up the organization to the 'buzz of what's going on out there that's interesting'.

2 The classic approach to the problem is called 'imitation', i.e. adapt any appropriate technology or innovation and improve upon it, then adopt it.

3 The 'risk aversion and fear of failure' syndrome. Some areas of innovation are inherently risky. Organizations that are risk-averse are therefore less likely to be innovative. Morden (1996) uses the Goldsmith and Clutterbuck (1985) sample of UK companies as a starting point for suggesting the areas of UK management that form key discouragements to innovation. He says:

- They insist on reviewing all risk decisions at a high level. As a result, managers 'pass the buck', knowing that some-one above will take (or 'chicken out' from taking) the responsibility.
- They impose excessive financial controls, coupled with the fact that managers do not have the discretionary spending power to take initiatives of their own accord.
- They have excessively rigid rules and procedures. Risk ventures, by their nature, involve a departure from the rules.
- They expect a guaranteed return. Risk ventures will not always come off.
- They penalize managers when the venture does not succeed. The manager whose risk venture fails may expect delayed promotion, to be shunted aside, or even to be fired.
- They do not provide enough rewards for success or adequate incentive to take risk. Similarly,
- By the example set by top management. If directors do not take the company into calculated risk, then people down the line are unlikely to stick out their necks. If they talk about success as simply hitting the budget, they will never encourage people to reach out to seize new opportunities. Morden (1993) suggests that inappropriate organization structure and culture can have a detrimental effect on technology development and innovation because:

1 Complex bureaucratic structures tend to encourage conformity, inertia and the maintenance of the status quo. Innovation may be perceived as a threat to the stability of such structures. The expectation in bureaucracies is that people will 'play by the rules' or 'manage by the book', not act creatively or 'rock the boat'.

2 Centralization acts to minimize innovative autonomy (or the opportunity for the exercise of internal entrepreneurship or intrapreneurship) and maximize central control and sanction. Centralized structures prescribe and limit the discretion of people within the hierarchy, and impose the values and culture of senior management in a 'top down' manner. Centralized structures may be unwilling to empower innovators, even if innovation is seen in general terms as 'a good thing'. Worse, in emphasizing expectations of conformist behaviour, the deviance or perceived failure associated with unsuccessful attempts at innovation or intrapreneurship may incur punishment. Centralized structures may demonstrate indifference or hostility to changes that are driven from the 'bottom up', precisely because centralized structures, by definition, are driven in a 'top down' fashion.

3 Hierarchical communication is a feature of centralized bureaucratic structures. Weak lateral communication links reinforce centralized direction and control, and give rise to what Kanter (1985) calls the 'dominance of restrictive vertical relationships', which, combined with:

4 Departmentalized and functionally centred structures make interdisciplinary or cross-functional communication and coordination difficult, let alone facilitating any kind of multi-functional project management. Kanter describes this situation in terms of 'departments as fortresses'.

5 Role cultures may have been established such that innovative or intrapreneurial activities may simply not have been prescribed. No organizational place may have been allocated to innovative activities within the standardized and formalized task. No allocations or job descriptions may have been laid down. Role holders may therefore respond to the issue of innovation in such terms as: (a) 'It's not my job', (b) 'It's more than my job's worth to suggest new ideas.' The risk posed to role structures by conditions of change and innovation have been documented by Burns and Stalker (1961) and by Handy (1985), who notes that: the role organization will

III

succeed as long as it can operate in a stable environment ... where economies of scale are [perceived as] more important than flexibility or where technical expertise and ... specialization are more important than ... innovation. [But] role cultures are slow to perceive the need for change and slow to change even if the need is seen ... the role culture is likely to continue to forge straight ahead confident in its ability to shape the future in its own image, then collapse.'

6 Internal orientations (for instance as described by Hampden-Turner and Trompenaars) tend to characterize centralized, bureaucratic or role structures. Such organizations are frequently unable or unwilling to look outwards and to absorb new ideas (the 'we have nothing to learn from them' syndrome).

SUMMARY

We have seen how leadership in a managerial context is about organizing, directing, guiding and helping people to do their work well.

There are several different leadership styles which managers may use to achieve this, ranging from an autocratic style, to a more participative approach as a facilitator. Each of these approaches will be effective in different situations: the mark of a good manager is knowing which style will be most effective in any given situation.

CHECKLIST: CHAPTER 6

After reading this chapter you will have knowledge of:

1 Theories of leadership:
- Personality
- Situational approach
- Contingency approach
- Action centred

2 Styles of leadership:
- Autocratic
- Democratic
- Independence of subordinates

- Likert's styles of management leadership:
  - Exploitative/authoritative
  - Benevolent/authoritative
  - Consultative
  - Participative
- Blake and Mouton's managerial grid
  - Impoverished
  - Enriched
  - Country club
  - Autocratic

3 Effective leadership:
- Reddin's 3D theory
- Vroom–Yetton model
- Management by wandering around
- Vision and holism
- Innovation

CHAPTER 7

Motivating

As well as leading and directing their staff, managers also have to motivate staff to work well in order to achieve the organization's objectives. In this chapter we will look at some of the problems that managers face in trying to motivate their staff, together with various motivation theories (from those concentrating on job content, to process and contingency theories), and some of the means that managers can use to motivate their workforce and subordinates.

WHAT IS MOTIVATION?

Motivation can be said to be the total propensity or level of desire of an individual to behave in a certain manner at a certain time. Within the context of the organization, motivation can be defined as the willingness of an individual to respond to the organization's requirements in the short run.

Everyone has what can be called latent energy, or motivation, within them which is *potentially* available. But this general state of being does not guarantee that an individual will behave appropriately in a given situation. The motivation within has to be directed towards a specific goal; it then becomes what is known as a 'motive for behaviour'.

Choices and priorities

Unfortunately, motivation is not quite so simple as that! It involves the person making choices from the available alternatives, about how best to allocate her energy and time. Most people are involved in many activities and groups, creating a multitude of relationships, and as the individual does not have unlimited time or energy, he must choose the activities on which to expend both. People tend to be more motivated in activities/relationships that offer the greatest perceived personal rewards or the fewest penalties, i.e. they will decide their own priorities.

It is important that managers understand this when they try to motivate employees, for from this it can be said that an individual who is not performing effectively within the organization is not necessarily lacking in motivation. Rather, the individual may not have been motivated in such a way as to give her role within the organization priority over other relationships and situations. Thus managers do not just have to motivate their subordinates; they have to motivate them in the right direction.

Motivation and personality

Motivation cannot be achieved in a vacuum independent of the individual's 'needs', 'wants' and 'fears'. Thus the central problem of motivation, as far as the manager is concerned, is how to induce a group of people with different needs, wants, fears and personalities to work together in order to achieve the organization's goals.

Needs and perceptions

The bases on which an individual's level of motivation is established are her needs and perceptions. Needs can be defined as desired, but as yet unrealized, goals; perceptions as organized impressions of her place in a particular environment, both as to the present and the anticipated future.

THEORIES OF MOTIVATION

Motivation theories can be divided into two types: content theories, and process theories. According to content motivation theories, which we will look at first, individuals are motivated by a 'package' of needs and wants which they pursue. Maslow's hierarchy of needs (1954), and Herzberg's two-factor motivation theory (1966) are examples of content theories.

In contrast, process theories of motivation examine the ways in which certain outcomes of events become attractive to people, and therefore are pursued by them. Process theories include Handy's motivation calculus, and Vroom's expectancy theory. Process theories differ from content theories in that they assume that individuals can choose their own needs and goals.

Management theories and motivation

The classical school of management theory assumes that workers are self-seeking, and only motivated by money, and so maximum productivity can be achieved by using assembly-line manufacturing processes with high rates of pay. However, breaking down tasks into their simplest elements, so that a day's work on (for example) a car assembly-line consists of repeating a task which has to be completed in under a minute several thousand times, creates mind-numbingly tedious jobs. Motivation will always be a problem in such industries, regardless of how much the employees are paid, and it tends to show itself in high staff-turnover rates, high absenteeism, and generally low morale.

The research of Elton Mayo in the early 1930s into productivity at the Western Electric Company showed conclusively that workers are not just motivated by economic motives, but that social contact and work-group self-government are also very powerful motivators.

Maslow's theory of human motivation

Abraham Maslow (1954) advanced a number of important propositions about human behaviour and motivation (Figure 7.1). First, he recognized that humans are wanting creatures, i.e. they want things, and continually want more. Even though specific needs can become

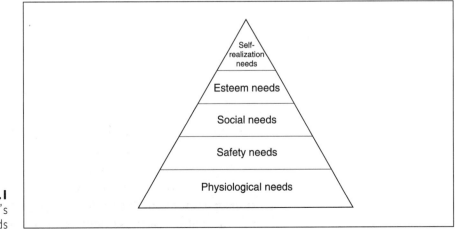

Figure 7.1
Maslow's
hierarchy of needs

satisfied, needs in general do not. Second, Maslow proposed that a satisfied need does not act as a motivator: only unsatisfied needs motivate behaviour. Third, human needs can be arranged in a series of levels — into a hierarchy of importance — consisting (in ascending order) of physiological needs, safety needs, social needs, esteem needs, and self-realization needs. As soon as needs on the lower levels of the pyramid are fulfilled, those on the next level will emerge as motivators and demand satisfaction:

1 *Physiological needs.* The lowest level needs are physiological ones. These are needs which must be satisfied to maintain life, and include the need for food, water, air, etc. Until these are satisfied they act as the primary motivators, taking precedence over any other needs. Thus a starving person will not be motivated by desires for self-fulfilment, but by the need to obtain food.

2 *Safety needs.* The next level of the hierarchy is that of safety needs. These come into operation as effective motivators only after a person's physiological needs have been reasonably satisfied. These take the form of the desire for protection from physical danger, economic security, an orderly and predictable world, etc.

3 *Social needs.* The third level is that of social needs. Once again, these only become effective motivators as needs for safety become reasonably satisfied. They include the need to belong to a group, to be accepted, to give and receive friendship and affection. Social needs act as powerful motivators of human behaviour, but may be regarded as threats by an organization's management in some instances. For example, managers may regard some informal groupings within a company as threats to the company's operations and so seek to break them up.

4 *Esteem needs.* Esteem needs form the next level of the pyramid. These include both the need for self-esteem and for the esteem of others. Self-esteem includes aspects such as self-confidence, self-respect, knowledge, etc. The esteem of others includes the need for their respect, recognition, appreciation, and for status in others' eyes. The competitive desire to excel is an almost universal trait. This is a major esteem need, and if properly harnessed by management can produce extremely high organizational performance. A manager's stimulation of these needs can bring feelings of worth

and value; if they are unfulfilled this can result in feelings of inferiority, helplessness and weakness. However unlike the lower levels of needs, esteem needs are rarely completely satisfied, and tend to be insatiable.

5 *Self-realization needs.* At the pinnacle of Maslow's needs' hierarchy is the need for self-realization. This is the individual's need for realizing his own potential for self-fulfilment and continued self-development; for being creative in the broadest sense of the term. The specific form of these needs will obviously vary from one individual to another.

Money as a need

You may have noted that Maslow did not include pay or money as a need in his pyramid. He considered money as a means of satisfying various other needs at the different levels, but not as a specific need in itself. Money is of course more important in satisfying the lower levels of needs in the hierarchy.

Qualifications of Maslow's theory

Maslow's theory of needs can be applied generally, but not specifically. It is a dynamic picture rather than a static one. In addition, it must be recognized that levels in the hierarchy are not rigidly fixed, but do tend to overlap. Another problem with the theory is that the chain of causation may not always run from stimulus to individual needs to behaviour. Although the theory states that a person deprived of two needs will want the more basic of them, the person may not act so logically, as other factors may also be having an influence.

Further problems associated with Maslow's theory are that the same need will not lead to the same response in all individuals. Individuals may develop substitute goals if they cannot satisfy a particular need directly; and many of the things which humans strive for are remote, long-range goals that can be achieved only through a series of steps.

Herzberg's two-factor theory (1966)

Herzberg has provided an alternative explanation of the ways in which factors such as salary, achievement, and working conditions affect people's motivation to work. He asked 200 engineers and accountants about the factors which improved or reduced their job satisfaction. Two distinct groups of factors were identified:

Hygiene factors	Motivating factors
Company policy	Achievement
Salary	Recognition
Supervision	Responsibility
Working conditions	Job itself

Hygiene factors

Hygiene factors were those factors which created a favourable environment for motivating people and prevented job dissatisfaction. They included company policy and administration, managerial supervision, salary, interpersonal relations and working conditions. If any of these factors were felt to be substandard or poor, there tended to be job dissatisfaction. However, the presence of such hygiene factors did not in themselves create job satisfaction.

Motivating factors

Motivating factors promoted job satisfaction by their presence, but only when hygiene factors were also present in satisfactory levels. Motivating factors included achievement, recognition, the work itself, responsibility and advancement. The common element in these motivators is that they are all related to the intrinsic nature of the work itself; they are not merely elements or circumstances surrounding the job.

Herzberg's work shows that satisfaction and dissatisfaction are not simple opposites. Each is governed by its own group of factors: satisfaction by motivating factors and dissatisfaction by hygiene factors. To remove the causes of dissatisfaction is not the same as creating satisfaction.

If this is correct, it has important implications for managers in general, and personnel managers in particular. For example, the provision of welfare services may improve the working environment, but will not in itself motivate people to work.

Maslow and Herzberg

There is a strong similarity between Maslow's hierarchy of needs and Herzberg's classification of factors influencing motivation and job satisfaction or dissatisfaction. Herzberg's hygiene factors correspond to Maslow's physiological, safety, and social needs, whereas motivating factors correspond to the higher personal growth needs in the hierarchy.

Self-realization Esteem needs	}	Motivating factors
Social needs Safety needs Physiological needs	}	Hygiene factors

McClelland – motivating needs

David McClelland identified three basic motivating needs which, to some extent, correspond to Maslow's social, esteem and self-realization needs. McClelland measured the levels of these needs in various individuals, discovering that the existence of one need did not mean that the other two did not exist; rather, that an individual could be strongly motivated by a combination of all three needs.

McClelland's three motivating needs were as follows:

1 *The need for affiliation.* People with a strong need for affiliation usually gain pleasure from a group within which they enjoy intimacy, understanding and friendly interaction, and are concerned with maintaining good relationships.
2 *The need for power.* Those with a strong need for power want to exercise influence and control. They seek positions of leadership and influence, and tend to be argumentative, demanding, forceful, and good communicators.
3 *The need for achievement.* People with a strong need for achievement have an intense desire for success, and an equally intense fear of failure.

Further research by McClelland showed that, as a group, managers have strong needs for achievement and power, but low affiliation needs. Although those managers who have strong achievement needs tend to advance faster than others, it must be noted that to be a successful manager requires other characteristics besides a burning drive for success and achievement. Managers normally spend their days interacting with other people, and they have to work and get on well with others. Therefore, a need for affiliation is also important in managers.

PROCESS THEORIES OF MOTIVATION

Herzberg, Maslow and McClelland's theories of motivation are content theories. We will now look at some of the more recent process theories of motivation.

Equity theory — Adams

In his equity theory, Adams (1963) puts forward the idea that the absolute situation of workers is less important than people's situations *in comparison* to other similar workers, or to what these people feel their situations ought to be. Any perceived inequalities, for example in wage levels, tend to create unease and dissatisfaction, and will thus affect the individual's motivation to work. This dissatisfaction caused by perceived inequalities is often demonstrated by workers when they compare their pay scales and living standards to other similar workers, e.g. the UK car industry has been renowned for leapfrog pay claims between Vauxhall and Ford.

Two important points should be noted. First, that the situation of the person may not actually be unfair, but is just *perceived* to be unfair. Second, this unease will be caused even if the inequality works in the individual's favour, as well as if he thinks he is getting a bad deal. If people do not think that they are being adequately rewarded for the effort they put into a job, either by money or recognition, they will reduce that effort to a level which they think is appropriate for the rewards they receive.

Expectancy theory — Vroom

According to expectancy theory Vroom (1964), the level of motivation that an individual feels for doing a particular activity depends upon the extent to which the results are expected to contribute to her own particular needs and goals.

Following on from this theory of expectation, it can be said that the strength of an individual's motivation is a factor of the strength of preference for the particular outcome, and the expectation that this outcome will occur if certain behaviour is used or actions carried out. This is shown in Figure 7.2.

$$M = P \times \left(\frac{Ex}{E}\right)$$

where M = strength of motivation
P = strength of preference for outcome
E = effort needed to secure outcome
Ex = expectation outcome will occur

Figure 7.2
Motivation
calculus

Normally, this calculation is not consciously made each time a person decides to do something. But certainly for major decisions, such as whether or not to change jobs, most people do at least weigh up the points for and against such a move.

The contingency approach to motivation

Theorists such as Kurt Levin point out that an individual's motivation cannot be looked at in isolation because people interact with life outside the organization, and also with others inside it. So the motivation of a person depends upon more than just his needs and expectations, and will change according to circumstances. Being complex, even fickle creatures, different people react in different ways to things, and an individual's level of motivation can change from day to day

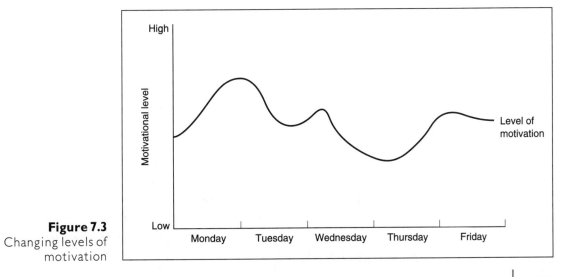

Figure 7.3
Changing levels of
motivation

and from hour to hour, depending upon how he feels. Figure 7.3 shows how an individual's level of motivation can change over a week.

WAYS OF MOTIVATING STAFF

Chris Argyris (1964) maintains that the work situation of an individual will affect the personal development and potential of that person. He identifies seven stages of development from infant to mature behaviour:

1 Infant passivity	$\longrightarrow$	Adult activity
2 Dependence	$\longrightarrow$	Independence
3 Limited behaviours	$\longrightarrow$	Many different behaviours
4 Erratic and brief interests	$\longrightarrow$	Stable deeper interests
5 Short time perspective	$\longrightarrow$	Longer time perspective
6 Subordinate social position	$\longrightarrow$	Equal/superior position
7 Lack of self-awareness	$\longrightarrow$	Self-awareness and self-control

Argyris argues that many organizations still do not encourage their staff to develop mature patterns of behaviour in their work: jobs are reduced to minimal routine tasks, wider thinking is discouraged, and most staff take no part in making decisions. In other words, the organizations are promoting and encouraging McGregor's Theory X management. (This was discussed in the preceding chapter.)

In contrast, Argyris would like to see companies practising Theory Y management: encouraging greater participation by their employees, better communications, and job enlargement and enrichment, so that people have the opportunity to develop as individuals. This would benefit the organizations as well as their employees by removing many causes of dissatisfaction, as well as helping to motivate people more by allowing them more responsibility and respect.

Job enrichment, defined by Herzberg as 'the planned process of upgrading the responsibility, challenge, and content of the work', can definitely increase a person's motivation, as it tends to give the individual involved more power over decisions which affect him, and generally adds to the interest and responsibility of the job. (Although, of course, the extra responsibility of the work has to be rewarded appropriately.)

Job enlargement increases the number of operations performed by one person in one task cycle. This is more of a hygiene factor, removing dissatisfaction, because it should help to reduce the repetition and boredom of the work, although it is unlikely to increase motivation among the workforce.

Unfortunately, there is no easy answer to give to managers on how to motivate their staff. Organizations try to increase worker satisfaction with pay incentives and bonuses, giving individuals a say in decisions which affect them, and increasing the interest and responsibility of jobs. Different companies, and different departments, will all need to use different ways.

Perhaps the best advice is 'do as you would be done by'. Consider which factors motivate you in your work – job satisfaction through responsibility, interest and variety in your work, recognition of your abilities and effort – and bear in mind that these factors will also probably be motivators for most other people, regardless of their position in your organization.

SUMMARY

Motivating employees in an organization is difficult, but very important, as people who are motivated and satisfied with their jobs work harder and are more productive than those people who are not motivated by their work.

People are motivated by a combination of needs, wants, and fears. Individuals will be motivated by different things at different stages in their careers and lives, as personal priorities change.

Job satisfaction and job dissatisfaction are not opposite sides of the same coin: removing factors which cause dissatisfaction, such as poor working conditions, will not increase job satisfaction, which is influenced by motivating factors such as responsibility and achievement.

CHECKLIST: CHAPTER 7

This chapter has given you knowledge about:

1 What motivation is

2 Theories of motivation:
   ■ Management theories and motivation

- Maslow's theory of hierarchical needs:
  - Physiological
  - Safety
  - Social
  - Esteem
  - Self-realization
- Herzberg's two-factor theory:
  - Hygiene factors
  - Motivating factors
- McClelland — motivating needs:
  - Affiliation
  - Power
  - Achievement
- Process theories of motivation:
  - Equity theory — Adams
  - Expectancy theory — Vroom
  - Contingency approach

3 Ways of motivating staff

CHAPTER **8**

Communicating

Communicating is a vital part of management. It links all the management processes together, and managers could not do their jobs without communicating.

Communicating can be defined as 'an attempt to achieve as complete and as accurate an understanding as possible between two or more people. It is an act characterized by a desire in one or more individuals to exchange information, ideas or feelings'. A more concise definition can be given as 'the process by which people attempt to share meaning via the transmission of symbolic messages'.

Communicating involves an exchange of ideas and information. This exchange takes place between the organization and the surrounding environment (here, communication can be seen as a way of connecting the organization with the outside world), and also inside the organization. Effective communications within a company are essential for the success of the organization.

In this chapter we will look at the links between communicating and the task of management, the communication process, communication channels in organizations, and the impact of IT on communication systems and on management.

MANAGING AND COMMUNICATING

Communicating is synonymous with managing: you cannot manage effectively without communicating. Managers spend their days communicating with other people: with subordinates, peers, superiors, customers, suppliers, and so on, by telephone, face-to-face meetings, electronic mail, written memos and reports, etc. One study by Rosemary Stewart of 160 managers over a four-week period found that on average they spent two-thirds of their working time with other people – attending meetings, giving and receiving information and instructions, discussing matters with colleagues. Most of their remaining time tended to be spent preparing and reading reports (Stewart, 1970)!

Communicating is also an integral part of the other elements of the management process.

Communicating and planning

We saw in Chapter 2 that planning is used to guide the organization towards its intended objectives and goals. Communicating information to managers is essential to the planning process. Without accurate information, managers cannot formulate relevant plans, and it is only through the communication process that plans are relayed down the organization to those subordinates and employees who have to implement the plans and meet the targets set out in them.

Communicating and organizing

Similarly, managers need to communicate in order to organize. Organizing is aimed at prescribing specific activities which are required to achieve the goals and objectives identified within corporate plans, and it is very dependent on effective communication. Communication is needed to provide managers with an understanding of the goals they are trying to implement. The entire purpose of the organizational structure is to create an effective communication system up and down the company's hierarchy.

Communicating, motivating and leading

In order to lead and motivate their staff, managers have to be able to communicate with them. Perhaps the aspect of communicating which is most important here is not the one normally associated with bosses and their employees, i.e. downward communication from the manager to subordinates, but rather, upward communication. Communicating is always a two-way process, and although the image of managers is normally one of initiating communications, with others listening and receiving information, managers in fact spend more time on the receiving end of communications. A good motivator and leader is one who listens to people.

Communicating and control

Control was mentioned in Chapter 2 when planning was discussed. It involves setting standards, monitoring performance and correcting deviations from these standards. Control depends upon feedback, which means accurate, timely and appropriate communication to the correct people. (The control process is discussed in the next chapter.)

Figure 8.1 is a model of the management process and summarizes the interrelationship between communicating and managing.

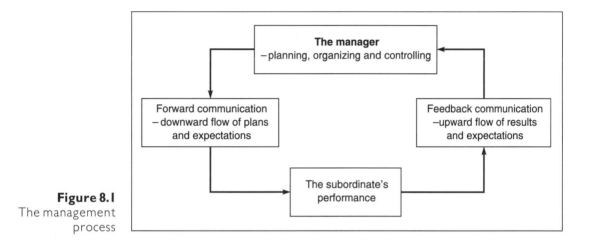

Figure 8.1
The management process

THE PURPOSE OF COMMUNICATING

To sum up the last section, there are a number of important reasons why good communications are vital for management. These include the following:

1 *Decision-making.* Management is concerned with decision-making, and the quality of those decisions depends to a large extent on the quality of the information communicated to the decision-makers.

2 *Organizing.* Communication is vital in starting the organizational processes. These processes are concerned with acquiring resources, developing them, and transferring finished goods and services to the customers. These all involve work teams and reporting relationships, and unless decisions are conveyed to and from the appropriate people, none of the organization's tasks can be accomplished.

3 *Influencing.* Communicating is all about persuading, informing, and educating. Therefore, its effect is to mould opinions.

4 *Activating.* Another purpose of communicating is to initiate action. Communication, in effect, acts as the regulating mechanism for beginning, continuing, and halting the company's business.

THE COMMUNICATION CYCLE

In order to use the resources at its disposal properly and effectively, management must carefully develop and maintain an adequate communication system. Certainly, one of the most basic skills that any management group must have is the ability to communicate.

The communication cycle (Figure 8.2) consists of five stages. All of these stages have to be completed for the process to be said to be a success:

1 *Perceive.* The communication process is centred around perception. This involves an individual assigning meaning to the signals he receives from the environment. The initiator of a message has received certain signals from the environment that he perceives as requiring attention. The purpose in communicating is to transmit information about initial perceptions to a second person. Therefore, the initiator must define clearly what he wishes to convey. If he is successful in structuring thoughts, the recipient of the message should in turn

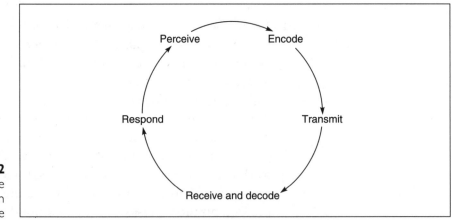

Figure 8.2
The communication cycle

perceive the need for action. However, the perception of two individuals is never identical; rather, the communication is understood in similar ways by both parties through the use of common symbols.

2 *Encode.* Once the individual originating the communication has clearly perceived the need for action, and defined the thoughts he wishes to convey, he has to put these thoughts into a code using communication symbols that will be understood by the recipient. It is important that he expresses thoughts, intentions, and impressions by means of symbols which accurately represent the message he wants to give to the recipient. These symbols can be written, verbal or any other symbols (such as expression, demeanour, etc.).

3 *Transmit.* Transmission is the sending of communication symbols from the message's originator to its receiver, either verbally or non-verbally. The selection of the method of transmission must be made after due consideration to cost, speed, accuracy, physical distance between the two parties, the need for 'personal' messages, and the type and quality of the transmission media available.

4 *Receive and decode.* Once the originator has sent out a message, the receiver must assign meaning to it. Thus the receiver must decode the message. This is essential, since the meaning that the message's receiver assigns to it governs the extent to which the communication process has been successful. If the receiver either does not or cannot understand what the sender of the message is trying to convey, then the process has not been successful.

5 *Response.* The final stage in the communication process is one of recycling. The receiver of the message considers the response he will make to the communication. This response will show just how well the original perception and message have been conveyed.

Data and information

It must be noted that, with regard to the human communication process, we have to differentiate between data and information. As far as human communication is concerned information can be defined as data which has meaning to the receiver. Data which does not convey meaning to the receiver is the equivalent of nonsense.

One purpose of communicating which has already been mentioned is to affect the behaviour of the message's receiver. It is therefore a mistake to assume that communication has been accomplished once the data has been transmitted. Transmission does not guarantee that the message's original intended meaning has been conveyed. Both the receiver and the person transmitting the message can affect the meaning ultimately communicated. The person sending the message has only limited control over what the person receiving it will perceive, while the receiver, because of a variety of reasons, such as personal background, psychological make-up, or 'noise' in the communication process, may see no meaning at all in the message, or assign to it a totally incorrect meaning.

HOW TO COMMUNICATE EFFECTIVELY IN ORGANIZATIONS

Although there are many possible standards that can be used to judge the effectiveness of a system of communication, speed, accuracy, and cost serve as representative measures. Businesses today need rapid and accurate communication and information systems. Decisions often have to be made at short notice because of the changing nature of the business environment. Nevertheless, these decisions must be based on adequate information. Therefore, an organization's communication system has to be capable of conveying large amounts of information quickly to and from the sources of the data and the decision-makers. At the same time, the system must be capable of transmitting accurate and timely information to the places at which it is required.

The principles of good communication

Effective communication is not solely a function of an effective communication system. We also need to look at the principles of, or criteria for, good communication, regardless of the system by which it is transmitted. The American Management Association (AMA) has suggested the following as principles of good communication:

1 The communicator must clarify ideas before attempting to communicate them.
2 The true purpose or message of each communication must be identified and examined.

3 The whole physical and human setting in which the communication is made must be considered carefully.
4 There needs to be consultation with other people when planning communications, so that conflicting or unintelligible messages are not sent.
5 The communicator should be aware of the overtones that are communicated in any message, as well as the message's basic content.
6 Every opportunity should be taken to convey something of help or value to the message's receiver.
7 Communications should be followed up in order to check that the intended meaning has been received and understood.
8 Communications need to be supported by the sender's actions, or else conflicting and contradictory messages will be transmitted to the receiver.
9 Good communications depend on a willingness to listen and understand, by both parties.

The following additional principles are also required for effective communications:

1 *Integrity.* Both personal integrity and integrity on the part of the organization. The integrity of the organization depends partly on supporting the position of middle- and junior-ranking managers. Since they occupy centres of communication networks, the organization should encourage them to use their positions for this purpose. Thus it is important that senior managers do not go over the heads of their subordinates and contact employees directly, unless it is unavoidable, because this risks undermining their subordinates' authority.
2 *Clarity.* The sender of a message is responsible for formulating the communication and expressing it in a clear and understandable way. If this is done, it should overcome some of the barriers to effective communication, such as badly expressed memos, faulty translations and transmissions, unclarified assumptions, bad handwriting, etc.
3 *Trust.* Trust is the key to effective interpersonal communications. Employees will not send accurate and open messages to their manager unless they trust the manager. They must have confidence that the manager will not use the information they have given her to the employees' detriment. They

must believe that the information will not be inappropriately or inaccurately transmitted to other people, and that the information they give to the manager will be treated fairly on its own merits.

BARRIERS TO EFFECTIVE COMMUNICATION

We have seen how important communication is for coordinating activities within an organization, and for bringing about action. Because of this it is very important to understand what sort of barriers may prevent effective communication, and how these barriers might arise. These may be identified and explained as follows.

Lack of preparation

Inadequate preparation reduces the effectiveness of any communication. This failure usually arises from a belief that there already exists a ready-made package of information, which needs only to be directed towards the appropriate recipients to bring about the required effect. This is a mistake. Time and thought needs to be given to communicating. The person initiating the message needs to be clear about objectives; needs to consider alternatives; and then select the form of the message. A conscious choice of communication techniques must then be made. For example, would a notice of redundancy be best conveyed in person, or by telephone or letter? A curt letter of dismissal would inform someone adequately that they had lost their job, but the same message delivered in person would normally soften the blow.

Lack of clarity

Another problem with communicating lies in a tendency for messages to be vague and lack clarity. This often leads to costly errors and costly correction procedures.

Lack of openness

A lack of openness on the part of both the sender of the message and the receiver is a frequent cause of poor communication. The sender of the message should not give only part of the information needed. In the same way, the message's receiver must be prepared to listen to the information, and to accept it, even if it is unwelcome. This is especially important when the information is given by a subordinate. If managers only accept information that they want to hear, then eventually they will either only receive messages which are untrue, or receive no information at all.

Assumptions

Unclarified assumptions which underlie many messages also cause problems and prevent effective communications.

Premature evaluation

Rodgers, in *The Seven Point Plan* (1970), points to the tendency to jump to conclusions prematurely when receiving information, instead of keeping an open mind and judging the message objectively.

Differing cultures and backgrounds

The problems caused by different social backgrounds, different cultures (both organizational and social), age differences, jargon differences, and so on, which prevent clear communications between parties, should *never* be underestimated.

COMMUNICATION CHANNELS

Organizations have two basic kinds of communication channel within their structures: formal channels and informal ones.

Formal communication channels

Formal communication channels are those which are officially designed and recognized by the organization for the transmission of official messages inside or outside it. The formal channels are determined by the organization's structure and the organizational chart, detailing the official lines of authority, reporting relationships, and where responsibility and accountability lie. All these relationships involve communication. For instance, the exercising of authority can be seen as a downward flow of information from a manager to a subordinate. Communication through formal channels can be complicated, however, by the fact that subordinates do not communicate in the same way with their managers as they do with their peers.

Informal communication channels

An informal communication network (or 'grapevine') is essential for the successful operation of a company. A typical informal network involves members within the same level of the organization, and (depending on how formal or informal the general organizational structure and atmosphere are) can also involve employees at different levels of seniority. It cannot replace the formal communication channels, but it can complement and enhance them.

The formal channels are often static, while the organization they seek to activate is dynamic and must react quickly to changing situations. The informal network is more flexible and is able to convey information with amazing speed and accuracy. Thus the informal communication channels act as very beneficial, rapid problem-solvers in many companies.

Team briefings

The formal and informal communication channels tend to merge in team briefing groups. These groups are small (usually less than 30 people) and are arranged on a regulated but informal basis. The communicator is of a higher status than the rest of the group – either a supervisor or manager – and the purpose of the meetings is to inform the members of the group of what is happening within the organization, what is expected of them, and so on. This downward communication is important, but so is the informal feedback which results from this face-to-face contact and discussion.

Team briefings and discussions also help to improve employees' morale and commitment, as they are able to feel that they can make more of a personal contribution to the organization.

INFORMATION TECHNOLOGY AND COMMUNICATING

The IT revolution has had a significant impact on communications within organizations and on their managers. At a very minimum, the latest communications and computer technology enable businesses to deliver information and data far more quickly to the people who need it, and at a lower cost, than they ever could before. The latest technology in digital computers can transmit everything – voice, data, or image – by converting them into a stream of computer on-off pulses, and communication networks are now being updated to become multifunctional links carrying everything from telephone calls to television pictures. At the same time, new ways of sending digital information are dramatically lowering the cost of sending messages over vast distances.

The spread of powerful personal computers throughout businesses and organizations, together with an array of sophisticated software packages, means that managers at virtually all levels have access to accurate, highly detailed information and figures (for example, on sales levels of product X, broken down into regions).

This *should* lead to better planning and decision-making, and tighter control over variances from those plans. However, managers often become swamped with too much information – simply because of the availability of the detailed figures – and poor communication systems which do not provide managers with the information reports appropriate to their needs, position, and seniority. The detail in reports, like the plans that the reports give feedback on, should be inversely proportional to the seniority of the manager. Details of weekly sales and calls made by each sales representative in an area should be provided to the area sales manager, not to the company's sales and marketing director!

SUMMARY

We have seen how good management depends upon good communications, both communication systems (providing information through formal channels up and down the company), and personal communication between peers, subordinates and superiors.

Barriers preventing good communications include lack of clarity in messages; badly prepared and thought-out communications; the different backgrounds of people, leading to misunderstandings; a lack of openness to information and suggestions; and the assumption that once a message has been given, it has been understood and the communication process has been successful.

The information technology revolution has meant that managers can get up-to-the-minute data and information on a huge range of company activities. However, it has also meant that managers are often swamped by the sheer volume of data, and so there have to be effective communications systems in place to make sure that the data that managers receive is accurate, timely, and, above all, appropriate to their needs.

CHECKLIST: CHAPTER 8

This chapter has provided information about:

1 Managing and communicating:
- Communicating and planning
- Communicating and organizing
- Communicating, motivating and leading
- Communicating and control

2 The purpose of communicating

3 The communication cycle:
- Perceive
- Encode
- Transmit
- Receive and decode
- Response
- Data and information

4 How to communicate effectively in organizations:
- Principles of good communication
- Check out AMA list 1 to 9

5 Barriers to effective communication:
- Lack of preparation
- Lack of clarity
- Lack of openness
- Assumptions
- Premature evaluation
- Differing cultures and backgrounds

6 Communication channels:
- Formal
- Informal
- Team briefings

7 Information technology and communicating

Control

The management process of control was mentioned briefly when we looked at planning in Chapter 2. Control is the measurement and correction of subordinates' activities and the production processes, to ensure that the enterprise's objectives and plans are being carried out. Here we will discuss the control process; control and information systems; control techniques; and quality control.

THE CONTROL PROCESS

There are three steps in the basic control process: the setting of standards; measuring the results achieved against these standards; and correcting any deviations which might occur. The process is illustrated in Figure 9.1.

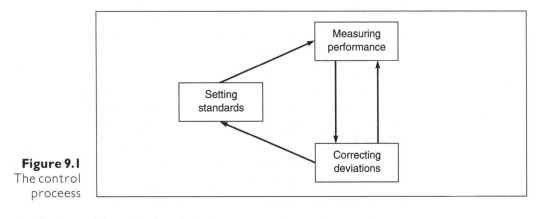

Figure 9.1
The control
proceess

Setting standards

Effective control procedures are dependent upon good planning procedures. Without planning there can be no real understanding of the results which the organization is aiming for. The first logical step in the control process is, therefore, to draw up organizational objectives and plans. However, since company plans vary in both detail and complexity, and since managers cannot usually monitor everything, special control standards need to be established.

Standards are simply criteria of performance. They are points selected in the planning programme where performance measurements are made, so as to provide managers with indications of how things are going without having to check every step in the process.

The criteria of performance vary in nature. Among the best are verifiable goals or objectives, whether stated in quantitative or qualitative terms, which are regularly set in well-operated management by objective systems. As the best measures of the achievement of MBO plans are their end results, they provide excellent standards of control. These standards can also be stated in physical terms, such as quantities of goods produced, and so can easily be checked.

Measurement of results

The measurement of results actually achieved against the standards set should (ideally) be on a forward-looking basis, so that any deviations from the standards may be detected in advance of their happening, and avoided by appropriate remedial action.

If standards are appropriately set, appraisal of actual or expected performance is fairly easy. There are, however, many activities for which it is difficult to develop accurate standards, and many which are difficult to measure. If an item is mass-produced, then it may be simple to establish labour–hour standards and to measure performance against them. But if the item is custom-made, the appraisal of performance is often a far more difficult task; for example, Wedgwood have tussled with the problem of production of a plate as opposed to design. The first is easily quantified; the second has historically depended on the skills and requirements of an artist. Moreover, in the less technical kinds of work, not only may standards be hard to set, but appraisal may also be difficult. For example, measuring the performance of the senior finance manager, or the industrial relations director, is not easy because definite standards are very difficult to establish.

Nevertheless, as managers at all levels develop verifiable objectives, stated in either quantitative or qualitative terms, these aims become the standards against which all position performance in the organization's hierarchy can be measured.

Any accurate performance measurement has to depend heavily on the relevance, accuracy and timeliness of control information, or feedback. Such information comes from a variety of sources within the organization. The single most important source is the management accounting department, which is responsible for producing regular operating statements, expenditure analyses, profit forecasts, cash flow statements, and other relevant information. We will look at control information and techniques in more detail later.

Correcting any deviations

The manager's task of correcting any deviations which may occur between the standard results and the actual results is made easier if standards are set which reflect the organizational structure, and if performance is measured in these terms, since in this case he will then know exactly where, in the assignment of individual or group duties, the corrective measures must be applied.

Once the deviations have been identified and analysed, the manager must develop a programme for corrective action, and implement this in order to arrive at the results required. The development and the implementation of corrective programmes are likely to be time-consuming tasks. For example, in the case of quality control, it may take a considerable time to discover exactly what the cause of factory rejects is, and more time to put corrective measures into effect. This time-lag in the management control process shows how important future-directed control is, if control is to be effective. What managers need for an effective control process is a control system that tells them, in time to take corrective action, that problems will occur in the future if something is not changed now.

Control as part of the management task

The correction of deviations in results is the point at which control can be seen as part of the whole system of management, and where it is linked to the other processes in the management task. Managers can correct deviations by redrawing their plans or by modifying their goals, or by exercising their organizing function, through a reassignment or clarification of duties. They may also seek to correct deviations by recruiting additional staff, by better selection and training of subordinates, or by firing employees.

CONTROL INFORMATION SYSTEMS

Effective control depends upon the generation and supply of relevant information. The qualities of good control information are as follows:

1 *Accuracy.* Accurate control information is needed to direct the manager's attention to those matters actually requiring control action. If the information is inaccurate, then the manager is liable to make incorrect and inappropriate control decisions.
2 *Timeliness.* The timeliness of information is important, since it is of little consolation to the manager to know that, although the information was accurate, it was received too late to make use of it! Timely information will avoid control delays and encourage prompt control action.
3 *Conciseness.* Management information systems can produce vast quantities of information, but the manager needs relevant information which highlights the exceptional items which require attention.
4 *Comprehensiveness.* The information presented needs to provide a complete picture of events in order to prevent inappropriate control decisions.

Management information systems

The provision of good quality information, thanks to IT innovations, and the great expansion in the use of microcomputers, has led to the development of management and control information systems. Management information systems (MIS) are essential for providing information for control purposes, as they allow access to greater databases and fast analysis of company results and possible future trends than was ever possible before.

One brief definition of an MIS is 'a system in which defined data are collected, processed and communicated to assist those responsible for the use of resources'. An MIS is a collection of functional information systems. Thus, within most organizations the most frequently used control systems are financial ones. This is because success is almost always measured in monetary terms.

Control reports

The purpose of control information systems is to produce control reports. The information contained within these should, first, have a purpose (and be relevant to that purpose), and, secondly, be tailored to meet the particular needs of the manager concerned. There should be a hierarchy of control reports, so that each manager in the organization has responsibility for the activities over which he or she has authority.

Control and feedback

The information generated by control systems is known as feedback. The actual results are recorded, and the information fed back to the managers responsible for achieving the target performance. Early feedback is essential for good control, especially where unexpected deviations have occurred.

To be effective, the system of feedback must be designed to provide quick, accurate reports of any serious deviations from the planned performance levels. The system must also supply reports to the correct organizational levels, and be phrased in the same terms as the original plan. In addition, the feedback must reflect the needs of the company. We can categorize feedback into the following two types:

1 *Positive feedback.* This type of feedback causes the system to repeat or to further intensify the particular condition being considered.
2 *Negative feedback.* This feedback causes the system to report and correct a trend by taking action in the opposite direction. A control system which uses negative feedback is often referred to as 'homeostatic' in character.

CONTROL TECHNIQUES

Although the fundamental nature and purpose of management control does not change, a variety of tools and techniques have been developed over the years to help managers in the control process. Some are quite basic, while others are more complex and sophisticated. Some measure the organization's financial soundness, while others are concerned with production efficiency. Still others deal with employee attitudes and perceptions. Although control techniques vary widely in their design and in what they measure, they all seek the same basic objective: to detect any variations from predetermined standards in order to enable managers to take the appropriate corrective action.

Budgetary control

A budget is simply a statement, usually expressed in financial terms, of the desired short-term performance of an organization in the pursuit of its objectives. Budgets form action plans for the company's immediate future, representing the operational and management sections of the corporate plan (see Chapter 2). Using budgetary control, the target standards are the desired performance outcomes. Information relating to actual performance is then collected systematically, and any variances between the two are identified.

A budgetary control system is built up from the following basic stages:

1 *Forecasts.* These are statements of probable sales, costs and other relevant financial and quantitative data.
2 *Sales budget.* The preparation of a sales budget is based on an analysis of past sales figures and a forecast of future sales levels in the light of a number of assumptions about market trends.
3 *Production budget.* This is prepared on the basis of the sales budget. It involves an assessment of the productive capacity of the organization in the light of the sales level estimates, and a consequential adjustment of either (or both) to ensure a reasonable balance between demand and potential supply. Production budgets will include output targets and cost estimates relating to labour and materials.
4 *Capital expenditure budget.* The capital expenditure budget specifically outlines proposed capital expenditure on plant, machinery, equipment, etc. Capital expenditure budgets should usually be tied in with long-range planning, because capital investments in plant and equipment usually require a long period for their costs to be recovered from operations which create a great deal of inflexibility.
5 *Cash budget* (Table 9.1). This is a forecast of cash receipts and outgoings, against which actual cash receipts and payments

Table 9.1
A cash budget

	Jan. (£)	Feb. (£)	Mar. (£)	Apr. (£)	May (£)	Jun. (£)
Receipts:						
Sales	8 000	8 000	10 000	11 000	14 000	14 000
Interest			500			500
Total receipts	8 000	8 000	10 500	11 000	14 000	14 500
Raw materials	3 000	3 000	5 000	6 000	7 000	7 000
Wages	1 000	1 000	1 500	1 500	2 000	2 000
Tax	5 000					
Dividends				1 000		
Capital outlay			2 000			
Total outgoings	9 000	4 000	8 500	8 500	9 000	9 000
Net cash inflow/outflow	(1 000)	4 000	2 000	2 500	5 000	5 500

are measured. This is perhaps the single most important control tool for an organization, as the availability of cash to meet obligations as they fall due is the first requirement of business existence.

Budgeted costs are calculated using a system of standard costing. Under this, costs of such things as materials, labour, production, etc., are worked out under set conditions. It is these standard costs which form the basis for the forecasted costs in budgets. Variance analysis is the process of examination and investigation of the factors which have caused any differences between the standard costs budgeted for and the actual costs incurred.

It has to be said that if budgetary controls are to work well, managers need to remember that they are designed only as tools, and not to replace managing! Moreover, they are tools for all managers, not just for the budget controller. It must also be noted that to be most effective, budget setting and administration have to receive the whole-hearted support of top management.

Break-even analysis

Break-even analysis is a valuable and relatively simple technique for managerial planning and control. A break-even chart (see Figure 9.2) shows how different levels of product sales will affect the profits of the business. The chart produces a break-even point, which is the level of operations where income and costs are equal. Sales figures above the break-even point are profitable, whereas sales levels below the break-even point are not.

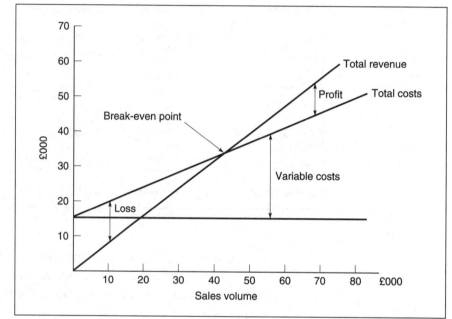

Figure 9.2
A break-even
chart

Certain assumptions have to be made when using break-even charts. Among these is the acceptance of a static, unchanging environment, when in fact the environment is more likely to be a dynamic one. There is also an implied assumption that the revenue-cost relationship is a linear one. Nor can the chart be used beyond the budget period of the firm. Despite these limitations, breakeven charts do have a basic practical value – if only as a first approximation of the profitability of a project.

Network analysis

The purpose of network analysis is to ensure that the shortest possible time elapses between a project's inception and completion, in order to keep delays and costs to an absolute minimum. To this end, a diagrammatic network of 'events' is drawn up in sequential order, with a timescale for each part. The total time of the project is found by tracing the shortest way to the finish, i.e. by taking the 'critical path'.

The network of events can be extremely complicated, the critical path threading its way through a maze of different channels to find the shortest sequence of significant events. Such a highly complex network usually requires the use of a computer for the assessment, analysis, and scheduling of input data.

Whatever the type of network, the programme or project must be effectively controlled throughout the sequence of scheduled activities to ensure that its progress is as planned.

Network analysis has five important advantages as follows:

1 It forces managers to plan, because it is impossible to make a time-event analysis without planning and seeing how the pieces fit together.
2 It forces the whole company to coordinate its planning, because each manager down the chain of command must plan the event for which he or she is responsible.
3 It makes forward control possible.
4 It concentrates attention on the critical elements that may need correction.
5 The network system, with its subsystems, makes possible the aiming of reports and pressure for action at the right spot and level in the organization's structure, and at the right time.

Network analysis will not make the control process automatic, but it does establish an environment within the organization where sound control principles are used. It is also less expensive than might be thought in relation to other planning and control techniques.

THE REQUIREMENTS FOR ADEQUATE CONTROLS

If the control process is to be effective, it must meet certain requirements. These are as follows:

1 The controls should be tailored to the organizational positions using them. For example, what will do for a senior

manager in charge of manufacturing will certainly not be appropriate for a shop-foreman.

2 Controls should reflect the structure of the organization. The more controls are designed to reflect the place in the organization where responsibility for action lies, the more they will enable corrective action to be taken as and when it is needed.

3 Controls should be tailored to the personalities of individual managers.

4 Controls should be flexible.

5 Controls should be objective.

6 Controls should be economical. Control techniques and approaches are most efficient when they detect and illuminate the causes of actual or potential deviations from organizational standards, with the minimum of costs incurred.

QUALITY CONTROL

The final aspect of control which we will consider is that of quality control. The assumption on which the control of quality rests is that in mass-production processes no two units are exactly identical. However, it is possible to mass-produce vast quantities of *almost* identical units. These units can be produced within certain tolerance levels, and a customer will accept variations between these tolerances, but not outside them. The role of quality control is to ensure that appropriate standards of quality are set and that variances beyond the tolerance levels are rejected. Quality control, therefore, is basically a system for setting quality standards, measuring performance against those standards, and taking appropriate action to deal with deviations outside the permitted tolerances.

Traditionally, quality control checking is very costly, and, since it represents an overhead in the production department, the amount of time and resources spent on it tends to be related to such factors as price, consistency, and safety and legal requirements.

One answer is for companies to start a programme of 'total quality control', such as has been part of many Japanese manufacturing companies for some time. Japanese firms, notably in the car industry, manage to instil a concern for extremely high quality throughout their production processes, and in all their employees. Each person on the shop-floor becomes personally responsible for checking and testing the quality of the goods that he or she makes, instead of using separate quality control inspectors. The aim, ultimately, is to achieve a level of zero defects in goods manufactured in their production process, making everything right the first time around. This means that the costs associated with rejecting goods and reworking parts which do not meet the given tolerance levels should be eliminated.

Of course, it is both costly and time-consuming to set up a system of total quality control. All the workforce have to be trained to check and inspect the parts and goods they make, and generally have to be trained to high standards of workmanship. Management also have to seek out and put right underlying causes of damage and reworking, instead of accepting wastage as unavoidable and inevitable, provided that it is kept below certain levels. However, firms that have set up such programmes have shown that in the longer term they allow the company to be extremely cost-effective and competitive, and that they can use the quality of their goods to a very effective marketing advantage.

SUMMARY

The process of control involves setting standards, measuring how far actual results meet those standards, and using this feedback to correct any deviations between the two.

Effective control is dependent upon accurate, concise, comprehensive and timely information in order to provide feedback reports.

Control techniques include break-even analysis, network analysis, and (the most used of all) budgets, due to the fact that most standards tend to be expressed in monetary terms – being a common, understandable and measurable unit throughout any organization.

CHECKLIST: CHAPTER 9

This chapter has given you knowledge of

1 The control process
- Setting standards
- Measurement of results
- Correcting deviations
- As part of the management task

2 Control information systems:
- Accuracy
- Timeliness
- Conciseness
- Comprehensiveness
- Management information systems
- Control reports
- Control and feedback

3 Control techniques:
- Budgetary
- Break-even analysis
- Network analysis

4 Requirements for adequate control:
- Tailored
- Reflect structure
- Flexible
- Objective
- Economical

5 Quality control

CHAPTER 10

Measuring performance

In order to achieve effective communication, motivation and control, it is necessary to have accurate performance measures in place. Historically, performance has been measured by financial criteria, but many companies have discovered the 'new' performance measures to be a vital part of any strategic management system: measures which are not only quantitative and financial in nature, and which are not geared solely to the maximization of future profits. Measuring performance by using information from existing management accounting systems has generated narrow measures which tend to look back and give a historical view of performance. There was a growing concern that these traditional models were failing.

WHY TRADITIONAL MODELS FAILED

As extensions to accounting systems, traditional performance measures produced information which was irrelevant to a strategic management initiative. The objectives of commercial strategy have changed from increasing throughput while keeping costs down to other fundamentals of product quality, timeliness and customer service. Traditional models provided information which was irrelevant and misleading, which would lead to poor decision-making, or at least would not contribute to good decision-making.

There were extended debates over the fundamental purpose of an organization, and for many years now the view that an organization exists merely to make money for its shareholders has been challenged. Rather, organizations may outline their function as meeting the needs of a number of different groups, which would include: customers; suppliers; and employees. The traditional way of providing financial measures required the processes within the organization to be interpreted financially so that performance measures could be applied. Delays and misinterpretation abounded!

In the past, individuals within an organization often viewed performance measures as a way of influencing behaviour, so that failure would be 'punished'. In reality, such a perception stifled innovation and experimentation, so that growth and development were difficult, if not impossible. Although this was not their intention, the perception of performance measures as 'big sticks' led to distrust and risk aversion which could devastate management strategies.

NEW APPROACHES AND MODELS FOR MEASURING PERFORMANCE

There are four approaches to measuring performance, which are in some respects interrelated. These are:

- Systems resource based
- Culture based
- Goal based
- Multi-actor based

The models that we will consider in relation to these approaches are:

- Total quality management (TQM)
- The performance pyramid
- Critical success factors (CSF)
- The balanced scorecard

Systems resource-based performance measures

Systems resource-based performance measures are based on the premise that the purpose of an organization is to survive, so performance measures focus on all key functions which contribute to the survival of the organization. In this type of measure the organization is a series of interactions with its environment. The criteria on which the performance measures are based are those which reflect the efficiency and effectiveness of the interface between the organization and the environment. Taking periodic measures provides a reading of the interface at that time, and a series of such 'snapshots' of performance in a changing environment enables remedial measures to be taken in between the snapshots.

Culture-based performance measures

Culture-based performance measures are closely associated with systems resource measures in that they relate to the factors which particularly distinguish the organization from others in its environment. The nurturing and improvement of its culture is what ensures the survival of the organization. The organization could be viewed as a living system of roles, norms and values which make up the specific culture – thus performance measures would include an assessment of the 'oneness' of the organization and the level of understanding between members.

TOTAL QUALITY MANAGEMENT

Total Quality Management (TQM) is a good example of these first two types of performance measure because TQM involves all members of the organization, and has been described as aiming to 'create constancy of purpose towards improvement of product and service with the aim of becoming competitive, stay in business and provide jobs' (Dewing, 1986). Everyone within the organization is involved in TQM, which employs a comprehensive approach to the activity of the organization. TQM demands continuous improvement; thus there is a need to assess current performance for comparative analysis.

TQM performance measures should lead to the identification of best practice, which will contribute to organizational performance above that of competitors and beyond previous organizational achievement. The key point is the improvement of the process as a whole. Performance measurement in the TQM context can be considered in three main areas.

Customer focus

The TQM view of an organization is made up of customer-supplier chains. That is to say that the raw material supplier is a supplier selling to the raw materials purchase department (customer), who provides the manufacturing process with materials. The raw materials department is now a supplier to the manufacturing department (customer), and this continues through the entire process until the final customer. Figure 10.1 demonstrates the links.

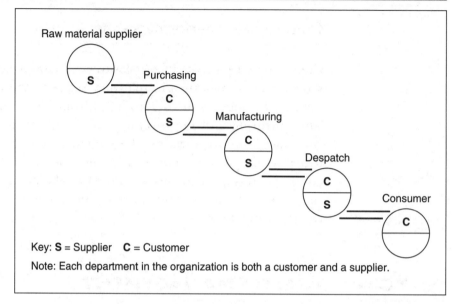

Key: **S** = Supplier   **C** = Customer

Note: Each department in the organization is both a customer and a supplier.

Figure 10.1
Customer supplier
chains

Every process within the organization needs to be able to identify who is their supplier and to whom they themselves supply. The points of contact between supplier and customer at each stage are crucial. Opinions can be formed of product, process and organization on the basis of these short contacts. One measure could be an analysis of customer defections. Reicheld and Sasser (1990) argue that such an analysis would highlight problems with the service offered.

Process focus

In Figure 10.1, the 'manufacturing' circle may encompass the conversion of sand into glass and, whether the glass is for internal or external use, the process provides a visible link in the customer-supplier chain. To achieve optimal performance, each link of the chain must perform to the highest standard.

Control measures are used to determine whether the process is achieving the required standards; if achievement targets are not reached the process is stopped and remedial action is taken. This is determined by analysis of the performance measures which indicated the process should be stopped. The failure may be due to a common cause (i.e. part of the process) and can be rectified by controls, but special or extenuating causes can only be controlled by taking action which prevents them arising again. For example, if power fluctuation causes the process quality to vary, then the process itself is not at fault.

Emergency alternative power supplies may well be sufficient to prevent the situation recurring.

Improvement measures would be geared towards optimizing efficiency, effectiveness, productivity and quality, whilst minimizing waste. *Effectiveness* measures actual output against expected output and determines whether objectives are being achieved. While effectiveness measures concentrate on the outputs of a process, *efficiency* measures focus on inputs and compare resources used with resources planned to be used. *Productivity* measures the use of inputs in producing the required output and may be expressed as actual or expected (actual output/actual resource consumption; and expected output/ expected resource consumption respectively). *Quality* measures are concentrated on the product or service and will reflect customer satisfaction. *Waste* is a measure of resources which did not add value to the product. An important measure in this instance is Cost of Quality (the aggregate cost of all activities to test, inspect and ensure the quality of the final product).

People focus

Owners and employees all have a role in the process of performance measurement. If the roles are optimized in the design and implementation of performance measures, then competent staff are motivated by the identification of best methods. TQM demands an ethos of innovation and continual improvement. Key areas of an organization which benefit from the TQM approach include:

1 High leverage process measures, which necessitate an intimate knowledge and understanding of the organizational process to be measured. The deeper the level of understanding, the more readily performance measures can be identified. Employees who work the processes on a day-to-day basis will bring a detailed insight to the measurement task, and definitions will ultimately be more useful and will lead to greater improvements.

2 There will be many employees within the organizational sectors (see Figure 10.1) who will never feel themselves to be in contact with customers. This may mean that they perceive their role as rather insignificant and unimportant in the process chain. If these same employees are concerned with the design of the TQM process then individual contributions to

customer satisfaction cannot only be identified but measured also.

3 Employee input into the design of measurement systems means that measurements will be in a language readily understood by the workforce and timed in a way to be useful in remedial action.

4 An organization instituting performance measures may face a range of employee reactions. Often these reactions can include misgivings and doubt, leading to a fear of the system itself. This may largely be because of a lack of understanding of the system and its purpose. Involvement in the design stages of the system can only increase understanding and reduce fear, resulting in a greater likelihood that the system will be accepted when it is in place.

5 One of the consequences of misunderstanding is employees' desire to manipulate the system to produce results they think the managers want to see. This means that measurements may be skewed or distorted to produce an erroneous impression. Decision-making based on the information thus produced must be of dubious value. Thus employee involvement in design and implementation will improve the measurement system's usefulness. This is not, however, to say that industrial relations can be based on this sort of cooperation. TQM can be used as a supplement to existing worker/management relationships.

There have been suggestions that TQM systems themselves should be subject to performance measurements to determine their own effectiveness. Although this is a time-consuming process, Philip Ullah (1991) argued that it was worthwhile because it enables, for example, production of information on cause-and-effect relationships between the organization's reward system and employee attitudes to quality.

Goal-based performance measurement

Goal-based performance measurement is the third approach to performance measurement. This approach presupposes that the organizational purpose can be translated into organizational goals by management. Another assumption it makes is that the levels to which these goals are achieved can be used as an indication of the effectiveness of the organization. The goals-based approach requires the goals of the organization to be common throughout the organization, and for all levels within the organization to have accepted the goals as targets for performance achievement. Gregory and Jackson (1992) described such an organization as a 'well oiled goal achieving machine'. Comparison of results allows actual achievements to be measured against targets and provides the necessary information for remedial action.

THE PERFORMANCE PYRAMID

The performance pyramid is an example of goal-based and systems resource-based performance measurement systems. Adhering to TQM principles in the context of strategic goals and objectives, the performance pyramid gives a performance model which is both a top-down and a bottom-up (strategic and process) performance measure. The pyramid allows translation of management vision into performance indicators and operational measures. See Figure 10.2.

The focus on strategy requires performance measurements to provide a continual comparison between estimated and actual gains in order to highlight necessary remedial action. New systems create their own enthusiasms which fade over time, but the system provides a climate of accountability and commitment to strategic goals which should be sustainable in the longer term. By providing information

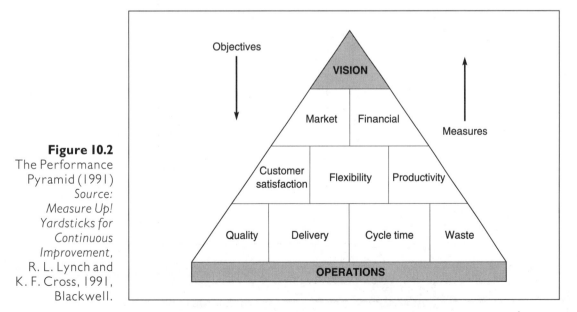

Figure 10.2
The Performance
Pyramid (1991)
*Source:
Measure Up!
Yardsticks for
Continuous
Improvement,*
R. L. Lynch and
K. F. Cross, 1991,
Blackwell.

on the effect of adopted strategies and highlighting individuals' contributions to the achievement of strategic goals (thus informing and motivating individuals) the comparisons of actual to expected outcomes are achieved.

Performance measures of strategic goals are essentially in a context definable by market and financial objectives. Measures include market share, cash flow, profitability and market position. Objectives laid down are achieved by improving customer satisfaction, organizational flexibility and productivity. Thus there are three key measures: customer demands need to be managed and satisfied; changes in customer demands need to be identified and met efficiently; and productivity must be effective. As the pyramid diagram suggests, the entire organization is monitored in this model, as opposed to individual units or departments. In contrast to the strategic focus, the process focus needs operational measures, which in turn require identifiable business systems. Lynch and Cross (1991) define a Business Operating System (BOS) as 'all the activities required to deliver a product/ service to the customer'.

The flow of work illustrated in Figure 10.3 is from left (Accept customer order) to right (Deliver to the customer) and crosses depart-

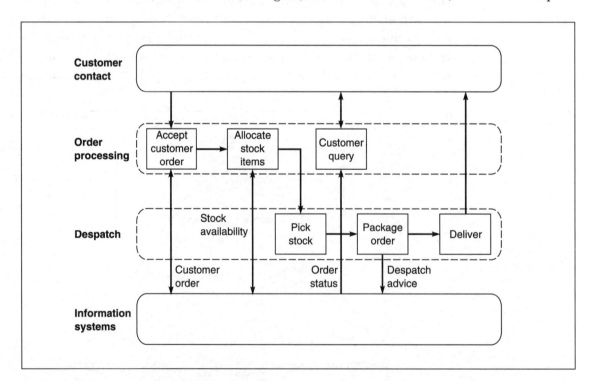

Figure 10.3
Business Operating System for simple order processing

mental boundaries (Customer contact/Order processing/Despatch/ Information systems) without hindrance. The map indicates not only the customer/supplier relationships but also the cost drivers which affect the process as a whole. In terms of performance measures, there are two key identifications made here. The first is to demonstrate the individual's responsibility for establishing day-to-day operational control measures. The second, by highlighting the customer/ supplier relationships, identifies activities which may usefully be measured. Measures would be geared towards maximizing quality and delivery whilst minimizing waste.

The balanced perspective of the diagram is achieved by the horizontal flow which reflects the cross-functional vision of the top level of the pyramid. The proponents of this type of model would argue that establishing measures at both operational and global levels makes a major contribution to the achievement of organizational goals.

THE CRITICAL SUCCESS FACTORS (CSF) METHOD

The performance pyramid is a combination of goals-based and systems resource-based models. However, there are approaches to measuring performance which are purely goal based. Of the two examined here, the first, the Critical Success Factors (CSF) method, is of the longest standing, being an early attempt at replacing cost accounting-based performance measures. The basic premise of the method is that concentration upon measures at a small level will increase the performance of the whole. Each area to be measured is known as a critical success factor, and can be measured at any level within an organization and will usually be unique to an organizational unit. Rockart (1981), a proponent of the CSF method, identified five main sources of CSF within an organization:

1 Organizations divided into industry sector will share CSFs that will be specific to that sector. For example, a factor affecting the automotive industry would be emission control standards, and all organizations within the industry would be required to meet standards, and common CSFs would be used to measure their performance against standards.

2 Some CSFs will be determined by the competitive strategy adopted by the organization. For example, if the strategy

adopted is cost-led, then CSFs would necessarily include cost control and pricing policy.

3 Pressures from outside the organization in terms of the political, economic, social and technological environment may also influence the choice of CSF. For example, an industry using a labour force in short supply may well find industrial relations critical to survival and success.

4 Within an organization there are factors which have an influence for a short time only. While accepting that such factors do not constitute a long-term difficulty, measures are required to confirm that action taken is correcting the current situation.

5 Managers of units within the organization can be critical to the success of the whole organization. This means that managerial positions are critical success factors in two respects: first, at the level within the organization at which the manager functions; and second, in the activities in which the manager's unit is engaged. In addition, a significant influence on the performance measures can be the manager's understanding of what constitutes success or failure within the unit.

Having identified the CSFs, the next stage is to consider specific indicators for each CSF Indicators will require the collection of information, both easily measured information and subjective assessments. There will tend to be a desire to use information that is easily collected – say from the accounting system. However, Rockart suggests that this is not a good source of information to use as the basis of the measures. It is clearly preferable for the measures themselves to drive the data collection process. This suggests a relatively high level of flexibility and change, given the list of CSFs above, which themselves are likely to change from time to time. Any measurement system must be able to respond quickly to any changes in the CSF. Flexibility is one of the key words and conditions for the success of the CSF method.

It should be noted that the basic premise that achieving low-level targets will lead to the high-level performance improving is not a universally held view, and has been subject to serious challenge. In fact, Blenkinsop and Burns (1992) and Harvey-Jones (1993) conclude that, rather than optimizing performance, managers become blinkered to opportunities for balancing performance across the chain of customer service. Difficulties occur in the simplification of the model to a point where it can no longer represent the real world

The third-sector organizations have market-place problems. Their administrators are struggling to keep them alive in the face of rapidly changing societal needs, increasing public and private competition, changing client attitudes and diminishing financial resources. The major requirement for survival has been propounded as follows: third-sector administrators must begin to think like marketers. Marketing is not just a business function, it is a valid function for non-business organizations as well.

Of all the classic business functions, marketing has been the last to arrive on the non-profit scene. As it has done so, it is evident that a number of non-profit-making organizations, for example a number of colleges, have equated marketing with intensified promotion. A number of American colleges and British universities have undertaken aggressive promotion, but such a policy carries a number of dangers, as follows:

1 Strong negative reactions among the faculty.
2 Aggressive promotion may turn off many prospective students.
3 Aggressive promotion can attract the wrong students to the wrong college.
4 This kind of marketing creates the illusion that the college has undertaken sufficient response to declining enrolment – an illusion which slows down the needed work on product improvement, the basis of all good marketing.

A genuine marketing response has been undertaken by a relatively small number of colleges. Their approach is best described as 'market-oriented institutional planning'. In this approach, marketing is recognized as much more than mere promotion and, indeed, the issue of promotion cannot be settled in principle until more fundamental issues are resolved. By doing its homework on market, resource and missions analysis, a college is in a better position to make decisions that improve student and faculty recruitment and institutional fund-raising.

Despite the growing interest in marketing, many non-profit organizations still resist it. Marketing will initially be viewed as advertising and promotion rather than as a revolutionary new way to view the institution and its purposes. A few institutions will lead the others in developing an advanced understanding of marketing. They will start performing better. Their competitors will then be forced to learn their marketing.

Steps in marketing planning

The relationship between market planning and corporate planning

A vice-president of the US Steel Corporation once stressed the relationship between market planning and corporate planning:

> Market planning is the starting point for all corporate planning. Whether your business involves a service or a product, it is based upon the existence of present and potential markets. Planning with respect to those markets is the basis for the extent and direction of all other corporate decisions.

It is not possible to state categorically where a company's strategic planning process ends and corporate planning for each functional area of the firm, including marketing, begins. Policy formulation, the setting of objectives and strategic planning do not occur in isolation from the activities of the marketing function – indeed, the planning processes of top management and the various functional divisions are inextricably bound up with others. The job of marketing planning is, broadly, to structure the future use of resources and, principally, the marketing mix, in order to achieve the objectives, goals or targets that stem from the firm's strategic planning.

The marketing plan

The process of marketing planning is a three-stage sequence involving environmental analysis, market target selection and marketing strategy design.

Analysis

This first step involves an appraisal of the extent to which the marketing environment and the company's marketing style are effectively matched and how environmental changes are likely to call for the new directions in marketing management; for analysis of market growth trends is therefore essential, as is detailed research into the economic, psychological and social backgrounds of the buyers. The analysis of the firm's competitive situation includes an appraisal of its competitive advantages which relate specifically to product marketing and, finally, the structure of marketing distribution channels, relations with distributors, stock financing, wholesalers' margins and financing arrangements must be monitored and future behaviour predicted.

The analysis of the firm's competitive situation can be made by means of a marketing audit. An audit is a systematic, critical and unbiased review and appraisal of the environment and of the company's operations. A marketing audit is part of the larger management audit and is concerned with the marketing environment and marketing operations.

Any company carrying out an audit will be faced with two kinds of variables. First, there are variables over which the company has no direct control. These usually take the form of what can be described as environmental and market variables. Second, there are variables over which the company has complete control. These we can call operational variables. There are two parts to the audit: the external audit and the internal audit. The external audit is concerned with the uncontrollable variables, whilst the internal audit is concerned with the controllable variables. The external audit starts with an examination of information on the general economy and then moves on to the outlook for the health and growth of the markets served by the company. The purpose of the internal audit is to assess the organization's resources as they relate to the environment and vis-à-vis the resources of competitors.

Finally, since the objective of the audit is to vindicate what a company's marketing objectives and strategies should be, it follows that it would be helpful if some format could be found for organizing the major findings. One useful way of doing this is in the form of a SWOT analysis. This is a summary of the audit under the headings of internal strengths and weaknesses as they relate to external opportunities and threats.

Market targeting

This step involves the selection of market targets, those segments of the overall population of potential customers towards which the firm intends to direct its marketing programme. Companies pursue one or more of three types of marketing effort: *undifferentiated marketing*, in which no attempt is made to modify the product or any other mix element on the basis of varying buyer characteristics or buying habits: the product is aimed at the entire population that is liable to purchase it without any attempt to offer different versions each of which matches a unique bundle of purchaser attributes; *differentiated marketing*, in which the firm provides a separate marketing mix for each identifiable segment of its market; and *concentrated marketing*, in which the company directs its marketing programme to just one segment of the overall market, preferring to specialize rather than try to offer differential marketing mixes. Market targeting depends on more routine sales forecasting; its success hinges on the skilful gathering, interpretation and application of knowledge about buyer behaviour and the social, psychological and economic forces that shape it.

Marketing objectives

The establishment of measurable, quantified, time-based, feasible objectives relating to the implementation of marketing strategy has two functions. First, it provides guidelines for the marketing programme and criteria for decision-making; and second, it sets out standards that can be employed in the control of marketing activities.

Marketing strategy

This section of the marketing plan indicates how each element of the marketing mix and each subdivision of the elements will be used to achieve marketing objectives. The detailed provisions of this part of the plan enable specific operations to be carried out by designated personnel in a definite time-span.

Marketing strategy has several aspects: product strategy; pricing; promotional activities; and selling and distribution.

Product strategy

Product planning is strategic because the efficiency of an organization depends largely on the development of new products/services, the elimination of outmoded or unprofitable lines, and the improvement of existing products/services to give better satisfaction to customers.

The development of a product line must be based on objective marketing research. A creative product strategy aims to build up a balanced product range that optimizes productive efficiency and marketing effectiveness. The marketing research will involve the following:

1 Appraising the products and their trends, in relation to those of competitors, as viewed by the consumer.

2 Analysing consumer needs and habits and evaluating them with respect to both present and possible future markets.

3 Preparing product specifications of performance, physical characteristics, quality level, dependability, serviceability, safety features, product identification, packaging and appearance.

4 Formulating prices with the targets of volume and profit in mind.

5 Controlling product lines by developing and administering policies, programmes and plans.

6 Processing product ideas to make plans for innovation.

7 Providing product information for manuals, advertising, etc.

8 Recommending design and redesigning.

9 Coordinating the plans and product programmes of the various chief management functions.

There are a number of special points that need to be considered relative to the firm's product policy. The basic marketing question is: what needs do the firm's product/services actually satisfy? Thinking about the needs satisfied by the product leads to consideration of the ways in which alternatives could present themselves to satisfy that same need. The question that follows is: could the market need be satisfied by other products currently available or potentially available as a result of foreseeable developments? It has been pointed out that ocean-going liners competed with each other to cross the Atlantic in the shortest time, yet their real competitors were the airlines. So to concentrate a study merely on existing competitive products is a mistake.

It is important that the marketing manager is aware of his product's life-cycle. The actual position of a firm's products in their life-cycles affects the forecast of their future profitability. Should a large number of them be at the end of their cycles, there is a clear need for new investment in new product development and some fall in sales is to be expected while these are developed and brought to the market. Ideally, a company will possess a balanced range of products passing through different stages in their respective life-cycles.

Products and services should also be analysed and assessed relative to competition and customer preferences, so that innovations are deliberately planned and introduced to occupy identified market positions. The concept of product positioning alerts manufacturers to the strengths and weaknesses of their products viewed against competitive brands.

Pricing

Pricing is a critical element in the overall marketing strategy. It is only one of the variables contributing to the marketing mix; it is inter-related with the other factors affecting buying decisions, such as product design, after-sales service and promotional efforts. Pricing cannot, therefore, be considered in isolation.

Pricing can be projected as an active, dynamic part of marketing strategy, planned to achieve certain corporate objectives, or it may play merely a subservient role in the marketing of goods and services.

Specific markets have particular pricing problems. One that is significant refers to the relevant demand–supply position. Another important factor that influences prices relates to the trading structure in particular industries. Price competition is affected significantly by the balance that exists between the various sizes of firms. The more suppliers that exist within an industry with an equitable distribution of market shares, the more marked will be the tendency for price competition to be active.

Pricing decisions are complex and should therefore be considered against the following factors:

1 Nature and extent of demand.
2 Competitors' activities.
3 Costs of production and marketing.
4 Pricing objectives.
5 Product life-cycle.

The creative use of pricing as a positive element of the marketing mix is rare. Judging price levels in terms of what customers will pay, perhaps in terms of what they want to pay, is not widespread because the fact that many customers judge quality by price and may there-fore derive greater satisfaction at a higher price is overlooked by businessmen.

Promotion

The third input to the marketing plan is promotion. In organizational markets, promotional inputs to marketing strategy are often under-rated and demoted to an inferior role. Marketers of organizational supplies and services should be prepared to spend time and effort in planning promotional inputs that will reinforce the overall marketing strategy. Promotional strategies themselves depend on the effective linking of several variables: media, timing, intensity, etc. These demand professional skills that may partly be available within an organization; more usually, however, they are drawn from the services of specialist advertising agencies. The essential point, however, is for marketing management to ensure that promotional specialists work closely within the general marketing plan. While creative flair should not be stifled, marketing management has the final responsibility for developing an integrated and coherent marketing plan in which the various inputs are balanced effectively.

Promotion has four fundamental reasons for its existence: communication, incentive, invitation and competition.

1 *Communication*. The idea that promotion is part of the firm's total communication function in marketing is quite new. In the real world the vast majority of marketing communication is promotional in content and in effect: promotion is the dissemination of ideas. By the use of promotion the company can gain the attention of the prospective buyer, thereby giving itself the opportunity to provide the information that will lead to the consumer trying the product.

2 *Incentive*. The promotion incorporates some sort of offer that equals extra value: something for nothing – if that message comes across then the incentive is greater. It may be that more goods are being obtained for the same price, that the price is less than normal, or that a future saving is being offered in the form of a coupon.

3 *Invitation*. Sales promotion includes a direct invitation to engage in the transaction proposed now.

4 *Competition*. Effective promotion provides an edge over competitors and makes the product being produced more competitive. Most marketing men believe that promotion gives drive and meaning to the marketing strategy.

Selling and distribution

The fourth main input to the overall marketing strategic plan is selling and distribution. Channels of distribution comprise 'all the institutions involved in moving goods or services from producer to end user or consumer.' Discovering a channel of distribution is not done independently of other factors. A central element in distribution strategy is the selection of the marketing channels that will be employed to move products and services to the next stage in the chain that links manufacturers with final customers.

A number of criteria are used in the selection of a channel of distribution, as follows:

1 Knowledge of the product. For example, questions need to be asked such as 'How does the product itself and the characteristics of the manufacturing firm constrain the methods?' 'Is it purchased frequently?' If the answer is 'yes', then a wide distribution is necessary. Wholesalers have to be used if this involves shops with low turnover. On the other hand, if sales are not so frequent, or to a limited number of people, the firm's own outlets may well be the answer.
2 Knowledge of alternative types of outlet.
3 Awareness of the 'ideal' channel. The characteristics would include such aspects as economy of use, easy access to consumers and links with associated products. The marketing manager must also consider whether immediate or long-term profit is to be considered paramount. If immediate profit is wanted, then the established channels are probably going to be developed rather than new ones set up. In a perfect world, most manufacturers would like complete control over their product and distribution to as few points as possible. The consumer's typical shopping behaviour, however, forces the manufacturer into a pattern of distribution points compatible with the goods to be supplied.

MARKET RESEARCH

Information for marketing decisions

Marketing information systems (MkIS) represent a new approach to the need for management information, which has been traditionally addressed by the company's marketing research function. The MkIS approach takes full advantage of managerial and buyer behaviour. Definitions of marketing research and of marketing information systems indicate that they are fundamentally directed towards similar objectives. Typically, definitions of marketing research depict it as 'that function in a business which is specifically charged with providing information to facilitate the making of marketing decisions'. On the other hand, MkIS may be defined as 'a set of procedures and methods for the regular, planned collection, analysis, and presentation of information for use in making marketing decisions'.

In view of the fact that these definitions clearly refer to the same thing, why is current marketing thinking emphasizing the MkIS rather than marketing research? This question can be answered in three interrelated ways, in terms of:

1 The inadequacies of the breadth of marketing research in practice.
2 The integrative value of a systems approach to the provision of marketing information.
3 The extended audience for marketing-related information in the marketing-orientated firm.

The fundamental problem with much marketing research arises from its underlying tendency to be 'principally a series of independent, uncoordinated activities scattered through the complaining companies'. The advantages of a systematic approach lie in the ability to integrate and coordinate separate activities to provide the information currently required for the decision-making processes in which managers are involved. In the marketing-orientated firm, this means more than the provision of information to marketing managers: 'it demands those integrated, analytic, systematic approaches which will identify, assemble, process and communicate payoff-relevant marketing information to the decision-makers.'

Management's need for information

Different types of information are required at the various stages of the continuous managerial decision process, as follows:

1 *Policy formulation and determination of objectives*. Here the purpose of information is the selection of ends: mission development, policy-making and objective-setting. The predominant source of information is SWOT analysis.
2 *Strategic analysis and corporate planning*. Here the purpose of information is the reduction of uncertainty and selection of means. The predominant sources are market research, technological R & D, and growth vector analysis.
3 *Operations and control*. Here the purpose of the information is monitoring and appraisal of activities and control. The predominant sources are internal feedback and external market research.

4 At the *evaluation* stage the purpose of information is overall performance appraisal in terms of policy and strategy, objectives and targets. The predominant sources of information are internal and external data collection, analysis, interpretation and reporting: the management information system.

Orthodox economic theory depicts businessmen as making rational decisions that are contingent upon their having full information about markets and competitors and of the future consequences of the actions that follow from their decisions.

In choosing among alternative strategies, information is required in order to reduce uncertainty about the overall number of possible outcomes and the likelihood of each outcome occurring. The generation of data to reduce uncertainty involves careful investigation of current and projected patterns of demand and competition and of the firm's capabilities to meet them both. It is at the stage of strategic and corporate planning that the search for reliable external information is most intense.

Marketing research: its role in marketing information systems

Collection of data from the environment should be undertaken on a planned and objective basis. Marketers largely control the destinies of their companies, and it is no longer defensible that their decisions should be based on inspired guesswork. Objective, systematic research into market opportunities should become the first step in forming the marketing plan. Research should include economic and business analyses, technological evaluations, assessment of competitors' activities, and analyses of political, social and other environmental factors.

Marketing research has a very practical purpose: to provide reliable knowledge about specific aspects of marketing. But its function is not just to provide intelligence or information, but to interpret these data. Marketing research is not a substitute for decision-making, it is an aid to making better decisions by providing additional information in defined areas of investigation. Marketing research applies in real-life conditions some of the techniques of scientific analysis to provide management with up-to-date marketing knowledge. It therefore forms the cornerstone of a successful marketing strategy; applying marketing research does not guarantee success, but it will narrow the field of uncertainty that surrounds many marketing decisions. Marketing research should not be regarded as a luxury service but as an essential method of acquiring facts that were not available beforehand.

Marketing research techniques can also be applied productively in the planning of non-profit-making activities such as the social services, some areas of public transport, education, health services, etc. Unless reliable information is used at the design stage of these services, it is clear that public resources may be unwisely committed. Objective research will also be of value in assessing the effectiveness of existing services and may identify new areas that could legitimately be the concern of public authorities. Far greater use of marketing research could therefore result in better utilization of scarce resources and improved benefits to the community.

Methods in marketing research

Marketing research is split between reactive and non-reactive marketing research. Non-reactive methods are based upon the interpretation of observed phenomena or extant data, whereas reactive research involves some form of proactive assessment in the market place.

The most widely used method of reactive marketing research involves the asking of questions by means of a questionnaire survey, which is indeed a ubiquitous and highly flexible instrument. It can be administered by an interviewer, by telephone, or it can be sent by mail, and so on. Yet the biggest potential pitfalls with the questionnaire lie in its design. Everyone knows about the 'loaded' question or the dangers of ambiguity, yet these are not always easily detectable. Such pitfalls can be reduced by pilot-testing it, in other words, by giving it a trial run on a subgroup of the intended sample to isolate any problems that may arise.

Depth interviews are a means of providing qualitative insights. These are loosely structured discussions with a group broadly representing the population in which the researcher is interested, in which a group leader attempts to draw from the group their feelings about the subject under discussion. Experimentation is another type of reactive marketing research which can provide a valuable source of information about the likely market performance of new products or about the likely effects of variations in the marketing mix. Thus different product formulations, different levels of promotional effort, and so on can be tested in the market place to gauge their different effects.

In contrast with such methods are those classified as non-reactive, in that they do not rely on data derived directly from the respondent. Best known among these are retail audits and consumer panels, both widely used by consumer companies. Retail audits involve the regular monitoring of a representative sample of stockists. The consumer panel is simply a sample group of consumers who record in a diary their purchases and consumption over a period of time. This technique has been used in industrial as well as consumer markets and can provide continuous data on usage patterns as well as much other useful data.

Finally, and in many respects the most important of all marketing research methods, is the use of existing materials, particularly by means of desk research, which should always be the starting point of any marketing research programme. When combined with internal sales information, this can be the most powerful research method open to a company.

The marketing information system (MkIS)

Information systems should never be allowed to become ends in themselves; it must always be borne in mind that 'the fundamental objective of a marketing information system is to help managers make better decisions.' To accomplish this, information systems must assemble, process and communicate information that is used by managers to reduce uncertainty.

In developing a marketing information system, it is useful to appoint a committee of senior executives who may be directly involved. The committee should study the existing information flows in the light of the information that is needed. Each manager should anticipate his or her information requirements before problems arise and must also state what information he or she must have if they are to know that the problem has arisen. Information should give a reliable indication of problems with maximum lead time.

In addition, the individual manager must determine the value of information and seek a balance between the cost of gathering more and more information and the quality of decisions made on the basis of this information. If the right kind of information is to be available to management, plans must be drawn up stating what information is required, how it is to be obtained and how it is to be used.

Having determined marketing information needs, within the framework of the overall system design, the intimate interactions of information requirements and collection must be considered. Usually the requisition and acquisition of information will be carried out by different people, with the result that the wrong information may be supplied if the information gatherer does not know the problem to be solved and the recipient does not understand how to use the information presented to them, or fails to appreciate its limitations. The need for good communications is vital.

It must be noted that the MkIS should be compatible with the company's management style. Also, few advanced marketing information systems can be justified on the basis of cost reduction, but that test alone is not an appropriate one. The main purpose of such systems is to help management to make more profitable decisions rather than to reduce data-handling or paperwork costs. An MkIS, therefore, should be evaluated in terms of its estimated effects on marketing efficiency and profitability. A comprehensive MkIS should accommodate forecasting data, marketing research data, statistical data, library facilities, and economic and other environmental information.

Determining how much a marketing information system can increase marketing effectiveness is not an easy task. The involvement of management in developing overall specifications should help in compiling estimates, however imprecise, of system benefits. Also, the determining of a budget for developing a marketing information system need not be made in one large step. It is better to attain system sophistication in discrete instalments that involve a series of smaller budgeting decisions and cost/benefit evaluations. It is necessary, nevertheless, to draw up the blueprint of the total system prior to piecemeal implementation.

Theories of buyer and consumer behaviour

Buying decisions

The buying decision is not necessarily a straightforward 'to buy' or 'not to buy'; a number of influences come into play and the buying decision can be divided into three types:

1 *Routine*, i.e. buying low-cost, frequently purchased items such as bread, toothpaste, soap, etc. The buyer has few decisions to make; frequently he or she will remain with the same brand but the choice can be influenced by special offers,

price reductions and large advertising campaigns. A desire for change will also come into play. Goods that fall solely into this class are often called 'low involvement goods'.

2   *Limited problem-solving.* The process of buying becomes more complex when the buyer is confronted with an unfamiliar brand in a familiar product. The new brand may offer different qualities which require the use of judgement before choosing. The buyer may consult available literature, read advertisements, etc., before making a decision, but the basic knowledge of the product field is such that the buyer will know what he or she wants.

3   *Extensive problem-solving.* The problem of buying is at its most complex when the buyer does not know anything about the product field, and does not have any brand knowledge. The decision to buy a Brother word processor may be made but the buyer neither knows what the brands are nor what they offer. The buyer will set out to gather information which will eventually result in an evaluation of the prospective purchase and a final choice.

The marketing person has three different problems to solve here to lead the buyer to purchase his/her product. In the first example, big advertising campaigns or special offers may switch the allegiance of the buyer from one brand to another. In the second example, information showing the attributes of the new product is essential, In the third example, the marketing man must provide a wide and accessible range of information comparable with that given by competitors, and sufficiently convincing and readable to sway the final decision. Salesmen, too, will influence the choice here and the marketing man must be aware of the need to convince and satisfy their information needs.

Consumer behaviour

A number of factors influence or determine consumer behaviour. Consumer 'needs' and 'wants' play an important role. Needs and wants may be defined as follows:

- A *need* is something that requires satisfaction.
- A *want* is a perceived need.

The fundamental objective of marketing is to satisfy consumer 'wants'.

Wants are perceived by the individual either within themselves or in his or her environment. Wants arising within the individual may be physical wants, i.e. the basic requirements that the human body requires to survive. It has been suggested by researchers that around 25–33% of all consumer expenditure is aimed at satisfying these wants. The mind also may cause some wants. Intellect, attitudes and perception have a bearing upon observation, interpretation and activation of wants that are recognized in the self and in the environment. The urge to satisfy curiosity leads the individual to explore something unknown, and to consume products so far not experienced. Human beings are entertained in various ways by intellectual activity and 'cultural experience'.

Wants arising from the environment reveal the influence of small groups, e.g. family, friends or work colleagues. Work colleagues and neighbourhood acquaintances often move in the same entertainment circle, live in the same sort of house, consume the same kinds of goods and services. This conformation to group standards is very typical of consumer behaviour, indeed without it the job of marketing manager would be impossible. It is not simply that the behaviour of the neighbour or colleague is copied, but that a communication pattern is established. Some persons are more communicative than others and they are the opinion leaders, so that their ideas spread rapidly and their views tend to be adopted. Identifying opinion leaders is the vital step in directing marketing effort towards them so that their influence on the rest of the group may result in a broader consumer acceptance.

Socio-economic grouping is an important consideration in any analysis of consumer behaviour. Six such groups are often identified, ranging from the aristocracy through upper class, upper middle class, lower middle class, ordinary working class, and 'the rest'. These groupings have different goals, lifestyles, aspirations and incomes which need to be considered by the marketing team in their campaigns directed at any particular group. For example, the upper three groups consist of most of the professions and senior managers. Such groups are light television viewers, consequently if they are the target market it does not make sense to advertise your product or service on TV. However, they can be effectively reached by means of certain newspapers and magazines, where they comprise the principal readership.

Marketing control

The purpose of control

The effective control that is an integral part of integrated marketing management may be viewed as a process of minimizing the deviations of marketing performance from planned levels of activity and result.

Control depends on being able to measure performance in terms of expenditure and results. The more precisely performance can be measured, the more precisely it can be controlled. A criterion by which many companies have judged marketing performance in the past is 'results for the comparable period of the previous year.' While allowing to some extent for seasonal fluctuations, this fails to account for other vital factors including the 'typicalness' of last year's results, or the behaviour of the market as a whole. A company with formal planning procedures converts company objectives into quantified targets for the short, medium and long term.

Marketing control contains three essential executive processes:

1 *Monitoring trends* in performance and company results with expectations.
2 *Judging* which levels of deviation from targeted performance can be tolerated and which call for intervention.
3 *Correcting* the deviations as necessary.

Planning and control

It is important to note, briefly, that effective control begins with marketing planning. Indeed, insofar as control involves re-planning and reallocation of resources, the two processes are often difficult to unravel.

The criteria for performance evaluation and control derive from the objectives established in the planning process. Control is thus facilitated by the setting of realistic objectives that are unambiguously capable of use as instruments for measuring progress.

The role of MkIS in marketing control

Marketing information systems play a most important role in the control processes by ensuring that the requisite information for appraisal and correction is available to the individuals responsible for control at the appropriate times. The effectiveness of control decisions is necessarily a function of the adequacy and quality of

information, and the sensible use of a marketing information system thus depends upon the prior determination of total information requirements, the uses of present reports, the frequency of reports, their speed of preparation and their destinations.

The main uses of a marketing information system in the control effort are as follows:

1 To spot things that are going wrong and to take corrective action before serious loss results, which constitutes the most fruitful and constructive use of control information.

2 To highlight things that have actually gone wrong and guide marketing management in either cutting the losses of failure or turning apparent failure to further advantage.

3 To determine exactly how and why failure or deviation from plan have arisen and to suggest steps that should be taken to prevent their recurrence, which is another highly constructive application since mistakes need not be repeated even if they cannot be avoided.

4 To find out who is to blame for failure which, if not done in the proper way and followed up by corrective action, is the least constructive of uses.

The role of accounting information in control

Accounting information is an important control tool within the organization because it provides one of the few quantitative, integrative mechanisms that are available. Accounting information is important in the financial control that needs to operate within the marketing function. Financial control is concerned with the regulation of the flow of money and, in particular, with ensuring that cash is always available to pay debts when they fall due.

Cost problems in marketing control

The marketing function is the most difficult area to plan and control since it is the source of sales forecasts and revenue estimates that can rarely be predicted accurately, and there is an additional need to plan and control expenditure.

The essence of marketing control, as in any other activity, is measurement. In relation to marketing costs, however, this measurement is not as straightforward as it may seem. The cost problems that are of decisive importance in exercising the necessary controls may be classified as follows:

1 The costs of promotion and distribution – the two main tasks of marketing – have different effects and must be treated differently. The minimization principle should be applied to distribution activities, whereby a given quantitative target is aimed for at the lowest possible cost. But this principle cannot be applied to promotion, since the relationship between promotion and sales means that a variation in promotional expenditure will affect turnover, so minimal promotion may mean minimal sales. Consequently, an optimization principle must be applied, and a balance struck between the desired level of sales and the level of promotional expenditure necessary to achieve that level of sales.

2 The special structure of marketing costs raises problems. The cost structure of every activity is related to the interaction of fixed costs and variable costs, and is reflected in the costs per unit produced or sold at different rates of activity. However, a large number of marketing costs are semi-fixed. These stepped costs of a semi-fixed nature determine the behaviour of other costs.

3 The allocation of marketing overheads raises questions that require solutions. Along with a general increase in the proportion of fixed overhead costs that exists in modern business, there has been an increasing adoption of direct costing systems which often result in overhead costs being ignored. The significance of marketing costs is so great that they must necessarily be subjected to detailed control.

4 Further cost problems relate to the greater number of essentially different marketing conditions that have to be controlled continually and rationally. Financial control in marketing is complicated because a number of factors are influenced by the costs incurred – the product, the territory, the customer group and the salesman's profitability.

5 Special cost-control problems arise in attempting to evaluate the results of each element in the marketing mix. It is almost impossible to isolate the role played by any one element in the marketing operation.

Methods of control

Various control techniques are available, some of which are essentially financial and others only loosely quantitative.

Budgeting. A budget is a quantitative plan of action that aids in the coordination and control of the acquisition and utilization of resources over a given period of time. Budgeting involves more than just forecasting, since it involves the planned manipulation of all the variables that determine the company's performance in an effort to arrive at some target in the future.

There are essentially two types of budget: the long-term and the short-term. Typically, however, budgets tend to be compiled on an annual basis, with this time-span broken down into perhaps monthly intervals for reporting. What is known as the operating budget is compiled within the yearly framework.

Ratio analysis. A technique for exercising control used by management is ratio analysis. Ratios and percentages permit the comparison of results over time on a common basis, but caution must be employed because ratios cover the events they are helping to control with a blanket of averages. A number of different ratios may be employed:

1 Liquidity ratios. 'Liquidity' refers to a company's ability to meet its current financial obligations as they arise, and thereby remain solvent. The importance of liquidity to marketing cannot be emphasized too much, in the light of the fact that the whole cycle of stock into sales, debtors into cash, and cash to creditors is concerned with the central question of liquidity.
2 Profitability.
3 Market standing.

Market segments

Market segments are portions of an overall market; they may be defined in various ways, such as by geography or the characteristics of the consumers in each segment. The purpose in segmenting a market is to measure and make comparisons. Marketing costs can be reasonably accurately allocated to segments. The provision of financial information on a segment by segment basis is of value in controlling an integrated marketing programme. Management accountants are becoming increasingly aware of the needs of marketing management for information of this type.

Managing the marketing mix: measuring effectiveness

We have already noted the elements that comprise the marketing mix: advertising, personal selling, sales promotion, pricing and channels of distribution. In managing that mix, and exercising control as part of that management, it is important to measure the effectiveness of each of the elements.

Advertising

It is not a simple task to measure the effectiveness of advertising. The relationship between advertising expenditure and resultant sales is difficult to define. The major difficulties in measurement of advertising effectiveness are fourfold:

1 Lack of stability in marketing operations.
2 The separation of the effect of advertising from the effects caused by other marketing and economic variables.
3 The time, effort and money required to sustain a programme of comparison for the purpose of measurement.
4 The patience and dedication needed by the researchers over the long period required to obtain meaningful data.

However, having outlined the difficulties, we can identify two main ways of looking at the question of advertising effectiveness. The first is to consider the results of the advertising in achieving target improvements in specific tasks, e.g. increasing brand awareness in a specific market. The second is to consider the impact of advertising on sales generally. It is extremely difficult to assess the impact of advertising on sales as a whole, because so many other factors, internal and external, are at work in the marketing process of an organization. It is easier to assess the impact of specific advertising campaigns on sales in specific product areas.

The evaluation aspect of advertising is an element of marketing that is remarkably short of measurement devices. The limited aids that are available are as follows:

1 Television audience measurement figures.
2 Information on the circulation figures for printed media.
3 Information concerning the readership of newspapers and periodicals.

4 Information on specific campaigns obtained by interviews and/or questionnaires.

The value of items 1–3 is restricted to quantifying or qualifying the market; item (4) offers more genuine guidance about the effects of advertising.

It must be noted that if marketing activities cannot be measured with any degree of objectivity, then, like any other aspect of management, their effectiveness can be judged only in an incomplete way. At present the assessment of advertising effectiveness can still be judged only in such an incomplete way.

Personal selling

Personal selling ranges from mere order-taking to the creation of new sales in a highly competitive market. Companies that utilize an aggressive policy, based on personal selling, are said to be adopting a push strategy; those that rely more heavily on advertising are described as adopting a pull strategy.

Whilst many organizations still see the prime role of the sales rep as that of generating sales, there is an increasing trend which sees the rep in a wider marketing role, which emphasizes the profit responsibility of the position. If sales are pursued regardless of such factors as costs and reputation, the value of the sales volume obtained can be severely reduced, if costs have been excessive and/or the organization's image has been tarnished by over-zealous reps. If reps are trained, however, to put themselves in their customers' shoes they are much less likely to put immediate sales gains before the prospect of much larger market opportunities in the future. In a sales-orientated approach the sales rep is focusing on his needs as a seller. By comparison, a market-orientated approach to selling concentrates on the needs of the buyer.

The effectiveness of sales reps can be measured in a number of different ways. Typical evaluation criteria include:

1 Net sales achieved.
2 Value of sales per call.
3 Call rate.
4 Sales expenses in proportion to sales achieved.

Sales promotion

Sales promotion activities are a form of indirect advertising designed to stimulate sales mainly by the use of incentives such as free samples, twin-pack bargains or temporary price reductions. The evaluation of a sales promotion is never a clear-cut matter, mainly on account of other variables in the overall marketing mix. The most popular method of evaluation is to measure sales and/or market share before, during and after the promotion period.

Pricing

A basic requirement of pricing policy is that the price fixed should be high enough to keep the business going. Beyond that, pricing in the marketing approach works on the basis that it should be what the customer will pay, with a healthy respect for other prices, especially those of competitors selling a similar product. Research into what the customer expects to pay is therefore a vital part of pricing policy. By and large, consumers tend to judge quality by the price charged; given a low price they may well wonder what is wrong with the product that can be sold so cheaply. Often the consumer will pay the higher price of two comparable goods, thinking that they are thereby getting better value and quality.

Channels of distribution

The channels of distribution normally extend from the manufacturer who sells to wholesalers, either direct or through agents, and thence to retailers. The wholesalers can be by-passed, as a matter of policy, by the manufacturer selling direct to retailers, and so can the retailers by selling direct to consumers. The channel of distribution used for products is largely dictated by the historical development of the type of product offered. People are used to obtaining these from certain sources, and so the supplier is obliged to accept this and conform to the buying behaviour pattern existing. There is continuous need to keep up with competitors and to check on what and how they are using the channels of distribution.

The marketing/finance interface in a corporate structure

The question of coordination and communication between marketing and the financial control function is of fundamental importance. The financial controller has a service function, through which he aims to develop information flows and reporting systems to facilitate improved planning, decision-making and control. In the marketing/ finance interface the controllership is concerned with the controller's service to marketing management, and this will become increasingly important as the marketing concept is more widely adopted and as marketing becomes more dominant within the typical company.

To offer the best service to marketing, the controller must study the company's marketing organization and its problems. The most effective communication tends to occur where members of the controller's staff are located within the marketing function with line responsibility to the controller but with a close working relationship with the marketing staff.

The finance/marketing interface is all part of the corporate approach to management in which the marketing plan is a means whereby the broad strategies of the corporate plan can be carried into effect on a year-to-year basis.

FINANCE

The finance function is responsible not only for controlling costs, paying salaries and creditors, and ensuring that sales invoices are paid by customers, but also for setting and monitoring the organization's annual budgets, longer-term capital expenditure plans, and borrowing levels. The finance manager is also responsible for dealing with the money that the company receives: making sure that profit targets and other earnings ratios are met, and investing spare cash in the money markets.

PERSONNEL

The personnel department has the job of recruiting new staff and training them so that the skills of the workforce meet the requirements of the organization. Training and developing a person's skills should be an on-going process throughout their career with the organization, and not just at the start of it. The personnel manager is responsible also for staff—management relations, grievance and disciplinary matters, and redundancy and dismissal procedures. The manager also has to ensure that the organization adheres to the equal opportunities and equal pay legislation, and does not discriminate against individuals because of their race or sex, or on the grounds of disability.

SUMMARY

We have looked at the marketing concept and at the implementation of the concept in a range of organizations, including the service sector and not-for-profit industries. We examined marketing planning and highlighted the key elements of a plan.

The role of marketing research was examined in relation to the manager's need for information. The market information system is an important tool for management developing a marketing strategy. The behaviours of many players in marketing were outlined and methods of market control reviewed.

CHECKLIST: CHAPTER 11

After reading this chapter you will be able to identify the functions of:

1 Marketing
2 Market planning
3 Market research
4 Market information systems
5 Market control

Part Four

The Managerial Environment

CHAPTER 12

The business environment

The manager's task has to be looked at in context. Both the organization and the work of its managers will be affected by the business environment in which they exist. This business environment has two forms: the external environment (common to all organizations); and the company's internal environment, or culture, which is unique to each organization.

In this chapter we will look at the internal and external business environments of organizations, and will then briefly discuss the management of environmental and business change.

THE EXTERNAL BUSINESS ENVIRONMENT

The external business environment in which organizations operate has a continuous and profound effect on their management. The different parts of this environment act both as constraints on business operations, and will present organizations with new opportunities to exploit. The way in which different organizations respond to these common constraints and opportunities determines which organizations are successful and which fail.

However, because organizations are open systems, importing resources from the environment (such as raw materials, finance, employees, etc.), and because organizations' activities are often subject to 'rights' or claims of interest groups in the environment, it is sometimes difficult to determine where the organization ends and the external environment begins. Therefore, the boundaries between the two are blurred. The company's employees are simultaneously involved in, and are a part of, the environment outside the company.

The boundaries between the organization and the environment are not static either. They are based upon relationships, rather than physical entities. Thus while certain fixed elements, such as its location, do have some impact on an organization's limits, it is the decisions of managers that really determine where the organization ends and the external environment begins. It can be said that different employees and their tasks are at the company's boundaries, depending on the activity at the time: sometimes it is the switchboard operator, while at other times it is the managing director.

Elements of the external environment

The external environment is made up of a number of different elements: the economic environment, the technological environment, the political and legal environment, and the social or cultural environment (see Figure 12.1).

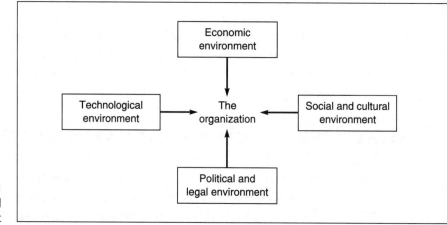

Figure 12.1
The external
environment

The economic environment

The economic environment affects the organization because of two reasons. First, it relates to the effect of changes in the level of prices on the company; and second, the level of general economic activity in the country indicates the likelihood of consumer incomes rising or falling. This in turn will affect company sales, costs and wage rates.

The parts of the economic environment

The economic environment is made up of several parts, which all have a greater or lesser influence on organizations and business:

1 *The supplier.* The supplier provides the organization with raw materials and the other components it needs. The organization has to purchase these at a price (and quality) which it can afford, while at the same time it still has to make a profit from selling the finished goods.

2 *Customers.* Customers form another part of the economic environment, and affect the organization in that their needs and demands determine what a company produces and sells successfully in the way of goods and services, and the prices at which they can be sold.

3 *The investor.* Business confidence and the willingness of banks and other investors to lend money to companies are closely linked to expectations about the future level of economic activity in the country. Thus, the state of the general economic environment determines the ability of businesses to borrow money for capital investment purposes.

4 *The government.* The government is a particularly important element in the economic environment. Government fiscal and monetary policies influence the organization in relation to the cost and availability of credit, the level of taxation, interest rates, exchange rates (if the company exports its goods) and general business confidence.

5 *Competitors.* A company's competitors are simply a 'threat' in the economic environment. Thus, for example, any advertising promotion of Peugeot would have an impact on the sales of Rover.

The legal and political environment

The legal environment is a very important external constraint on organizations. The law sets out the operating conditions of most businesses, ranging from specific bans on certain kinds of behaviour, to regulations requiring the reporting of income and staffing at various times of the year.

Companies have to comply with laws setting minimum health and safety standards; laws on employment practices; laws banning discrimination on grounds of race, religion, sex, and marital status; trade union laws; and a whole host of other regulations specific to individual industries and businesses. Again, car manufacture provides a useful example, where Saab were using as part of their 1993 advertising programme the fact that they already comply with California car emission controls for 1994. With the introduction of improved technology, Saab continued to promote the environmental benefits of their products in the second half of 1996.

However, the legal environment has to be considered alongside the political environment, because it is the political environment that is responsible for bringing about the enactment of new laws and regulations.

The political environment consists of the government and parliament in the UK, together with the Commission, Council and Parliament of the EU. These bodies pass the many, many laws and regulations which affect the way organizations function. The network of laws, regulations, directives and court decisions presents a highly complex environment in which all companies and organizations must operate. The way in which an organization responds to this environment may well determine its success or failure.

An organization can respond to these constraints by studying prospective rules and legislation, in order to develop a business strategy which will deal with the new legal framework within the necessary time-span. For example, car manufacturers who have developed engines with the capacity to run on both leaded and lead-free petrol, before leaded petrol has been either totally banned or priced out of the market in favour of unleaded fuel, have neutralized this potential threat to their business.

You should note, however, that there are political influences on organizations and their managers regardless of any legal obligations. For instance, strong political pressure brought by conservation groups concerned about potential pollution risks have affected industrial companies (such as chemical manufacturers) independently of any legal ramifications.

The political environment is closely linked with the social environment. Laws are often passed as the result of social pressure on the government. The ability of political parties to make laws also depends upon popular acceptance of their social and economic ideas and policies at the polls at election time.

The social or cultural environment

The social or cultural environment is the third major element of the external business environment. It is made up of the attitudes, customs, beliefs, education, etc., of people and society at large. The most important determining factors of this social environment are the class, culture, age, sex and political beliefs of the people in it. The social environment has a significant influence upon organizations and the ways in which they are managed, because the organizations themselves are made up of people who are part of this external environment. An example of the social environment influencing business behaviour is found in W. H. Smith deciding to restrict selling publications likely to be viewed as degrading.

Closely linked with the social environment is what may be termed the 'ethical environment'. This consists of a set of well-established rules of personal and organizational behaviour and values. The ethical environment of organizations refers to justice, respect for the law and a moral code. The conduct of any company will be measured against these ethical standards by the company's customers, suppliers and the general public. The problem with 'moral ethics', however, is that the organization's view of the world may not always be in accordance with society's normal codes of morality! A number of unit trusts have been set up as 'ethical trusts' investing in companies who have equal opportunities policies, and no links with the armaments industry, etc.

The technological environment

The final element of the external environment is the technological environment. Recent developments in technology have had an enormous influence on the ways in which companies operate. Computers have revolutionized product design and manufacture; for example, the introduction of sophisticated automated or robotic machinery in the car manufacturing industry can now enable a group of people to do what required a mini-organization to do even just a few years ago. It has also changed work patterns away from the assembly line and back to the 'gang' or 'work group'.

Volvo in Sweden experimented with allocating teams to the construction of individual vehicles. Advances in technology have also made it possible to open up new markets which were previously unexploited, either because the technical 'know-how' was lacking, or because the costs involved were prohibitive. Offshore oil and gas exploration is just one example of this.

Technical developments and innovations can present enormous opportunities for companies. But there is a down-side risk attached to this. The rapid pace of technological change does mean that, unless businesses are careful, they can find their products and manufacturing processes becoming obsolete very quickly. Therefore, it is vital for organizations to pay a lot of attention to monitoring the technological environment and to try and forecast possible medium- to long-term changes in it.

THE TYPES OF ENVIRONMENT

The different elements in the external business environment tend to relate to each other in different ways, bringing about a particular set of circumstances which the organization has to react to. Emery and Trist (1965) called this the 'causal texture' of the environment.

Environments are considered to be made up of various 'good' and 'bad' elements, which have an effect upon the organization. Emery and Trist identified four types of environmental causal texture, each of which affect the organization and its management in very different ways:

1 *The placid randomized environment.* An environment in which the good and bad elements are relatively unchanging in themselves and are distributed randomly. In such an environment the organization need hardly plan strategically at all, and is able to act purely on a tactical basis.

2 *The placid clustered environment.* An environment in which the good and bad elements are not randomly distributed, but relate to each other and are grouped together in certain patterns. An organization must respond to this kind of environment with strategic, long-term planning, rather than merely short-term tactics. The tobacco industry often finds social, political and economic factors combining together.

3 *The disturbed reactive environment.* In this type of environment there is more than one organization of the same kind; indeed, the dominant characteristic of this type of environment is that several similar organizations exist together. In this environment each organization does not simply have to take account of the other competing organizations when they interreact at random; it also has to consider that whatever information it has may also be known by its competitors. Examples here include supermarket chains, where the policies of Sainsbury have an impact on Tesco, etc.

4 *The turbulent environment.* In this environment, dynamic processes, which create significant variances for the organizations which exist within it, arise from the environment

itself. The organization operating in this type of environment thus faces a large degree of uncertainty, with the consequences of any actions becoming increasingly unpredictable. Markets which are subject to taste variations such as popular music suffer from this type of environment.

THE INTERNAL BUSINESS ENVIRONMENT

The internal environment, or culture, of an organization is made up of the unique combination of values, beliefs, behavioural patterns, and so on, which characterize the manner in which groups and individual employees of that organization work together in order to achieve their objectives. The individuality of businesses is thus expressed in terms of their differing cultures.

Four major types of organizational culture have been identified by Charles Handy (1984): the power culture; the role culture; the task culture; and the person culture.

The power culture

In this business culture power rests with a central figure of authority who exercises control through the selection of key individuals. An organization with this kind of culture operates with few written rules, and decisions are often taken according to the balance of influence at the time, rather than in accordance with logic or procedure.

The main strength of organizations with power cultures is that they are able to move and react quickly to any threat. However, whether the company does move quickly – or in the right direction – depends upon the person or persons in control. The success of organizations with power cultures therefore largely depends upon the quality of the individuals in control: the power culture puts a tremendous amount of faith in the individual. Such a culture is often found in new companies controlled by their entrepreneurial founders.

Size and growth do pose problems for organizations with power cultures. Often, successful businesses with this culture and dynamic founders grow comparatively quickly, and often rapidly become too big to be manageable by one person. If such a company is to remain a cohesive, controllable entity, it should really either create other subordinate organizations or develop a modified power culture whereby some standard management procedures are introduced to complement the existing control structure. Otherwise, such organizations risk becoming victims of their own success.

The role culture

The organization based upon the role culture is structured according to functions or expertise, for example the finance department, the personnel department, etc. Each of these departments is strong in its own right, but is coordinated by a small group of senior managers by means of set written rules and procedures, such as:

> Procedures for tasks/roles (i.e. job descriptions).
> Procedures for communications.
> Rules for settling disputes.

It is these rules and procedures which are the major source of influence in a role culture. This type of culture is perhaps better known as 'bureaucracy'.

In the role culture the role (or job) is the factor which is important; the individual is a secondary consideration. People are selected in order to perform a particular job and that job is usually described in such a way that a variety of individuals could do it. The organization's efficiency therefore depends not so much on the quality of individual people inside that organization – as in the power culture – but on the rationality of the allocation of work and responsibility.

The success of a role culture organization depends upon a stable environment. It will then provide security and predictability in terms of the acquisition and promotion of specialist expertise without risks. The drawback of role culture organizations is that they tend to be slow to perceive any need for change, and are slow to change even if that need is recognized. Organizations based upon the role culture tend to be found where economies of scale are more important than flexibility, or where technical expertise and depth of specialization are more important than product innovation or product cost.

The task culture

In contrast with the role culture, where the emphasis is on *how* something is done, rather than what is done, the task culture emphasizes the accomplishment of the task or project. In order to do this a task culture organization seeks to bring together appropriately qualified personnel in a team, and gives them the resources they need to do their jobs. The task culture provides team members with a substantial amount of control over their work, and employees also enjoy mutual respect within the group, based upon capability rather than age or rank. This culture harnesses the unity of the work team, with its goal of completing a particular project, in order to improve efficiency, and to identify the individual with the objectives of the organization as a whole.

Managers have the power to allocate projects, people and resources, and so they maintain control in the task culture. However, this is not control on a day-to-day basis; team members retain substantial control over their work, and indeed any attempt by senior managers to exercise closer everyday control would not be acceptable in this type of culture.

It is when there is a scarcity of resources that management often feels a need to interfere in the control of the project teams' work. Team leaders also start to vie for what resources are available, and, consequently, the task culture begins to change to a power culture.

The task culture is very adaptable and is, therefore, appropriate where flexibility and sensitivity to the market or to the external environment are important (i.e. where the market is competitive and the product life is short). Conversely, the culture is not suitable in situations which require economies of scale or great depths of expertise.

The task culture is popular with managers. According to Handy it is:

> the culture most in tune with current ideologies of change and adaptation, individual freedom and low status differentials.

Even so, it is not always the most appropriate culture for the prevailing climate and technology.

The person culture

In the person culture the purpose of the organization's existence is to serve the individual. The individual is therefore the central point in this culture. Organizations based upon the person culture are rare — usually they are family firms. Instead, one tends to find within another culture a person whose behaviour and attitudes reveal a preference for the person culture. A popular example of this is the person culture-oriented professor working within a role culture. The professor does what is necessary under the contract, teaching when required, in order to retain a position in the organization. Essentially, however, he looks upon the university or college as a base on which to build personal career and interests. These may, indirectly, add interest and value to the organization, although that would not be the professor's main motive for pursuing them.

Factors influencing organizations' cultures

The culture of an organization is a matter of its own choice. There are a number of factors which will help determine this choice, such as the following:

1 *Size.* This is a very important variable influencing an organization's choice of culture. The larger an organization, the greater the tendency towards formalization and the development of specialized coordinated groups. Therefore, a growth in size generally influences an organization towards a role culture.

2 *Technology.* In general, routine programmable operations are more suitable to a role culture than to any of the other cultures, as are high-cost technologies which require close monitoring and supervision and depth of expertise, and technologies where economies of scale are available. However, power or task cultures are more suitable where organizations are involved in unit production and non-continuous operations. These latter two cultures are also more suitable when technology is changing rapidly.

3 *History and ownership.* Where there is centralized ownership of organizations, i.e. in family firms, there is a tendency towards a power culture. Diffused ownership allows diffused influence, based upon alternative sources of power.

4 *Goals and objectives.* Quality objectives can usually be monitored more easily in role cultures, while growth objectives are usually more appropriate in power or task cultures.

5 *The people.* The availability of suitably qualified people is a significant factor in any choice of culture. The individual preferences of key people in the organization will also have a large say in determining the dominant culture, irrespective of what it actually should be for the good of the company!

6 *The environment.* The final important factor influencing the choice of culture is the external environment. An unstable, changing environment requires an adaptable, responsive culture, i.e. a task culture, whereas a more stable environment may lead an organization more towards a role culture.

Differentiation

An organization might have a structure which reflects a single culture. On the other hand, different structures reflecting different cultures might exist side-by-side in separate departments of the same organization. This is known as 'differentiation', and should help the organization to adapt to changes in its external environment better and more quickly than it perhaps would if it had just one organizational culture.

However, to be successful, differentiation has to be both co-ordinated and integrated, or else there is a danger that the organization's staff will not work together towards any common aim or goal.

INVESTIGATE

What sort of culture does your company, college, or an organization with which you are familiar have? And what degree of differentiation, if any?

MANAGING CHANGE

The ability of organizations to manage change effectively has become more and more important recently because of the rapid advances in technology and the increasing uncertainty and risk associated with the business environment. Companies that want to survive and prosper are having to be very much more receptive to new ideas and practices, and very much more responsive and adaptable. In order to manage change, the organization must be properly prepared for it, from the top management team downwards. (This is often the sticking point — a board of directors or a chief executive who are isolated from what is really happening in the company by layers of management.) A climate of change can really be successful only if it has the overt backing of the senior executive. This is why change is usually easier to accomplish in task or power cultures, rather than in role cultures.

Managing change requires flexibility, a good planning and decision-making system and an efficient management information system. A contingency approach to management, to leadership, to motivation, and so on, is one of the more flexible and adaptable ways of managing people — the idea that what is the right answer in some circumstances is not necessarily the right answer in others. This approach also promotes an openness to different ideas and concepts. Systematic planning and information systems also help by enabling the manager to take decisions in the confidence that uncertainty and risk have been accounted for and minimized as much as is possible.

The possibility of change tends to provoke resistance among the people it will affect, due to a very natural fear and mistrust of the unknown. This resistance will show itself in different ways, ranging from an outright refusal to cooperate to a covert undermining of the proposals. (It should be noted that these reactions can be found all through the organization, from senior managers to workshop employees.)

This mistrust and resistance have been found to be best overcome by a deliberate policy of keeping people informed of what is being proposed, and getting them involved, as far as possible, in the discussions and decision-making. If someone has been able to suggest a new way of doing a task, or has at least been asked his or her opinion, they will be far more likely to be willing to give the solution a fair trial than if it has just been imposed. However, these discussions should be genuine ones, and not held merely for form's sake, with no account taken of what is said by the people taking part.

Causes of change

There are a number of causes of change, and they fall into two main categories: *internal* and *external*.

Some of the internal causes of change are more obvious than others. If an organization performs poorly and is neither successful nor profitable, then in order to survive at all, some change will be inevitable. Studies by Huczynski and Buchanan (1991) suggest that the desire to improve performance may drive the desire for change. The trigger for such improvements may be, as suggested above, a requirement for increased efficiency, or others including benchmarking and cultural influences.

Some external causes are listed by Morden (1996) as:

■ Market competition, which affects market offer, the product or service portfolio, costs and prices, etc.
■ Technological change and innovation, for instance as illustrated in the dynamics of S-curves.
■ Re-engineering, by which changes in the perception of best, most cost-efficient or most appropriate practice are implemented.
■ Internationalization, globalization and cultural differences.

Externalities include:

■ The need to manage diversity.
■ The need to manage in a socially responsible and ethical manner.
■ The need to manage strategically.

Other external drivers of change include:

■ Changes in competition policy and regulations (especially towards free trade in Europe, NAFTA and Australasia), and the effects of WTO/OECD.
■ Demographic changes.
■ Changes in consumer tastes and social attitudes.
■ Changing attitudes towards the environment.
■ Changing legislation.

The management of change is closely linked to the 'innovator' role as outlined in the competing values framework developed by Quinn (see Chapter 1). Quinn *et al.* (1996) include an exercise for evaluating personal acceptance of change. That exercise is reproduced here as Table 12.1. Spend a few moments completing the table and then interpret your answers.

Different elements of change may lead to a variety of reactions. Change that is planned and even anticipated can be a very different experience from those that are sudden, unplanned and possibly unwelcome too. Planned and unplanned changes can result in both anticipated and unanticipated consequences. The results we planned for sometimes do not come about. Similarly, unplanned changes can bring welcome and unwelcome results.

Table 12.1

Directions:

The following questionnaire will help you assess your personal acceptance of change. Consider carefully the following list of changes. List any others that are applicable. Which of these changes have occurred in your life in the past five years? As you consider each change, recall your resistance to change when it happened.

In column A, place a number reflecting your resistance at the time of the change. Next, in column B, place a number reflecting your current level of acceptance of that change. If you did not experience the change, place a '0' in both blanks.

Scale A	No Resistance							Strong Resistance
		1	2	3	4	5		
Scale B	No Acceptance							Strong Acceptance
		1	2	3	4	5		

A	B	
—	—	1 You were married or engaged.
—	—	2 There was a death in your immediate family.
—	—	3 You moved to a new location.
—	—	4 You enrolled in a college or university.
—	—	5 You had a personal health problem.
—	—	6 You began work at a new job.
—	—	7 An important relationship in your life changed.
—	—	8 Your income level changed by over £6,500 a year.
—	—	9 You were divorced or separated.
—	—	10 A close friend or relative was divorced or separated.
—	—	11 Other (List):

Interpretation:

What do your responses reveal about how you deal with change? As you look at each item, note the difference between the number you placed in column A (resistance to change) and the number in column B (acceptance of change). A large difference (4 is the maximum possible) indicates that your ability to accept change is strong.

1 Which changes did you strongly resist at first, but now accept? Think of as many reasons as possible why you now accept these changes. Identifying these reasons may help you identify your strengths in acceptance of change.

2 Based on your responses, do you consider yourself to be open to change, or do you find change difficult to deal with?

3 Are there any events which you strongly resisted, and which you now have difficulty accepting? Seek to identify the reasons for your non-acceptance. As you compare strongly resisted events which you accept with those you do not, you may find valuable clues to your ability to cope with change in your life.

Morden (1996) highlights the differences between planned changes and unplanned changes:

1 Planned change carries a more positive connotation than unplanned change.
2 Planned change tends to involve a sense of gain; unplanned change tends to involve a sense of loss.
3 Planned changes can be anticipated; unplanned changes are sudden.
4 We are active participants in planned changes; we see ourselves as passive receivers of unplanned changes.
5 Planned changes are usually less stressful than unplanned changes.

Organizations can use both culture and style to help employees cope with change. Organizational culture reflects both philosophy and mission and can influence the way members of the organization interact with each other. In addition, organizational culture affects the way individuals within the organization interact with outsiders.

In some circumstances, the culture of an organization can be a hindrance to managing change – for example, in an organization where the philosophy is that the way it has always been done is the best and the only way to do things, this will seriously stand in the way of flexibly adapting to change. In your own organization, try to identify elements of the culture that build resistance to change and those that actively enable change to be managed.

In coping with change, flexibility and adaptability are key skills, and need to be encouraged long before the crisis of unplanned change occurs. Another way to improve the adaptability of an organization is to encourage employees to participate in changes as they take place and as they are being planned.

In times of change, employees can be a source of creativity. If the manager can tap into such creativity it not only helps the employees and managers to identify key values and strengths but also demonstrates the values that help to cope with unplanned changes.

Resistance to change

Is resistance to change inevitable? When there is a move to change, whether voluntarily or forced, there would always appear to be elements of resistance. Think of times of change in your own life when you have been able to welcome or even instigate the change. Think also of changes you have experienced which you resisted. The reasons for resistance are many and varied, and will differ for individuals as their own circumstances change. Morden (1996) lists a number of potential causes for resistance to change of which managers should be aware. They are:

1 Inertia, for instance caused by a long time period unaffected by significant change. Similarly, a long-established and stable workforce dominated by older managers and staff (perhaps with only a few years to go before retirement) may be strongly antipathetic to the need for change. This may be related to:

2 A preference for stability, and a low tolerance of change. This is a natural human reaction. The prospect of change may, at the very least, be inconvenient.

3 Custom and practice; habit and conformity. People become habituated to doing things in certain ways. Custom and practice becomes convenient and easy; habits are hard to break.

4 Inflexible attitudes, structures and practices. Inflexible attitudes, mechanistic structures and 'bureaucratic' practices are all likely to be hostile to changes that may have a potential impact on them.

5 An installed base of thinking. Hamel and Prahalad (1994) suggest that 'what prevents most companies from creating the future is not an installed base of obsolete capital equipment ..., not an installed base of end products that must be maintained and updated ..., and not an inefficient base of distribution infrastructure.... What prevents companies from creating the future is an installed base of thinking – the unquestioned conventions, the myopic view of opportunities and threats, and the unchallenged precedents that comprise the existing managerial frame of reference.'

6 An inappropriate organization culture. Values and priorities may be incongruent with the needs of change. Inward-looking or production-orientated cultures may, for instance, find it hard to come to terms with external market pressures for drastic improvements in customer orientation and customer service.

7 An inappropriate leadership or management style. Authoritarian styles may attempt to impose change, only to

find, for instance, that the lack of employee commitment to, or ownership of, these changes results in implementation failures.

8 Denial. There may be an outright refusal to admit to the need for change; a refusal to accept the nature of the problem; or an unwillingness to agree to a definition such that a solution cannot be identified. Denial is a negative form of reaction.

9 Opposition, in which an attempt is made to stop the change at source, for instance through legislative means, lobbying, removing individuals associated with the proposed change, etc. Opposition is a positive form of reaction.

10 The use of countervailing power, for instance through group solidarity and prestige, customer inertia, trade union power, or standards institutions.

11 The use of ritualized behaviour, for example the formalized use of rules, procedures and committee structures, the bureaucratic or hierarchical referral, the referral (and slowing down) of all change issues to negotiating procedures in which trade unions, staff associations or mediators are involved.

12 Departments as fortresses. Ritualized behaviour and countervailing power are described by Kanter (1985). Strongly established functional departments (such as those in some French organizations) may be so powerful that they can block changes that are likely otherwise to affect (or reduce) their authority and autonomy.

13 Protection of self-interest. This is threatened by change. This is similar to point 14 below.

14 Perception of change as a threat to economic interest, job security, status or prestige. Resistance to change will be seen as a logical strategy by which to protect self-interest threatened by that change. This is related to:

15 Fear of the unknown, or reluctance to accept new experiences. Change may be perceived as 'an unknown quantity' and therefore to be resisted. New experiences may be good, but they might equally be bad.

16 Misunderstanding. People may simply not understand what is likely to be involved in the change or its outcome, particularly if there has been ineffective communication between the proposer of the change and those who will be directly affected by it. This may be related to:

17 Conflicting perceptions, in which different people assess (and communicate) the costs and benefits of the change in different and conflicting ways. Change is likely to be resisted where people cannot agree on its character or its consequences.

18 Lack of trust in the proponents of the change. People are hardly likely to have faith in a proposal for change when they distrust its proponents. The establishment and maintenance of trust within the enterprise will be a prerequisite to the effective implementation of ongoing programmes of change and innovation.

GM's unrivalled size and success made it easy for us to ignore the significance of change and the signs of potential future problems. The lesson we have learnt is that for unrivalled leaders, success itself breeds the roots of complacency, myopia and ultimately, decline.

(Jack Smith, chief executive of General Motors. *Financial Times*.)

Models of change

Take some time to reflect on the changes you have experienced in your organization and consider how they may or may not fit into the models of change as described. An early model by Lewin still forms the basis for many but not all later models, in that Lewin argued that organizational behaviour was essentially stable and the stability was maintained by the effects of two opposing sets of forces. One set works to maintain things as they are, the status quo, whilst the other set pushes for change. When the opposing sets work with force about equal to one another, then the organization's behaviour is maintained in a state of system equilibrium. Lewin argued that an imbalance in the forces would result in change. He further argued that reducing the forces working to maintain the status quo would be more easily accepted and produce less tension than increasing the forces for change. This, he went on, would result in a more effective strategy for change.

Lewin's model comprises of three steps which are:

1 '*Unfreezing*', that is, reducing the forces that keep the organization in its current behavioural state.

2 'Moving.' This process moves the organization's behaviour to a new state and will involve the setting-up and implementation of new values, attitudes and behaviours.

3 'Re-freezing.' This occurs when the new behaviour is established and reinforced by the revision of structures, cultures and processes.

Although many more recent models criticise Lewin's model for being too 'linear', even some new models have an element of unfreezing, moving and re-freezing within them. These three elements are worth further consideration as they form the basis of motivation.

Motivation

Unfreezing

This process may be stimulated or motivated by one or some of the following:

- Resistance; the causes and sources of resistance to change, as outlined above, can be addressed by seeking out and responding to them. Strategies used here could include: invoking higher authority; overcoming, mitigating or blocking the resistance; appointing intermediaries who may be able to persuade those who resist; waiting for resistance to subside; engaging in a strategy to defeat those who resist.
- Another course of action can be to describe the changes in terms of benefits to those affected by them. Improvements in customer service can also mean that there is a substantial benefit in terms of job security and employer commitment to workforce and location.
- Communication remains of vital importance. The searching out of views and distribution of reasons for and methods of change to those involved will be more likely to result in the acceptance and even ownership of the proposals for change.
- Personal motivation of those affected can be enhanced by elements such as increased personal satisfaction, commitment to and identification with their organization. There could also be increased remuneration, improved conditions,

reduced supervision, etc. There are negative aspects to personal motivation too which would include fear of redundancy, etc.

- If the individuals recognize a crisis, then they will better understand that a reaction (change) is necessary. In addition, if the workforce senses that they are pulling together in the face of a crisis, then they could react more positively when facing it together rather than as individuals.

- Forcing compliance to change does not necessarily result in people believing in what they are doing or in being particularly committed to it.

- Managers as leaders can have a significant impact upon the acceptance of change. Techniques employed include: communicating their vision; championing the change; establishing role models; using management by wandering around (MBWA). Morden (1996) describes MBWA as:

---

to spread the word, to persuade and exhort, to encourage and support, and to make themselves visible as 'generals leading their troops by example' rather than hiding behind committees and consultants. Sam Walton, the founder of the North American retail chain Wal-Mart, was for instance celebrated for his 'punishing schedule, visiting store after store ... in his aeroplane ... motivating staff.' (*Business Age*, April 1994)

Armstrong (1990) suggests that resistance to change will be less if those affected by change feel that they can accept the project as their own, not one imposed upon them by outsiders; the change has the whole-hearted support of management; the change accords with well-established values; the change is seen as reducing rather than increasing present burdens; the change offers the kind of new experience that interests participants; participants feel that their autonomy and security are not threatened; participants have jointly diagnosed the problems; the change has been agreed by group decisions; those advocating change understand the feelings and fears of those affected and take steps to relieve unnecessary fears; and it is recognized that new ideas are likely to be misinterpreted and ample provision is made for discussion of reactions to proposals to ensure complete understanding of them.

New patterns

The establishing of new patterns was identified by Morden (1996) as a series of identifications, definitions and evaluations, thus:

1 Identify, define and diagnose the change problems or issues to be dealt with.
2 Define and agree the desired outcomes of the change process, and the objectives that must be achieved in order to attain these outcomes.
3 Define and evaluate the likely degree of resistance to the change.
4 Define and agree the strategies and means by which change may be motivated, and the unfreezing process facilitated.
5 Define and agree the strategies and means by which new patterns may be established and formalized (re-freezing).
6 Define and agree the transition state commitments and activities required to meet the change objectives, and to implement the necessary strategies. The change process may be carried out by the managers and staff directly affected by it. Or, in addition, it has become a received wisdom that this process may be assisted or 'facilitated' by the use of third parties. Such third parties may be internal or external consultants, or 'change agents'. Their role is to act objectively as process supporter and motivator. Alternatively, the change process may be facilitated by three of the team roles identified by Belbin (1981). These roles are the chairperson, shaper and plant. These roles can literally be used as the movers and shapers of change within the organization.

The introduction of a movement towards new patterns will involve a number of people within an organization. These individuals and teams are involved in a number of processes that lead to the new pattern becoming established.

There will be a period of consideration during which the key issues involved in change are identified, defined and analysed. All the parties involved in the change will have to communicate with one another. This element returns again and again in all discussions on management and cannot be over-emphasized. It is almost certain that there will be an element of advice in the introduction of changing patterns. An adviser who is strong and gives guidance on how to proceed is more likely to be followed than an adviser with a weaker approach. Part of the motivation process may involve the application of some pressure, as was discussed above on overcoming resistance to change. Types of pressure can vary from subtle to overt, but all varieties can form part of the process of establishing new patterns within an organization. Linked closely with the advice given, those holding authority in the organization will be able to indicate a direction to be taken by the staff, and the nature of the processes to be established. There are occasions when the management of an organization fails to achieve a consensus. Huczynski and Buchanan (1991) say, "This may happen where there is a profound disagreement between those concerned with a change, and where there is little or no chance of anyone altering their views. The result is the use of force or threats ... [and an] offer to fire, transfer or demote individuals or to stifle their promotion and career prospects.' This is termed by Huczynski and Buchanan as coercion, which seems to suggest that if people will not change willingly then they will be changed. A wide consultation with all those involved in the change is likely to identify a broader range of problems to be addressed, and will also increase the capacity for finding solutions to them. The involvement and participation of all levels of the organization in the formulation of new patterns, and the processes by which the enterprise moves towards them, through negotiation and agreement, will further enable the transition to take place. Many changes will necessitate education, training and staff development. New skills and competences may be required.

For example, British Airways put its entire workforce through a major customer service training programme in order to reinforce its strategy of improving service quality and customer perceptions of the airline's service offer. Individuals may be overwhelmed by the new pattern process and may not think themselves able to handle it. In such cases, part of the process should include support in the form of assistance, guidance and reassurance to individuals and groups involved in implementing the change.

Armstrong (1990) comments that 'people support what they help [to] create'. Commitment to change will be greater if those affected by change are allowed to participate as fully as possible in planning and implementing it. The aim should be to get them to 'own' the change as something they want and will be glad to live with. Getting involvement in the introduction of change will only be effective in gaining commitment when management is prepared to listen and to change its plans if there is a clear message that they are unworkable, or if the plans could be made more acceptable without prejudicing the objectives of the change programme.

The techniques and processes described in texts on management, including this one, are not guarantees of success. There are many 'excellence' programmes that have failed, and have reduced businesses to a shadow of their former selves. In 1994, Furlong identified a number of factors that had contributed to programme failures in Canadian, British and US companies. They included: wrong or no execution, i.e. the implementation failed because of inappropriate levels of effort and resources, or by trying to fit new patterns into old structures; top management lack of involvement meant there were no role models of sufficiently high standing to enable to process to work; lack of management know-how — managers may not have sufficient training to enable them to cope with the ambiguities of change; managers have a real desire for a 'quick fix'. She says that because managers often receive accolades for achieving ends quickly, the desire for speed in fixing things is reinforced. Thus a programme that may take three years to produce results does not fit in with the Western culture demand for speedy solutions. She argues that solutions may not fit in tidily with a fiscal year, which is an entirely artificial time frame, but need to be applied 'slowly and progressively'. New processes and their implementation are often not accompanied by appropriate rewards and recognition; when employees are not heavily involved in the planning and implementation process, the effectiveness of the change can be seriously reduced. Change programmes should be done with employees rather than done to them. This level of involvement calls for a shift in power towards employees, but if the change is to be effective it needs to be done.

The establishment of new patterns or re-freezing is achieved, according to Morden (1996), by the combination of one or more of four key influences: structure, culture, style and process. The following paragraphs are from his book *Principles of Management.*

Structure

Organization structure and process may be adapted or changed to meet the requirements of change. The structure might be made:

- More responsive to customers, with an enhanced focus on customer service.
- More flexible and adaptable, for instance through decentralization and devolvement.
- International or global in scope and scale.

227

- More effectively controlled with the implementation of a package of simple and universally applied performance measures.
- More capable of innovation and intrapreneurship.

The process of restructuring may be part of a wider programme of re-engineering of structure and process set in train as a result of the change decisions made by the enterprise, The process of restructuring may instead be managed on the basis of organization development or OD.

Culture

Change processes may result in the eventual development of new organization culture, for example, moving towards any of the person-centred or intrapreneurial, the task, the tough-guy, the bet your company, the turnaround, the team, the excellence or the partnership cultures.

The proponents and managers of the change process may need to take into account those features of national culture that are likely to help or hinder the change process, or influence the establishment of new patterns.

Styles

The role, process and style of management may be adapted to meet implementation needs associated with the change process. The same is true of leadership. Leaders may be of particular importance in reinforcing and consolidating the new patterns of performance and behaviour, especially during the initial stages when structures and processes are new; when learning and experience are being accumulated; when things can be expected to go wrong; and when staff may become discouraged, frustrated or disillusioned.

Processes

A variety of processes will be used to establish and re-freeze change. These include:

- The re-engineering of human resource management (HRM) practices, and enterprise personnel policies.

- Recruitment, by which new staff may be brought in who have no experience of pre-change conditions, and who therefore do not have to go through an adaptation experience.
- Training and development, by which to put in place the new knowledge, skills and competences required by the new conditions brought about by the change being implemented.
- Remuneration and reward, by which to motivate or incentivize (*sic*) staff adoption and implementation of change. The new realities will be reflected in the pay structures and in the terms and conditions of employment. At the same time, however, key individuals and groups of staff may have to be awarded incentive or bonus payments to 'ensure loyalty' during a critical but difficult period, and to discourage them from leaving.
- Changing the people who will not, cannot, or do not want to change. This may require an adequate resource commitment to financing payoffs or early retirements, etc. The crude use of sackings (firings) or redundancy is likely instead to create an atmosphere of fear and mistrust among staff, and may make them inclined to resist the next proposal for change even more fiercely and effectively.

Pause for thought

MAKE A CHANGE! (from Quinn *et al.*, 1996). Identify a change you would like to make, either in your personal life or at work. On a clean sheet of paper write today's date and a description of the change. Determine when you will start implementing the change. The format should be as follows:

Today, write: Today's date.
Description of a change you wish to make.
Implementation target date.
Design of the change.
Strategies for implementing the change.

On the implementation
target date, write: Description of your experience to date and an evaluation of your plans.
Target completion date.

On the target completion
date write: Description of your experience, evaluating the strategies you used.

Now, answer the following questions:

1 How did you feel once you identified the change and the implementation date?

Many people feel vaguely dissatisfied with themselves when they want to change something and often think the dissatisfaction will remain until the change is completed. However, as you probably experienced in this activity, when we take action towards change, the dissatisfaction with ourselves often diminishes, and we are thereby encouraged to continue our plans.

2 What difference do you note in writing down your proposed change, with its accompanying dates, rather than merely having these ideas in your head?

Writing down the proposed change is a clarifying effort, and by so doing you tend to increase your belief that it will happen.

INTERNATIONAL STYLES AND CULTURE

In an organization the term 'culture' can be used to represent the collection of expectations, values and beliefs that affect if not govern the methods and ethos of management practice. In many ways, management culture will reflect the culture in which and with which it operates. Management cultures can be changed and developed, they are not written on tablets of stone. There is a wide variety of management cultures, and in this section we shall look at some of them and consider how knowledge of different cultures should help the management of an organization.

INVESTIGATE

Would you eat my horse or turn him into glue?

How do cultural values attached to the use of animals vary between countries?

Note down a few ideas before continuing.

Culture has a variety of meaning depending upon where and when you are. Different attitudes and histories produce a wide variety of development, philosophies and practices. The concept as a whole is more important now than previously because of increased interest and value credited to 'culture' in the light of transnational and global organizations.

Cultures change and develop over time and organizations working within national cultures find themselves adapting so that human resource management, among other aspects of management, can be used most effectively, economically and efficiently. On a personal level, managers dealing internationally experience the cultural influence/differences in interpersonal and inter-group relationships and communication. Organizations will perhaps choose to communicate through a local agent who has experience of dealing both with the local culture and within the culture of the multinational. The awareness of each others' expectations can be mediated by agents. 'Swiss and American businessmen get frustrated at the lack of punctuality of the Brazilian colleague and the English manager is confused and embarrassed at the personally persuasive compliments of the Egyptian counterpart and an Indian manager loses some respect for a Swedish director who openly seeks his assistance in making a decision which he confesses he finds very difficult' (University of Durham Business School, 1995)

In earlier chapters we have seen that there is a wide variety of factors influencing managers. The impact of specific influences will vary from time to time, but Laurent (1983) argued that nationality has three times more influence on managerial behaviour than any other characteristic. Laurent's survey produced some very clear national distinctions when asked what characterized an organization that was running well:

- Germany − creative and appropriate decisions being made by professional and well-qualified individual managers.
- Britain − a network of relationships where influence and negotiation get things done.
- France − a pyramid with differentiated levels of power to be acquired or dealt with.

Earlier, Sirota and Greenwood (1971) identified the following:

- English-speaking − high value on achievement and a low value on job security.
- Japan − little importance on individual achievement and much importance on a friendly working environment,

where most employees expected to spend the rest of their working lives.

■ Southern Europe – high value on security.

These few examples begin to show that a wide variety of cultures will affect organizations not only within the cultures identified, but having contact, trade or communications with different cultures.

Some countries show a wide human diversity of culture and accepted behaviour within their own borders: countries such as the USA, the Netherlands, Canada, the UK, Australia and New Zealand, France, Israel, Brazil, South Africa, Kenya, Nigeria, India and the West Indies. Morden (1996) states that this human and cultural diversity that characterizes these countries is one of their most important assets. 'It is a source of new ideas and new human capital. But it is also a source of challenge for the management process. In particular, it has a number of major human resource management implications.'

Before considering some individual national characteristics as they affect management, we will set down a framework for managing diversity within an organization. The following components are likely to form part of the management process (Morden, 1996):

1 Analysis and evaluation of the degree of diversity that characterizes the enterprise and its immediate environment. Enterprise management may from time to time re-examine these variables to ensure that it understands any changes that are taking place, for instance in terms of employment or customer expectations, or changing social and political attitudes.

2 Understanding the legislative and regulatory context within which the enterprise operates. Management may periodically need to review:

(a) The degree to which it meets the current requirements of employment law, equal opportunities expectations, or relevant codes of practice.

(b) The implications for the organization of ongoing developments, new laws, and future expectations (for instance those that result from EU policies, or from the further refinement of national or provincial charters of obligations, rights and freedoms).

3 Defining the actual incidence or potential sources of discrimination within the enterprise and its immediate

environment. Management will need to understand the degree to which discrimination occurs, or has occurred within the organization, and what were the reasons for that discrimination. This is evidently a potentially highly sensitive process. It is likely to require the championing, commitment and support of the highest level of management.

4 Defining the functional and operational impact of the need to manage diversity. The consequences may affect policies and practices for:

(a) Human resource planning, for instance in remedying actual or perceived 'imbalances' in employment categories such as the number of women in management positions, or the proportion of ethnic minorities employed.

(b) The formulation of job descriptions and personnel specifications, such that potential discriminatory features are eliminated 'at source'.

(c) The recruitment and selection process, such that all types of applicants are sought and selected within the spirit and requirement of prevailing laws, codes of practice and company statements of purpose (for instance to act as an equal opportunity employer).

(d) Training and development processes and opportunities, such that no eligible person is excluded on non-relevant grounds.

(e) Performance appraisal, such that evaluation criteria are relevant and appropriate, and based on merit; that they are clearly communicated to all; that they are applied to all, equally and without favour; and that there are no discriminatory criteria applied to individuals undergoing appraisal. This is also relevant to

(f) Promotion, such that no eligible person is excluded from consideration on non-relevant grounds, and that the criteria for success are clearly understood and non-discriminatory in all cases (unless agreed programmes of positive discrimination or affirmative action are in force).

(g) Remuneration systems and compensation programmes, such that payment and reward are based on skill, performance, length of service or seniority, etc., and not on discriminatory variables such as sex or race.

5 Defining the consequences for line managers. The need to manage diversity, and to remove discriminatory practices, will have a direct influence on the tasks and responsibilities of line managers. It will have at least two effects, as follows:

(a) The policies by which managers direct their work, and that of their subordinates, will be shaped by considerations of diversity and discrimination defined for them at a corporate or enterprise-wide level.

(b) It may be implicit that the implementation of diversity management programmes will be supervised and monitored by the use of the functional authority. In this case, functional specialists may have the right to give orders to line managers, who will be obliged to comply, in order to achieve a consistent application of the diversity management and anti-discriminatory policies across the enterprise. Line managers are likely, therefore, to have to undergo some level of diversity management and anti-discriminatory training. The needs of diversity management programmes may also be reflected in line management performance evaluation, remuneration and reward, and promotion policies.

6 Dealing with discriminatory behaviour and harassment. Policies and practices will have to be implemented by which discriminatory behaviour, sexual harassment and forms of intimidation may be identified and dealt with. This will be a mandatory requirement in those countries where employment law holds the employer to be responsible for the actions of employees within the work environment. Dealing with discriminatory behaviour and harassment may be a function of staff communication and training. It is also likely to have consequences for grievance, disciplinary and dismissal policies.

7 Establishing strategies by which to deal with discrimination, discriminatory behaviour and harassment, such that consistent management action may be achieved across the organization, and the letter of the law achieved.

8 Establishing strategies by which to implement equal rights and equal opportunities, such that consistent management action may be achieved across the organization, and the spirit of expectations, codes and laws achieved.

Influences on business practice

Having identified the areas that will have an influence, we now need to consider the effects on business practice. Peters and Waterman

(1982) suggest that successful organizations find ways of rewarding and motivating staff so that they see themselves as winners.

INVESTIGATE

How do you like to be rewarded?

An example of appropriate rewards:

Foxboro:
The firm Foxboro desperately needed a technical breakthrough and one evening a scientist rushed into his boss's office with the answer. His boss searched his drawer, found a banana and gave it to him. This firm now awards a gold banana pin as the highest accolade for technical achievement.

Writing about the Japanese, Nancy Adler (1991) describes how promotion and reward may be avoided as it will separate an employee from his colleagues and this would actually demotivate him.

The point of this illustration is that even though increasing globalization may lead us to think that organizations are becoming more similar, research shows that ethnicity remains a fundamental influence on organizational behaviour. So the banana badge will not work everywhere! Laurent found that employees in multinationals strengthen their cultural differences. Germans became more German!

Hofstede's (1980) extensive study of 150,000 managers in over 50 countries indicates that national culture explained more in work-related values and attitudes than did position, profession, age or gender.

Individualism dimension

Individualism was found to be largely a cultural value of Western nations whereas the Far East, South America, Greece and Turkey were typically collectivist in outlook. In a collectivist society the individual is expected to put the corporate interest first, before any individual priorities are considered. The return of this is that the corporate body will look after the individual interests. This could also lead to strong mutual obligations between employer and employee. For example, Hampden-Turner and Trompenaars (1994) demonstrate this relationship of obligation using Sony:

> Akio Morita recalled an occasion when he complained to American colleagues about a particularly exasperating employee: 'What can I do with this guy?' I asked one day. They all looked at me as if I was slow-witted. 'Why, fire him, of course', they said. I was stunned by the idea. I had never fired anybody and even in this case it had never crossed my mind. But to solve the problem by firing the man was the American system.

Morden summarizes: 'Ultimately in collectivist cultures, the demands and responsibilities of workplace relationships may come before task achievement.'

INVESTIGATE

What difficulties would this present in your organization?

Individualistic societies expect employers and employees to view their obligations towards each other as instrumental or legalistic – as based upon a contract. Hofstede suggests that in such societies the task or outcome may take precedence over the character of relationships.

Power distance dimension

Power distance is a term that Hofstede used to indicate the extent to which subordinates accept the power of the boss. Japan, France, Belgium, Spain and Italy with bureaucratic organizations preferred high power distance. In such an organization, by-passing one's immediate superior to get the work done would be unthinkable. The USA, Australia, Britain, Germany and Scandinavia were examples of low power distance behaviours. 'Large power distance societies stress inequality; develop systems where everyone has a place and knows it; and reinforces the status quo'.

Morden summarizes thus: 'Societies associated with large power distance will exhibit a high degree of centralization of political authority and economic power. They will favour autocratic and authoritarian styles of leadership and management. This may result from either:

- a traditional role-resource control relationship (the priest, warrior, landowner, farmer, miller, trader, lawyer, accountant, etc.); or
- the traditional pre-eminence of one class or ethnic group (e.g. Brazil, Serbia); or
- greed and ruthlessness of those in power (e.g. dictatorships in Africa, South America and the Middle East; Stalinist-type regimes).

Small power distance societies regard social inequality as undesirable and try to reduce it. The exercise of power by one person may be looked at by others with scepticism or suspicion (as in Holland), or even open resistance.'

Uncertainty avoidance dimension

This factor reflects the extent to which a culture will try to control the future and is more likely to be found in new democracies (Italy, Japan) and where efficiency is highly valued (Germany). Countries like Canada, Britain, the Netherlands and the USA were lower on this scale.

Strong uncertainty avoidance societies try to anticipate the future and create institutions that establish and reinforce security and stability. This may show up in education – for example in France and the USA there is a strong application of mathematics and statistics, and in the Netherlands risk analysis is emphasized. The legal framework can also be used to lock nations together (as in the European Union). Economic and market power, military power, control of resources or access to resources (e.g. gold, diamonds, oil) can also be useful tools.

Morden uses Switzerland as an example: 'Switzerland, for example, has sought to minimize the uncertainties that derive from her geographical position (in the middle of a continent with a turbulent and bloodstained history), her ethnic diversity, and her lack of resources. She has exploited the defensive possibilities of her mountainous geography; maintained political neutrality; established strong decentralized regional governments (the cantons) which are not dependent upon each other or the political centre; and established a unique banking and financial services industry. At the same time the country has developed highly specialized and globally marketable competences associated with hydro-technology, electric power generation and transmission; cable car and lift/elevator technology; railway technologies; air treatment; and financial treasury management.'

Hofstede suggests that some societies, such as Switzerland, Germany, Austria and Israel, in which uncertainty avoidance is strong, are also characterized by high levels of anxiety and aggression, and a strong inner urge in people to work hard.

Weak uncertainty avoidance societies instead encourage people to tolerate uncertainty, to accept what the day brings, and maybe to take risks. Such people can tolerate behaviour, values and opinions different from their own. They do not feel threatened by the cultures of others. More negatively, some weak uncertainty avoidance societies are associated with low expectations and a fatalist outlook.

Masculinity/femininity

Masculinity is related here to assertiveness and acquisition of money. Concern for people is a low priority. Feminine-style cultures are represented as regarding good relationships between people as essential and the overall quality of life is valued above efficiency and material concerns. Japan and Austria are strongly masculine, the USA slightly masculine, with Scandinavian countries being the most feminine. In America, for example, women are encouraged to work and nurseries are provided. In Sweden women are expected to work and paternity leave is as accessible as maternity leave.

Figures 12.2 and 12.3 show the relationship between the Hofstede primary dimensions and also indicate some of the countries that fit the analysis.

INVESTIGATE

Consider Figures 12.2 and 12.3 and identify the characteristics of each country that place it where it is in the figures.

Do you think the figures are correct for: (a) your own country? (b) another country?

During the third quarter of the twentieth century, Japan, Hong Kong, Singapore, South Korea and Taiwan exhibited impressive economic growth. The original explanations offered for this success by analysts were only partial. In summary they consisted of cheap labour and transport, government involvement and subsidies.

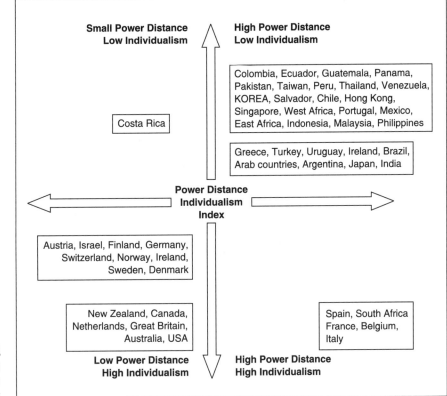

Figure 12.2
Power Distance
Individualism
Index

INVESTIGATE

What evidence can you think of to indicate these explanations are only partial?

The Hofstede dimensions already discussed are not uniquely Western, although uncertainty/avoidance is unique to Western culture. In the West, which includes the religions of Judaism, Christianity and Islam, the search for truth is fundamentally different from the East, where there is no assumption that any one human being can have a monopoly on truth. Indeed it is not uncommon for Hinduism, Buddhism, Taoism and Shintoism to cooperate in moral and ethical issues. In some Japanese households, Shintoism and Buddhism coexist in families. Given this social and religious context, it is less surprising that a non-religious ethical system like Confucianism, which became a moral and religious system in China, can become a cornerstone of society in contrast to the West where ethics are derived from religion. A key goal of Confucianism is the achievement of social harmony and

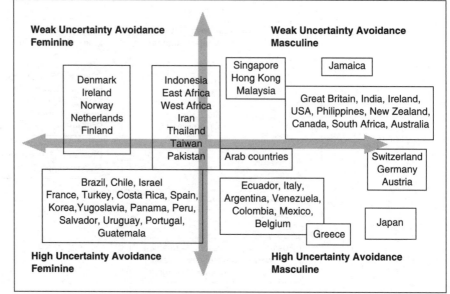

Figure 12.3
Uncertainty /
Masculine-
Feminine Index

order within a hierarchically based society. Confucius believed that mankind was divided into two: inferiors, whose task was obedience, and superiors, whose task was to provide for the common welfare. The doctrine may be summarized as: there is an obligation on those at the top of society to look after their inferiors, and on those lower down the strata of society to toil cheerfully in pursuit of the greater good.

The following abbreviated set of key principles of Confucius written fifteen hundred years ago are still easily discernible in Eastern attitudes and behaviours:

- Stability based on unequal relationships with mutual obligations.
- The family is the prototype of all social organizations where harmony, respect, prestige given and keeping face 'are vital elements'.
- Treat others as you would treat yourselves (except loving enemies; if you did that, what's special about friends?).
- Effort is an important virtue in acquiring skills, education and perseverance.
- Moderation, not losing one's temper, in a general pursuit of virtue rather than a pursuit of the truth.

Some Western organizations have had limited success when trying to adopt some Eastern cultural features such as consideration and service for customers and the current interest and emphasis on Total Quality at all levels of a company. It is possible to initiate changes by modest procedural alterations and, on occasion, powerful persons may affect change with innovative ideas. Taiichi Ohno lead Toyota from obscurity to the world's number 3 vehicle manufacturer with his Just in Time (JIT) stock supply system. This was a technical advance but securely based upon service to customer and high quality values.

INVESTIGATE

Can you think of an occasion where dependence upon JIT led to difficulties?

A look at individual countries

Having identified the general principles and key indicators of cultural influence upon organizations, we will now consider a few management styles of different countries.

France

Hampden-Turner and Trompenaars (1994) comment: 'France defies easy categorization. ... Despite a fiercely insurgent history, with successive uprisings from below, unleashed in the name of equality and fraternity, France remains one of the most hierarchical and least egalitarian of Western democracies. Can any centralized state have been challenged and replaced so frequently and yet have remained so powerful and centralized? A passionate belief in personal liberty vies with a cultural enthralment with great leaders who have periodically saved France and/or plunged her into disaster.'

Barsoux and Lawrence (1990) identify the following motivations of French employees:

- The desire for personal independence and autonomy.
- The desire to avoid conflict.
- The desire to avoid unpredictability.
- The desire to be protected from arbitrary decisions.
- The preservation of individual dignity, value and feelings of self-worth.

■ The desire to avoid the kind of 'manipulation' that the French (with suspicion) associate with the cordial and informal work relations practised in the UK or the USA.

Hofstede (1980, 1991) categorizes the French as having:

■ High power distance level.
■ High uncertainty avoidance level.
■ High individualist level.
■ Low masculinity level (strong on service, placing emphasis on leisure and the quality of life).

Morden (1996) comments that 'the high power distance score seems paradoxically to indicate a significant tolerance of inequality of power on the part of the French, who at the same time are reluctant to take orders! And the high uncertainty avoidance score also contrasts with French reluctance to accept orders. A standard remedy for reducing personal uncertainty is to accept orders from a superior, and to cast all the responsibility for the outcome on him or her! Thus, French attitudes to orders are negative; and to power distance are positive. And while the desire to avoid uncertainty is positive, there is a negative attitude towards the uncritical acceptance of orders as a means to this end.'

Barsoux and Lawrence (1990) categorize French work relations (and their management) as impersonal, formal, hierarchical, partitioned and subtly politicized. In addition, Hampden-Turner and Trompenaars (1994) state that French managers personalize authority and interpret rules flexibly, and take a rationalistic, holistic and communitarian view of their role.

Morden (1996) characterized management style in the a variety of countries as follows:

The Netherlands

The decision-making process is slow, formal and deliberate. All the appropriate group members are expected to make a contribution. Expertise, objectivity and pragmatism are as important as seniority in achieving an effective outcome.

The Dutch preference for examining every angle, coupled with the basic dilemmas (tensions) that underpin Dutch thinking, have for instance led Royal Dutch Shell to pioneer the development of scenario planning as a decision-making tool within the strategic management process. This rational and analytical approach reflects the ability of the Dutch to manage uncertainty.

Similarly, the Dutch apply an analytical and objective approach to risk-taking. Risk is an entity to be managed, while experimentation and innovation are encouraged within a proper framework of analysis and control. The lack of fear of unwanted take-overs also encourages a degree of long termism [*sic*] in the approach to R&D and innovation. Once a decision is made, implementation is fast and effective. All are committed to the chosen course of action.

Management style emphasises Theory Y and Theory Z. Informal and participative relationships are practised where possible. Use is made of teamwork. Management by walking about (MBWA) is encouraged as a mechanism of disseminating information, facilitating consultation and building consensus. Trust is implicit in the decentralized and autonomous approach to task completion that is favoured.

The manager is not seen as a figure of authority but as a co-ordinator and facilitator. This fits in with Dutch attitudes towards the nature and function of the organization, and accords with the prevailing scepticism about leadership as a concept and a practice.

Dutch managers may be slow to acknowledge poor staff performance, and tend not to fire people. There are two reasons for this. First, dismissal is legally and procedurally difficult. It may also cost a great deal in financial compensation. Second, in order to fire someone the manager would have to make a personal value judgement about the individual in question. This conflicts with a Dutch conviction that it is wrong for one individual to judge the actions of another. For instance, a former accountant is quoted as saying that he quit the profession because he did not like the judgement and criticism that is implicit in the auditing process.

An effective manager is described by the Dutch as *handig*. This can be translated literally as 'handy' or 'smart'. Its real meaning in the context of Dutch enterprise is the manager's ability to bring people together, to persuade and convince others, to get others to agree, or successfully to do deals. In essence, the *handig* manager is a good negotiator. He integrates well, is task-orientated, and makes good decisions. But in bargaining he achieves results by lightness of touch and tactical know-how. He does not pull rank or exercise his authority unless absolutely necessary, since these are not seen as effective ways of carrying everyone along with the decision that has to be made, and to which all should agree in order to achieve consensus.

Spain

Planning and decision-making processes are centralized, carried out on a top-down basis within the organizational hierarchy or web. Strategy and business plans tend to be formulated by senior management on an individualistic basis. Intuition and 'common sense' are used, perhaps backed up by consultants' reports. Information is gathered from personal contacts and networks as a matter of daily routine, without necessarily hinting at why that information is sought or what its purpose might be.

There is scepticism in Spain about the French and American belief in quantitative data as the bedrock of strategic decision-making. Improvisation is perceived as an art. Implementation problems then occur because middle-level managers have not been party to decisions affecting their departments, and because they lack the skill, authority and coordination to turn strategic directions into cohesive and integrated functional plans.

The role of the meeting is perceived as one in which views are canvassed, cases are presented or instructions given. The meeting is a tool of management manipulation or control, not of communication, consultation or decision-making. Communication is instead carried out on a verbal, personal and face-to-face basis.

While Theory X tends to predominate, managers will take a pragmatic view as to what will work best in any situation. They will also take opinions more readily from those staff that they know best and trust most. In other words, the prevailing style of management is personalized and humanistic.

Leadership tends to the authoritarian, as would be expected in a country with high power distance. It is the role and the responsibility of the leader to initiate strategy and take care of business risk and uncertainty. It is the right of the boss to exercise his authority and to expect conformity from others. The sharing of decision-making with subordinates is seen as a sign of weakness. Managers should not give away too much authority and may minimize delegation (where necessary delegating the most to those they trust the most). Managers may exercise control through: (i) the delegation of specific tasks with relatively short-term time frames; and (ii) the issuing to subordinates of detailed instructions as to how these tasks are to be carried out.

Direction and control should remain with the manager. Traditionally, the leader is seen as a benevolent autocrat who should display *valiente* (courage) in his dealings with others, and should be conspicuous in looking after the interest and security of his 'family' of employees

Germany

German managers tend to see the enterprise in holistic terms as a community of individual people working together. This communitarian and individualistic view sees its expression in a participative and Theory Z style of management. The role of the enterprise is to seek a position of competitive advantage through design and production activity. Thereby the enterprise creates value and security for its community; profit and shareholder benefit is secondary.

The uncertainty associated with business risk is minimized by the exercise of industrial skill and competence (international buyers do often perceive German products as better or more up to date and are therefore prepared to pay a premium for them). Uncertainty is also minimized by the taking of a long-term view of business activity, relatively untroubled by stock market pressures, and assisted by close relationships with banks as key sources of finance. Relationships with banks are well informed. Borrower and lender are locked into mutual dependency upon each other, and have to develop long-term trust. Such trust, lower expectations of return than elsewhere (for instance because of the low rates of inflation and the high value of the Euro) and German distrust of 'speculation' all reinforce the strong position of banks, not the stock market, as the financial bedrock of the economy. The strategic management process may, therefore, be concentrated on technological advance, operations and human resource management. The issue of dealing with potential predators, or business development and expansion in the case of the *Mittelstand* (middle class), do not necessarily arise.

Decision-making is slow and methodical. Information is shared and participative processes used. Group consensus is sought. Planning and problem-solving processes are logical and comprehensive. Once decisions are made, sufficient resources will be allocated in order to ensure success; Germans aim to dominate by shaping or specifying their markets in their own interest, and by picking winners for those markets.

Low power distance and high uncertainty avoidance lead to a high work rate and inner anxiety as a motivating force. German subordinates look to their managers to lead by example. Technical or managerial skill (and therefore status) are defined by functional efficiency and achievement, and the professional recognition that go with them. The nature of the role is defined by the competence required to fulfil it. Leaders are also expected to be decisive within a context where people have the right to have their own say; that is, interpersonal skills of communication, negotiation and persuasion may be required.

Conversely, the process of delegation is clearly defined and associated with the subordinate's own functional development. Delegating authority does not undermine the status of the superordinate; it reflects positively on his role as an instructor and guide.

The Far East

China. Chen (1995) notes that the dominant managerial ideology of the Chinese family business is patrimonial. This concept covers a wide range of themes such as paternalism, hierarchy, mutual obligation and responsibility, familialism, personalism and connections. Several interrelated influences are derived from these themes: the notion that power and authority are closely connected to ownership; autocratic leadership (which may or may not be benevolent); the role of the *taipan* (big boss); and a personalized style of management.

Organization structure in the Chinese family business is simple, informal, web-like and centralized. The proprietor holds the power to make decisions. This right is not delegated until the organization grows too large for personalized control. At this point, family members and long-term, trusted employees take on key roles in the business. Thus, the business becomes a social organization orientated to connections. This reflects the relatively high context character of Chinese culture. Due to the lack of formal structure and rules, personal relationships and feelings about other people are likely to take precedence over more objectively defined concerns such as organizational efficiency. As a result, the Chinese family business becomes an organization where who one knows tends to be more important than what one knows. One consequence is the suppression of professionalism. Setting up a personnel department, or hiring a financial analyst, is tantamount to inviting challenge to managerial authority. Expert power threatens the power of patronage and personal relationships.

The leadership style is authoritarian. In order to maintain his power, the boss controls information and transmits it piecemeal to subordinates so that they become dependent and unable to outperform him. The amount of information given to a specific subordinate depends on the degree of trust that the leader has for that individual. With this control of information, subordinates have frequently to ask the boss for instructions, thereby increasing their dependency on him. The boss's concern with the retention of power is also reflected in the careful maintenance of a large power distance. The boss should not openly be questioned or challenged by his subordinates.

Since the proprietor regards the business as the private property of the family, the formulation of objectives and decision-making are treated as the responsibility and preserve of the family. The financial situation of the Chinese family business (CFB) is in particular regarded as a private family matter. Those who are not part of the family are regarded as tools of implementation; their job is to implement the decisions made. Decision-making within the CFB is based on intuition and experience. It is also opportunistic in character.

Motivation is personalized. Given the family ownership, the corporate and personal goals of key executives from the family and its network are the same, thus making for a strong motivation to achieve organizational goals.

Performance assessment and reward are also personalized. Chen comments that because of the lack of structure and rules, the authority and responsibility of roles within the CFB are not clearly defined. Therefore, it is difficult for managers to make objective assessments about performance. Consequently, the top management in the CFB often pays special attention to the degree of 'manager loyalty'. For those highly loyal to top management and capable of special skills integral to the business, the boss will give substantial personal rewards in the form of year-end bonuses and/or a 'little red bag' (containing money). For those deemed 'less loyal' or less competent, any reward is correspondingly lower. For those having no special relations or special skills that the business depends on, the boss will typically employ them with lower wages and may not even give them 'face' by refraining from public humiliation.

The influence of personal relationships extends to the management of external business relations. The CFBs are linked together in networks, like a spider's web. (There are parallels with the networks described in earlier chapters of this book.) Business contacts are based on personal relationships, whether they are with relatives, friends or business acquaintances.

The business relationship is informal, with oral agreements. The connection network is also flexible and opportunistic. Networks of CFBs, each with an inherently fast decision-making capability, are able to respond rapidly and flexibly to changes in market demand and international trade patterns. The network is established and consolidated on the basis of *xinyong*, which refers to available credit. This concept of available credit has two components. The first is the provision of goods and services offered against the promise of future payment, as a customary basis for financing trade. The second is the concept of 'creditworthiness', 'trustworthiness' and 'future potential' of the person with whom additional or expanded trade is proposed. *Xinyong* oils the wheels of ongoing trade. And it offers a business development resource by which to further develop that trade. Business connection networks and *xinyong* synergistically make up for the limited resources of each family business. Institutional financial support (e.g. from banks in the absence of shareholders) for expansion or business development may not be needed.

Japan. Chen notes that, as with Japanese society, Japanese corporations are rigidly organized and hierarchical. At the top of the organization is the *kaicho* (chairman), who is followed by the *shacho* (president). Within the organization, each department constitutes an independent power centre. For this reason, the *bucho* (department manager) often commands the same level of respect as the president of a small company. In most companies, however, the day-to-day operation is accomplished at the level of the section manager (*kacho*).

Planning and decision proposals are circulated to all relevant persons and functions. Their views are taken on board, and potential problems addressed. A consensus must be reached before the proposal is recommended to senior management for final decision. Once the decision is taken, rapid and effective implementation should result. All parties will be expected to be committed to the decision as a result of the lengthy consultation and discussion associated with it, and of the establishment of consensus and agreement about it.

The system is criticized as slow and cumbersome. It can be used to block proposals. But it must be seen in the context of the need to achieve harmony within the group.

Manufacturing and operations are based upon the rational implementation of systems of operations management, supply chain management and quality management developed in the West but adapted to meet Japanese requirements (and then subsequently refined). The results of such a process include systems of *kanban* (developed by Toyota) and the concept of World Class Manufacturing (WCM).

Leadership (and hierarchical position) has traditionally been achieved on the basis of age and seniority, although there is now increasing correlation with performance rather than age and seniority alone. Management style can be described as being 'beyond' Theory Z. The achievement of harmony and consensus within the work group or department in attaining functional objectives for output and quality is as important as deference to management hierarchy, even though there is a large power distance and expectations of conformity. Tasks and work flows are carried out in an orderly and disciplined manner.

Employees are to a degree self-controlling, carrying out their work on the basis of mutually shared and internalized rules and culture. If something needs doing, then it is the responsibility of the individual to do it (and not wait until a supervisor tells him or her to do so).

Managers are responsible for ensuring that employees know what to do in any given situation, for training them adequately, and for ensuring that individual behaviour and group dynamics are satisfactory. Thereafter the work-group team, or cell, takes on a communal responsibility for ensuring that performance achievement and conformance are to standard, making such operational decisions or recommendations to management as are necessary. This process takes place at all levels in the hierarchy, and implies collective, not individual, responsibility as found in Theory Z

Korea. The organizational structure of many Korean companies is characterized by a high degree of formalization and centralization. Authority is concentrated at senior levels in the managerial hierarchy, with major decisions (especially financial ones) requiring a formal procedure of approval from top levels of management which involves taking many personal stamps of approval. Chen comments that 'the Samsung group in the past used a process of twenty-one chops, which took several months to get a project approved. After Kun Hee Lee took over the group, he demanded that these twenty-one chops be cut down to three.'

South Korean companies usually have a 'tall' hierarchical organization structure. Chen notes that executives tend to be supported by deputies and assistants in line positions, and that this increases the layers of vertical hierarchies conducive to a centralized and tall organizational structure.

Another outstanding organizational feature of Korean companies is that their vertical and hierarchical control is supported by strong functional control from staff departments like planning, finance and personnel. Korean companies attach great importance to functional specialization, allowing the planning and finance departments to exercise significant functional control under the leadership of the chief executive. Many family-owned conglomerates have a planning and coordination office under the group chairman, which is responsible for allocating major internal resources within the group. Therefore, many Korean companies have a combined organizational structure placing a vertical concentration of decision-making power at the senior levels of management and a horizontal concentration of functional control in staff departments.

Leadership and decision-making are influenced by family tradition. Korean corporate leaders, especially founders, tend to manage on the basis of principles governing the family or clan system. In the traditional Korean family, the father is the unquestioned and respected head. He has almost absolute power to wield if he so wishes. The traditional Korean father also had full responsibility to feed the family and to decide the future of his children. One legacy of such a family tradition for business leadership in Korean companies is the strong authoritarian style of superiors in the managerial process.

Chen comments that a top-down decision-making style is fairly typical; usually, 80 per cent of the authority lies in the upper management level, with middle or lower level management having very limited authority. Nevertheless, the authoritarian style is not despotic. Corporate leadership in Korean companies is also heavily influenced by a key value of Korean behaviour, which is defined as harmony and is similar to the Japanese. However, Korean harmony does not emphasize the group element, but rather emphasizes harmony between unequals in rank, power and prestige.

Korean managers cherish good interpersonal relationships with their subordinates and try to keep the needs and feelings of subordinates in mind. Korean managers tend to make decisions with the consultation of subordinates. The Korean process of informal consensus formation has similarities to the Japanese. Chen notes that 'managers maintain various interactions on an informal basis with subordinates as a way to achieve harmony-orientated leadership, which is based on mutual trust and benevolent authoritarianism'.

SUMMARY

We have seen how the organization is affected by its external environment because, as an open system, it interacts with it, taking inputs from the environment and returning goods and people out into it again.

The external environment consists of economic, technological, legal and political, and social or ethical elements. These elements present both opportunities and threats to businesses, and combine to form different environment types: placid randomized; placid clustered; disturbed reactive; and turbulent.

There are four types of internal organizational culture: the power culture; the role culture; the task culture; and the person culture. Organizational culture choice is influenced by the organization's size; previous ownership; the technology it uses; its objectives; the environment type it operates in; and the people in it. Often an organization may have more than one culture in its structure at the same time – this is called differentiation.

The management of change has become more and more important, and is best achieved through a flexible and open system of management.

The chapter continued with a review of international styles and culture in terms of expectations, values and beliefs that affect management practice. The practical difficulties faced by countries that have within them a diversity of culture were also considered. This was linked with a framework for managing diversity within an organization.

Having looked at factors that have an influence on culture, the chapter then considered the effects on business practice, with particular reference to Hofstede's 1980 study and the 'primary dimensions' within his model. Eastern nations have a very different outlook and it was shown that the key principles of Confucius are still discernible in Eastern attitudes and behaviours.

The chapter concluded by looking at management styles in a few selected countries from Europe and the Far East.

CHECKLIST: CHAPTER 12

This chapter allows you to identify:

1 Business environment:
- External
- Economic
- Legal and political
- Social or cultural
- Technological

2 Types of environment:
- Placid randomized
- Placid clustered
- Disturbed reactive
- Turbulent

3 Internal business environment:
- Power culture
- Role culture
- Task culture
- Person culture
- Factors influencing organizations' cultures
  - Size
  - Technology
  - History and ownership
  - Goods and objectives
  - People
  - Environment
- Differentiation

4 The management of change

Part Five

New Developments in Management Thinking

New Developments in management thinking

INTRODUCTION

How new is new? The inherent difficulty in using terms such as 'new' or 'modern' is that by the time the work is published and read, the items described are neither new nor modern. However, in this chapter the title refers more to ways of management thinking that do not draw on traditional or historic bases of management theory. There are challenges to conventional thinking that are addressed by these 'new' developments.

The chapter begins with humanism, asserting the essential dignity and worth of a person – a key feature of management in Spain, for example, and perhaps a key element in the traditional family business or cooperatives. We consider the family business and cooperatives in the Basque region of Spain.

Social theory suggests four key perspectives on an organization: objectivist, subjectivist, radical humanist and radical structuralist. The chapter then looks at the New Entrepreneurial Challenge, which essentially questions the assumption that large Western companies will outperform the competition. The post-entrepreneurial organization is characterized by examination of which elements of work are best done by partners and which can be done independently. A key word often heard in such organizational thinking is 'synergy'.

The chapter concludes with a table that presents the best and worst interpretations of the 'post-modern' organization.

HUMANISM

Humanism can be defined as a philosophy that asserts the essential dignity and worth of man. In 1994 Lessem and Neubauer, whilst examining the management systems of Spain and Italy, identified humanism as a key feature of management style. In broad general terms, humanists believe that mankind should seek to satisfy individual needs at the same time as meeting the needs of the community as a whole.

INVESTIGATE

One company's motto used to be 'Working together for the common good'. Could such a philosophy be successful? What do you think would contribute/diminish the company's operational achievement?

Because individuals perform better in small groups, the management style based on humanism demands a small-scale community or network within which managers operate. The small size makes the network manageable in scope and scale so that everybody can relate to, and communicate with, the other members. Examples of franchises kept deliberately small would include Benetton and Body Shop retail. Lessem and Neubauer found central and north-east Italy and the Basque region of Spain to be good examples of humanism in management.

Morden summarizes humanism in business thus: 'The family business lies at the heart of a Humanistic approach to business. Family businesses have a particular character in that they are composed of a flow through time of people with common (and conflicting) needs, concerns, abilities and rights who also share one of the strongest bonds human beings can have, that of a family relationship. A family business is more than an economic enterprise. It is a "stew" of family relationships, based on love, sharing, necessity, resentment and jealousy. Blood ties, moreover, are not the only qualification for membership of this family business. Business "relatives" are the long-term employees who become like blood relatives to the founder and family because they grew up in the business together. This "extended family" or employee network will require the same care and attention that the founder and the family expended on developing their own children for the future well-being of the family enterprise. For many Italians and Spanish, the family is effectively a substitute for the State. Loyalty is centred on the family and its members. The family may be perceived as the only institution that can be fully trusted and relied upon. Some loyalty may be devoted to one's native town or village, or to the region, but the first allegiance is to the family. What follows, particularly in the case of Italy, is that the capacity for motivation of people for work is greatest if it is for the family business, and only less so if it is for a large corporation or the State. The position of the family business is reinforced where the family is the banker. Italian enterprises often use family finance (perhaps made available at low or zero interest rates) rather than finance obtained from banks (which are associated with high interest rates and bureaucratic delays). After all, extended family incomes may be very substantial. This collective income may be treated as a family not an individual resource.'

The best example of humanistic business ventures in Spain are the cooperatives of the Basque region – the 'Mondragon Cooperatives'. Lessem and Neubauer describe the main elements as:

- Each worker-member must purchase (invest in) a significant stake in the particular enterprise of which he or she is a founder or member. The value of this personal/family investment will vary over time with the varying fortunes of that cooperative.
- A significant proportion of the cooperative's capital remains collectively owned by the community and indivisible.
- While the independence of each individual cooperative is guaranteed, all of the cooperatives are integrated on a group basis within the community.
- Management control within each cooperative rests with that cooperative's General Council, to which all its worker-members belong.
- All the individual cooperatives are ultimately responsible to the Mondragon community's General Assembly, to which all worker-members belong.
- Wage and salary differentials are set to take account of both market factors and the community's needs for solidarity.
- Each individual cooperative enterprise has continuous access to Mondragon's communal resources of professional advice, investment capital and skilled human resources.

The Mondragon Cooperatives represent a large-scale amalgam of small to medium-sized personal and communal enterprises, operated within a technical and financial infrastructure. Ownership and control are both individual and collective, but all are ultimately responsible as a whole for maintaining the prosperity and progress of the wider community that the Mondragon Cooperatives support.

Lessem and Neubauer characterize the Italian small and medium-sized businesses as bound in a web of competition and cooperation. Their characteristics are:

- A traditional 'communitarian' focus on the family and the local community.
- A communal, networked business orientation.
- An evolution from family business to socio-economic network.
- Localized kinship bonds of the extended family have been transformed into communication and transaction linkages of an extended business and communal network within an entire region. Lessem and Neubauer give the examples of Prato (textiles), Sassuolo (ceramic building materials), Como (silk fashion products), Reggio-Emilia (farm machinery) and Bologna (motorcycles).
- Innate individualistic and egalitarian attitudes. The individualistic and egalitarian philosophy of the Italian implies a character rebellious to any powerful machine bureaucracy or hierarchically organized collective life. Such forms of 'mechanical' collectivism may be seen by the humanist as the connecting of individual lives to a system of cogs and gears that (like the machine in the film *Metropolis*) will devour and obliterate individual personality and existence.
- A consequent antipathy to large-scale mass-production methods, and therefore to the structures of organization and management that are typically associated with them.
- A consequent dislike of formalized bureaucratic structures or hierarchies (which have the additional disadvantage of being negatively associated with State institutions). This dislike is reinforced by the fear that such structures, once established, will be open to politicization and corruption by people who are outside the influence and control of the family and its local community. Italians, having bitter experience of large-scale corruption and crime being carried out within such organizations, naturally fear that such outsiders will manipulate the organization for their own ends.

SOCIAL THEORY

The Burrell and Morgan model and the notion of paradigms propose that organization studies, which includes organizational behaviour, are dominated by seeing the world through only one perspective, i.e. the 'structural-functionalist paradigm'. The aim of the model is to propagate a wider knowledge of social theory and to appreciate other forms of analysis that have generally been neglected in organizational analysis. The model attempts to achieve this by highlighting 'blind spots' in each paradigm.

Assumptions and models about the nature of organizations, whether held explicitly or implicitly, form the basis of our understanding and analysis of organizations. It is the acknowledgement of this fact that is the foundation of this approach.

There are four key perspectives to consider:

The objectivist standpoint

This perspective focuses on the needs of the organization to achieve consensual and collegiate processes. It refers to a particular managerial approach, a top-down view of maintaining social order. Functionalism refers to a methodological and theoretical orientation in which the consequences of a given set of empirical phenomena, rather than its causes, are the focus of analytical attention.

Theory is viewed as neutral and value-free. The rationality of this perspective sees the structuring and ordering of the social world as being similar to the natural world and that can therefore be studied objectively from the position of the observer rather than the participant. The approach is anti-humanist in that the conscious, purposive actions of individuals and social groups are generally excluded from analysis. It focuses on 'structural causality' and 'purposive rationality'. To expand upon this, structural functionalists draw on the analogy of a biological organism and incorporate concepts such as structure, functions and needs, holism and interrelationship between parts. Conflict is viewed as dysfunctional and should be avoided. Its existence is rationalized as a breakdown or pathology that requires treatment (e.g. by training, better communication) so that harmony and normative behaviour can be resumed. The approach assumes an agreed all-consuming ideology that is adhered to by everyone because there can be no credible grounds for opposition to management.

Systems theory falls into this perspective. Systems thinking has had a major influence on the analysis of organizations and incorporates a set of assumptions about interdependency, synergy, boundary to delineate the organization from the wider environment, and a common binding ideology to provide a rationale for legitimizing the role of managers as coordinators within the system. It is the system, not the people, that does things in organizations.

The subjectivist standpoint

The subjectivist perspective is concerned with the interpretation of actors together with a focus on how order is maintained within organizations. However, this interpretative perspective does not view organizations as having a concrete existence prior to the involvement of actors but rather views organizations, their departments and hierarchies as being the creations of the actors involved.

Organizations are therefore viewed as 'structures in process', the creative fiction of the actors involved. People in their various ways interpret situations and in the process attempt to construct and reconstruct the organization to reflect these interpretations. Reality is socially constructed. 'Human social order is produced through interpersonal negotiations and implicit understandings that are built up via shared history and shared experience. What sustains social order is at least partial consensus about how things are to be perceived and the meanings for which they stand' (Hatch, 1998). Reality here is not objective but objectified – it appears to be objective.

By examining the subjective, this approach focuses on the social foundations of organizational realities and draws attention to the conscious participation of actors in the organizational process. The main problem with this view is that it allows the interpretation of situations but only within the bounds of a 'pre-determined plot' and fails to conceptualize the power relations between actors. A key strength of the approach is that it highlights the importance of the individual's subjective interpretation of reality.

Radical humanism

This perspective can be defined as radical change from a subjective 'consciousness' position – a critique of the status quo. It takes a reflective critical theory approach that attempts to place organizations in their wider social context. It disputes the neutrality of general investigations into organizations as being objective and subject to confirmation or denial by measurement. It argues that theories of organizations can only be understood as the outcome of a range of influences.

Its main focus is to gain wider understanding that organizations are complex and contradictory structures. Through this understanding, critical theorists seek change and emancipation. It takes the position that the consciousness of human beings is dominated by the ideological superstructures with which they interact and this creates a cognitive barrier between them and their true consciousness causing 'alienation' or a 'false consciousness'.

Freedom from this condition is to provide a critique of the status quo and bring about change through alteration to patterns of thought and consciousness. This perspective reflects an interest in the dynamic analysis of organizations.

Critical theorists seek to understand the political economy of organizations as structures located within a complex network. Through this they attempt to trace and understand changes in the forms and sites of the labour process. The radical humanism perspective views organizations as:

- sites of domination;
- displaying key characteristics such as hierarchies based on power relations and which are political;
- workers being dominated by the state so that economic interests are safeguarded at the organizational level – managers have to attempt to reconcile conflicts, ambitions and problems;
- not assuming an overall consensus to sort out political conflicts;
- forging links between structure and action.

The radical structuralist perspective

This advocates change from an objectivist standpoint focusing on structural relationships of the social world. The radical structuralist perspective examines organizations within the wider societal context and questions and demands a fundamental change in the form of both management and organization. This is in direct contrast to the consensus approach and argues that:

- Power is less evenly distributed in society.
- Power structures are difficult to shift, even if employees collectively join together, because the power structure reflects the interest of the more powerful groups such as the State and the larger financial system that regulates and controls business activities.
- The State is not a disinterested observer of management and employment relationships but plays a key role in maintaining and reproducing the power structures. The State can play a more direct role in disciplining and controlling the work force.
- Extreme radicals propose that the appearance of competition and debate between interest groups is barely changing the real power structures and only disguises the considerable inequalities within organizations, which are reflected in the wider society. Formal employees' rights are inadequate since they lack economic or political muscle because they fail to address the power imbalance at the centre of employee relationships; profit is the result of 'surplus value' extracted from the workers.
- Those who own the means of production wield power and therefore working under such conditions 'robs workers of their humanity' by causing alienation and exploitation at work; the focus in this perspective is what society does to people. Social action is marginalized or idealized. The approach focuses on the big issues and is not concerned with minor conflicts such as those between managers.

INVESTIGATE

Spend a few minutes thinking about your own organization. Note down any ways the four perspectives (if any) apply to it. Then note how the application of one or more perspectives may assist your organization.

NEW ENTREPRENEURIAL CHALLENGE

The global nature of markets has challenged the long-established position of US and Western corporations at the top of the industrial tree. The assumption that large Western companies will outperform the competition is no longer valid. Kanter (1990) describes the increasingly competitive and complex market conditions facing US and Western companies in terms of 'global olympics', where the place of Western businesses is much less assured than it used to be. Kanter suggests that what is necessary to be effective in the global market is to act like organizations that are smaller and more flexible. Businesses need to adopt a mission statement that includes the imperative to do more with less and to do it in cooperation with a number of other stakeholders, namely, employees, customers and suppliers. Kanter also argues that the other stakeholders in the activity are to be in the form of partners. Morden (1996) summarizes thus: 'Kanter suggests that neither the traditional, large hierarchical corporation nor the pure entrepreneurial firm is the answer to conditions of increasing technological complexity and international competition.'

Kanter identifies the solution to this problem as the 'post-entrepreneurial corporation', which is an organization that combines the best entrepreneurial approach with the best aspects of an 'agile and innovative' corporation – discipline, focus and teamwork. This hybrid organization will also have 'the appropriate level of requisite bureaucracy to ensure effective functioning, cost efficiency and financial control' (Morden, 1996).

The post-entrepreneurial organization does not blindly follow this strategy, but begins by considering what can be done independently and what needs to be done in partnership with others. In order to increase effectiveness, the hierarchy of a large organization will need to be 'flattened', i.e. have a few layers removed. Authority and responsibility may well be decentralized and staff may be associated with a particular profit or investment centre rather than with the corporate centre. Ordinary staff, especially those who deal directly with customers, should be empowered on a Theory Y or Theory Z basis. The part of the organization involved in a project would become focused on the market and customer segments in which it operates. Companies that have diversified may find themselves concentrating on core activities – Kanter refers to this as 'sticking to the knitting'. Service to the customer becomes the basic business rationale, 'giving the customer what they want' rather than 'offering them what we have'. The post-entrepreneurial organization would also have to take advantage of contracting out (to partners) and maximizing flexible patterns of employment described. Finally, the need for close monitoring of unit performance is essential, in order to be responsive to current situations and performances. An example of such monitoring is described by Hendry et al. (1993).

This 'restructuring' may be achieved not only by working with partners, but also by mergers between companies, or even by acquisition. This could have the additional benefit of getting rid of the competition. Another advantage of merger or acquisition is that an organization can become a global player quite quickly. However, Kanter suggests there should be two key reasons for the restructuring outlined above. Morden (1996) summarizes these as: 'First, the enterprise seeks to add value through the achievement of synergy. The restructuring may be designed to yield combined expertise, and gains in efficiency and experience (i.e. movement down the experience curve). Market intelligence can be combined and refined. And market benefit can be gained from the combination of product mixes and the opportunity for cross-selling between ranges.

'The second objective of restructuring is to achieve a better use of resources. This implies that the post-entrepreneurial corporation must add more value per unit of resource for its stakeholders than its predecessors were capable of doing. This second objective itself has two implications:

1 That traditional hierarchies and structures of management were ineffective (too expensive) in their use of resources, or worse, lost value (consumed resources) rather than creating it.

2 That the classic lack of necessary structure (requisite bureaucracy) in traditional entrepreneurial structures may render such organizations ineffective. Such organizations are also prone to periodic and sometimes catastrophic losses in stakeholder value, and in their continuing ability to generate value.'

The second characteristic of the post-entrepreneurial organization is that of cooperation and partnership. The fact that Western businesses have become more outward-looking is due, in Kanter's view, to the requirement to 'do more with less'. This increasingly outward-looking view finds its expression in a changing attitude to competition and cooperation, and in an increasing belief in the value of partnership arrangements.

Morden states that 'partnership arrangements allow corporations to combine resources, gain synergy, and move down the experience curve. They also allow the participants to achieve critical linkages of capacity and competence; to combine management expertise; and to jointly exploit opportunities which would otherwise be unavailable to any one enterprise on its own. Within an international context they also permit cooperation between enterprises whose ownership structures (and local company law or government policy) make it impossible to achieve merger or acquisition as an outcome.'

Kanter identifies three main types of partnership. These are:

1 The opportunistic alliance or joint venture that is formed to achieve rapid, if perhaps temporary, competitive advantage, or is instead used to counter an immediate competitive threat.

2 The multi-organization or consortium constructed by a number of independent enterprises. The consortium takes the form of a new company that is capable of making available products or services that would otherwise be beyond the resources of any one participant. Such consortia are for example to be found in the global construction and electrical, electronic and aeronautical engineering sectors.

3 The stakeholder or strategic alliance between the otherwise independent constituents of a supply or value chain.

Kanter suggests that successful partnerships are characterized by six I's:

1 The relationship is *important* and therefore receives adequate resources and management attention as a matter of priority.

2 There is agreement among the parties about the necessary *investment*, and about the sharing of returns therefrom.

3 The partners acknowledge their *interdependency* and the mutual need to share information, costs and benefits.

4 Relevant *information* is actually shared equally among the partners.

5 The cooperating organizations are *integrated* such that there are appropriate levels of communication, coordination and control.

6 The partnership is *institutionalized* within an appropriate framework of supporting legal, language, social and cultural ties.

The need to embark upon innovation and intrapreneurship can lead to a management dilemma. As described above, there is a need to concentrate on the core business and technology — what Kanter decribes as 'mainstream' — but this requirement could be in conflict with that associated with the creation of new ventures and technologies, which Kanter refers to as 'newstream'.

Is there a dilemma here? If 'yes', how could an organization separate the management of new ventures from the day-to-day maintenance of existing mainstream activities?

Morden (1996) highlights Sony, as being 'focused and disciplined in their management of mainstream activities. They are capable of intrapreneurship and innovation. They can manage technological discontinuities. They can develop new products and processes when they are needed. And they can deliver these new products or processes, in a tried and tested format, when and where they are needed, and within budget.'

Kanter contends that encouraging newstream activities helps companies to become innovative and intrapreneurial, but reduces their control of people. For a new venture to succeed, an identifiable and separate set of structures, cultures and systems may be required. Innovators and intrapreneurs may be free to use or ignore mainstream services, as they wish. As a result, newstream activities may loosen the traditional respect for hierarchy and authority, for bureaucratic procedures (for instance associated with financial control), and for corporate commitment. Staff in the newstream ventures may become increasingly committed to themselves and their project. Intrapreneurship may awaken and develop latent entrepreneurial skills. Staff and managerial identification with the parent mainstream may weaken, making it difficult for people to re-enter it. In order for the post-entrepreneurial corporation to succeed, it may therefore be necessary to operate in both modes at the same time, and to achieve a balance between the two. Kanter suggests that the successful post-entrepreneurial manager must be capable of operating in both a mainstream and a newstream manner, switching between the two as the situation demands.

THE POST-MODERN ORGANIZATION

Table 13.1 represents the 'best' and 'worst' interpretations of the 'post-modern' organization. Consider the table and think about elements that may apply to your own organization.

Table 13.1

Interpretations of the post-modern organization

Dream	Nightmare
Individuals are valued as ends, for their unique contributions: playfulness and quality of life are central.	Individuals are valued as a means to serve organizational goals; team processes and group tyranny dominate.
Hierarchical controls are eschewed as inconsistent with shared power; emphasis is on egalitarian relationships.	Unobtrusive controls substitute for bureaucratic controls. Meanings negotiated within teams enforce conformity.
Change is expected and celebrated. It is a source of renewal and creativity for organizational members.	Constant change reduces individuals' feeling of security and stability, producing alienation and frustration.
Diversity is valued, everyone has a voice and all the voices are heard. Difference is sought after as a valued attribute. Diversity of all types — gender, age, ethnicity, and culture — abounds. Difference of opinion is expected; emotions are encouraged.	A cacophony of voices erupts as political correctness stymies open discussion and supplants purposeful work. Contention is pervasive and members are on the defensive. Noise dominates and individuals are frustrated at not being heard.
Leadership is diffuse and distributed among all who seek it. Collaboration and consensus are put into practise and trust and confidence soar. All members help to construct and implement a vision into which diverse realities from inside and outside the organization are integrated.	Leadership is absent or manipulative. Either no one is in charge, everyone feels abandoned, and there are no answers without experts, or leaders practise manipulative and subtle forms of seductions. Form dominates substance and deviant views are censored or coopted.
Needs govern the choice of technology instead of efficiency. Technological determinism is challenged, as is the idea that people serve technology.	'New' technologies are used to control, e-mail becomes a means of surveillance and telecommuting a source of isolation and powerlessness.
Members have holistic and global views of the organization, the business, and the social and physical environment. They are comfortable with the idea that the organization has multiple identities and yet represents a holistic entity of which they are an architect/designer.	Local meanings and multiple identities confuse members. The picture is so fragmented that they are unable to make sense of it. Incompatible messages confuse and different parts of the organization cannot communicate.
Individuals experience a sense of fulfilment; their work provides different challenges and allows them sufficient autonomy to reconcile them; a personal life is enhanced by and enhances work life.	Individuals are torn apart: their work life makes incompatible demands of them which they find difficult to reconcile and their personal life intrudes uncomfortably into their work.

■ SUMMARY

This chapter addressed new developments in management thinking and focused on key characteristics of post-industrialism. There are some philosophies that have affected management systems and style. One of the major examples of this is humanism, and the chapter looked at management style in Spain with specific reference to the influence of humanism.

The chapter also examined social theory, proponents of which sought to widen the forms of analysis used by organizations by moving away from the 'structural-functionalist paradigm'. The four perspectives suggested are: objectivist standpoint, subjectivist standpoint, radical humanism and radical structuralist.

The New Entrepreneurial Challenge indicated that the assumption that large transnational corporations would always outperform the competition was no longer a valid view. The 'global olympics' of competition and complex market conditions requires a whole new set of assumptions — requiring, in many cases, fundamental restructuring of organizations to combine the best of an agile and innovative corporation with the best entrepreneurial approach.

The chapter closes with a look at the main features of a post-modern organization and presents a table that should help identify elements within your own organization that may be worth attending to.

CHECKLIST: CHAPTER 13

After reading this chapter you will be able to:

1 Identify key characteristics associated with post-industrialism
2 Understand what is meant by 'modernism' and the 'enlightenment project'
3 Discuss the post-entrepreneurial challenge
4 Consider possible applications of new developments in management thinking to your own organization

Part Six

Conclusions

Summary and conclusions

Over the preceding chapters we have looked at the management task from several angles. We have put the manager's task into its historical context, seeing how different management theories evolved and how they still influence current practices. We have seen how all organizations, regardless of whether they are profit-making or non-profit-making organizations, manufacturing companies or providers of professional services, have certain core departmental functions in common. The majority of managers will, at some point of their careers, be involved in one or another of these functions – production, marketing, finance or personnel – to some degree.

However, this is a non-function-specific book because, as we have discussed, there are certain key characteristics of the management task which apply to each and every management job.

'Management' is about planning on both short- and long-term bases; it is about making considered and judged decisions; it is about organizing the necessary resources (in terms of raw materials, machinery and people) in order to carry out the organization's plans; it is about motivating and leading staff to facilitate their work; and it is about monitoring and controlling all the processes in its responsibility.

To achieve all this, managers have to be able to communicate with their subordinates, bosses and peers effectively, to be able to look ahead and assess the future rationally and realistically, and they have to be able to guide and motivate those people around them to work well together towards stated objectives.

EFFECTIVE MANAGEMENT

A manager's effectiveness, or otherwise, can be judged not by what is done, but by what is achieved. Reddin (in *Managerial Effectiveness*,

1970) contrasts an effective manager with one who is merely efficient. An effective manager will do the right things, will produce new alternative solutions to problems, will optimize the utilization of the company's resources, will get new results, and will concentrate on increasing the company's profits. An efficient manager will merely do things the correct way, will solve problems as they occur, will safeguard the company's existing resources, will carry out set duties, and will concentrate upon lowering the company's costs. This is not bad management, far from it, but it is not truly effective management which helps the business to grow in strength and to expand.

It is the systematic making of profits by which management performance is ultimately judged.

Bibliography

Adair, J. (1974) *Management and Morality*. David & Charles.

Adair, J. (1985) *Effective Leadership: a self-development manual*. Gower.

Adair, J. (1986) *Effective Team Building*. Gower.

Adair, J. (1988) *Developing Leaders: the ten key principles*. Talbot.

Adams, J. S. (1963) Wage inequalities, productivity and quality. *Industrial Relations,* vol. 3, pp. 261–275.

Adler, N. J. (1991) *International Dimensions of Organizational Behavior*, 2nd ed. PWS-Kent.

Argenti, J. (1980) *Practical Corporate Planning*. George Allen & Unwin.

Argyris, C. (1964) *Integrating the Individual and the Organization*. John Wiley.

Armstrong, M. (1990) *How to Be an Even Better Manager*. Kogan Page.

Attwood, M. (1989) *Personnel Management*. Macmillan.

Barsoux, J.-L. and Lawrence, P. (1990) *Management in France*. Cassell.

Belbin, R.M. (1981) *Management Teams*. Heinemann.

Bennis, W. and Nanus, B. (1985) *Leaders: The Strategies for Taking Charge*. Harper & Row.

Blenkinsop, S. and Burns, N. (1992) Does your organisation get a clean bill of health? In *Journal of General Management*, vol. 18, no. 2, Winter, pp. 14–27.

Burns, T and Stalker, G. (1961) *The Management of Innovation*. Tavistock Publications.

Campbell, J. P., Dunnette, M. D., Lawler, E. E. and Weick, K. (1970) *Managerial Behavior, Performance and Effectiveness*. McGraw-Hill.

Carnall, C. and Maxwell, S. (1988) *Management: Principles and Policy*. ICSA Publishing.

Chen, Min (1995) *Asian Management Systems*. Routledge.

Child, J. (1984) *Organization: A Guide to Problems and Practice.* Harper & Row.

Clarke, P. (1972) *Small Businesses — How They Survive and Succeed.* David & Charles.

Cole, G. A. (1986) *Personnel Management: Theory and Practice.* D. P. Publications.

Cyert, R. M. and March, J. G. (1963) *A Behavioural Theory of the Firm.* Prentice-Hall.

Deming, W. E. (1986) *Out of the Crisis, Quality, Productivity and Competitive Position.* Cambridge University Press.

Drucker, P. F. (1955) *The Practice of Management.* Heinemann.

Drucker, P. E (1967) *A Theory of Leadership Effectiveness.* McGraw-Hill.

Drucker, P. F. (1985) *Innovation and Entrepreneurship.* Heinemann.

Eccles, R. G. (1991) The performance measurement manifesto. In *Harvard Business Review,* Jan–Feb, pp. 131–137.

Elbing, A. O. (1980) *Behavioural Decisions in Organizations* (2nd edn), Scott Foresman.

Emery, E. E. and Trist, E. L. (1965) The causal texture of organizational environments. *Human Relations,* February.

Fayol, H. (1949) *General and Industrial Management.* Pitman.

Fiedler, F. E. (1967) *A Theory of Leadership Effectiveness.* McGraw-Hill.

Furlong, C. (1994) Why excellence programmes fail. In *BC Business,* November.

Goldsmith, W. and Clutterbuck, D. (1985) *The Winning Streak.* Penguin.

Gregory, A. J. and Jackson, G. (1989) The internal information systems function as a service operation. In *Systems Practice,* pp. 37–39.

Hamel, G. and Prahalad, C. K. (1994) *Competing for the Future.* Harvard Business School Press.

Hampden-Turner, C. and Trompenaars, F. (1994) *The Seven Cultures of Capitalism.* Piatkus.

Handy, C. (1984) *Understanding Organizations.* Penguin.

Handy, C. (1985) *Innovation and Entrepreneurship.* Heinemann.

Hendry, J. *et al.* (1993) *European Cases in Strategic Management.* Chapman & Hall.

Herzberg, F. (1966) *The Motivation to Work.*

Herzberg, F. (1966) *Work and the Nature of Man.* Staples Press.

Herzberg, F., Mausner, B. and Synderman, B. (1960) *The Motivation to Work.* John Wiley.

Hofstede, G. (1980) *Culture's Consequences.* Sage.

Hofstede, G. (1991) *Culture's Consequences.* Sage.

Howe, W S. (1986) *Corporate Strategy*. Macmillan.

Huczynski, A. A. and Buchanan, D. A. (1991) *Organizational Behavior*. Prentice-Hall.

Humble, J. W. (1972) *Improving Business Results*. Pan Books.

Jacques, E. (1961) *Executive Leadership*. Blackwell.

Janis and Mann (1977) *Decision Making*. Free Press.

Jennings, E. E. (1977) *Routes to the Executive Suite*. McGraw-Hill.

Kanter, R. M. (1990) *When Giants Learn to Dance*. Routledge.

Kanter, R. M. (1985) *The Change Masters*. Routledge.

Kaplan, R. S. and Norton, D. P. (1996) Using the balanced scorecard as a strategic management system. In *Harvard Business Review,* Jan–Feb, p. 75.

Kaplan, R. S. and Norton, D. P (1992) The balanced scorecard – measures that drive performance. In *Harvard Business Review,* Jan–Feb, pp. 71–79.

Kast, F. E. and Rosenzweig, J. E. (1974) *Organization and Management: A Systems Approach*. McGraw-Hill.

Laurent, A. (1983) The Cultural Diversity of Western Management Conceptions. *International Studies of Management and Organization,* 13, 75–96.

Lawler, E. E. (1978) *Motivation and Work Organizations*. Brooks Cole Free Press.

Lawrence, P. R. and Lorsch, J. (1967) *Organization and Environment*. Richard D. Irwin.

Lessem, R. and Neubauer, F. (1994) *European Management Systems*. McGraw-Hill

Likert, R. (1967) *The Human Organization*. McGraw-Hill.

Luthaus, F. (1981) *Organizational Behaviour*. McGraw-Hill.

Lynch, R. L. and Cross, K. E. (1991) *Measure Up! Yardsticks for Continuous Improvement*. Blackwell Publishers.

McClelland, D. C. (1967) *The Achieving Society*. Free Press.

McClelland, D. C. (1969) *Motivating Economic Achievement*. Free Press.

McClelland, D. C. (1972) *Motivation Workshops*. General Learning Press.

McClelland, D. C. (1985) *Human Motivation*. Scott Foresman.

McGregor D. (1960) *The Human Side of Enterprise*. McGraw-Hill.

March, J. G. and Simon, H. A. (1958) *Organization*. John Wiley.

Maslow, A. H. (1970) *Motivation and Personality*. Harper & Row.

Mintzberg, H. (1973) *The Nature of Managerial Work*. Harper & Row.

Mintzberg, H. (1983) *Power in and Around Organizations*. Prentice-Hall.

Mintzberg, H. (1989) *Mintzberg on Management.* Free Press.

Morden, T (1993) *Business Strategy and Planning.* McGraw-Hill.

Morden, T (1996) *Principles of Management.* McGraw-Hill.

Peters, T. J. (1985) *Thriving on Chaos.* Pan.

Peters, T. J. and Austin, N. (1986) *A Passion for Excellence.* Fontana.

Peters, T. J. and Waterman, R. H. (1982) *In Search of Excellence.* Harper & Row.

Pratt, K. (1988) Performance management. In *Management Services,* Dec, pp. 6–11.

Quinn, R. E., Faerman, S. R., Thompson, M. P. and McGrath, M. R. (1996) *Becoming a Master Manager.* John Wiley.

Reddin, W. J. (1970) *Managerial Effectiveness.* McGraw-Hill.

Rees, W. D. (1984) *The Skills of Management.* Croom Helm.

Reicheld, F. F. and Sasser, W. (1990) 'Zero Defections: Quality comes to services. In *Harvard Business Review,* Sep–Oct, pp. 105–111.

Revans, R. W. (1971) *Developing Effective Managers: A New Approach to Business Education.* Longman.

Rockart, J. F. (1982) The changing role of the information systems executive: a critical success factor perspective. In *Sloan Management Review,* Fall.

Rodger, A. (1970) *The Seven Point Plan.* National Institute of Industrial Psychology.

Simon, H. A. (1959) *Administrative Behaviour.* Macmillan.

Stewart, R. (1977) *Managers and Their Jobs.* Macmillan.

Stewart, R. (1979) *The Reality of Management.* Pan Books.

Storey, D. J. (1982) *Entrepreneurship and the New Firm.* Croom Helm.

Tavsky, C. and Parke, E. L. (1976) Job enrichment, need theory and reinforcement theory. In R. Dublin (ed.) *Handbook of Work, Organizations and Society.* Rand McNally.

Taylor, F (1911) *Principles of Scientific Management.*

Trist, E. L. *et al.* (1965) *Organizational Choice.* Tavistock.

Ullah, P. (1991) The psychology of TQM. *Managing Service Quality,* pp. 79-81.

University of Durham Business School (1995) *Organizational Behaviour,* Stage 1, Unit 2.

Urwick, L. (1952) *Notes on the Theory of Organization.* American Management Association.

Urwick, L. (1958) *The Elements of Administration.* Pitman.

Vroom, V. H. (1964) *Work and Motivation.* John Wiley.

Woodward, J. (1965) *Industrial Organization: Theory and Practice.* Oxford University Press.

Yetton, P. W and Vroom, V. H. (1978) The Vroom–Yetton model of leadership – an overview. In B. King, S. Strenfert and F. E. Fiedler (eds), *Managerial Control and Organizational Democracy.* John Wiley.

Zaire, M. (1992) *TQM based performance measurement practical guidelines.* Technical Communications (Publishing) Ltd.

Index

Page references in italic indicate figures